THE GREEN DESK

THE GREEN DESK

JEANNETTE MALOY

joY

Canandaigua, NY

Published by joY

This work is a memoir. It reflects the author's recollections and interpretations of experiences over time. Individuals, events and dialogue are portrayed only through the lens of the author, and were at times compressed or altered for literary purposes.

Cover Art by Julia Maddalina

ISBN: 978-0-578-95880-4

If you are reading this book,
then it is dedicated to you.

CHAPTER ONE
Call It Off

October 21, 2005

"Call it off!" I scream at my sister on the phone. "Just call it fucking off."

"Okay," she says, quickly and quietly. "I'm sorry. I'm just making sure this is what you want."

"Well it's not what I want!" I yell, because I have to. I have to yell.

"Not what you want to do, but you know what I mean," she says, trying to mask the strain in her voice, trying to soothe me. "I want to make sure it's really what you're *going* to do."

I get up from the chair and walk back and forth in front of it, back and forth, back and forth. The phone is in one hand and the other clutches my bangs in a fist.

Back and forth and back and forth. It's always been like this. Back and forth.

My sister waits, and finally I reply.

"I'm sorry," I say. "I don't want to take this out on you. I just can't think anymore." My voice is twisted in fear and pain. I don't recognize it.

"I don't know what to do," I tell her. "I just don't know."

I do though. We both know. We know, but we are silent because some things are just too hard to say out loud and you think that if you keep them quiet they won't be true. We've kept this quiet for a long time, yet still it is true, and we both understand that this has to be the last time.

It has to be.

Through my haze of utter despair, I hear her speak softly, so softly.

"Are you still there?" she asks.

I whisper that I am, and I feel her trying to hold onto me. My sister. She is trying so hard and I am too, but this pain is killing me. It is so bad and it is killing me.

I return to the chair. I sit back down and look across the room and I am startled, totally shaken. I had forgotten. I'd completely forgotten.

He is sitting there. He is sitting on the couch across from me just watching, silently watching me go through this. For a very long time he's been there, silently watching me go through this. For years even.

Suddenly, I want to curl up in a ball and cry myself to death. It seems to hurt that much, enough to be gone. Then again, I want to grab everything off the shelves. Every single thing. I want to take each item one at a time and throw it as hard as I can at the floors and the walls and the windows and at him. I want to throw things at him as he sits there just looking at me.

Of course I won't though. I won't because I don't like anything out of place. Things have to be where they belong. I don't like messes or brokenness. But that's what we are. We are messes. We are brokenness.

Then all at once I feel painfully sick with knowing, knowing that this is over. I know it like the kind of knowing that comes at you undeniably and fierce, knowing that refuses to let you ignore it. I take a deep breath. I say my sister's name, then look at him with a sad mix of disgust and love as I tell her, "Just do it, okay?"

She sighs and I hear a catch in her breath as she tries to swallow this pain of mine, this pain that has become hers too. I'm still looking at him, holding his gaze as I say to my sister, "Send the notes. Tell everyone."

He continues to stare at me and I stare back and then he looks away and it hurts. It hurts that he looks away first, that perhaps he always has.

My sister waits a beat of my own heart, then whispers, "Okay."

"It's over anyway," I whisper back, bangs clutched in my fist again. "I don't know what I'm trying to do."

Tenderly my sister tells me that she is sorry, that she is as sorry as she has ever been about anything, and I know that she is. This sister of mine who has her own life and her own heartache, is as sorry as she has ever been about anything, and I love her.

"Thank you," I say, through jagged tears that cut at my throat. "Just send the notes, okay? Send them."

I repeat myself, sealing it all just like she'll seal the envelopes of the simple messages she'll be sending, the ones we talked about a week ago when we thought this might happen. They are the ones from Martha Stewart's website in the section about proper etiquette for calling off a wedding. They are the ones I tried not to write.

My sister begins talking to me then, but I can no longer stand to listen. I cannot stand to listen or to talk. I cannot even stand.

"Take the phone," I say, holding it out to him. "Take it!"

But he continues to just sit there listening and watching and twisting his hands and biting his bottom lip. He looks at me, but he doesn't move forward or say a word. He just sits like he's in a hospital waiting room and he's scared to find out if I will live or die.

And I wonder now which one he hopes for.

Finally I get up. I step across the room and thrust the phone into his uncertain hands. He fumbles with it and I try to yell at him, but my words come out as only choked whispers. Despair has lodged in my throat and I can't speak, can barely find the strength to turn and leave the room.

Somehow my feet carry me though, and I move in the direction of our bedroom. As I walk, I hear him start talking to my sister, but I don't hear the words and I don't want to. They won't matter.

I enter our bedroom. I step up to the bed and crawl slowly onto it, wondering if I will make it all the way to the pillows or all the way through the night. I wonder if I will make it through the next two months, the two months before what would have been our wedding.

This is it, I think. This is what happens when you say out loud what you have known inside for so long, for so much longer than you will ever admit.

The pain. It comes from somewhere so deep inside that there is no proof the place even exists. There are just quiet stories among those of us who have felt it, a tiny crack having started long ago. It is like the line in a windshield made by a pebble, so small that at first you think it might not even be there. But it is. It is there and it spreads slowly across your whole heart, your whole life, until one day when it suddenly reaches the edges, your edges, and it all just shatters.

Finally I am at the pillows and the tears come hard and big. They are so big that I must make room for them, and so I fold my arm and rest my forehead in the soft place made by the inside of my elbow. Soft places. I seem to have too many of them and the pain is severe then. It is so bad that I have to shift onto my side and fold my legs, bring them up toward my heart. I tilt my head in the direction of my knees and I grieve. I grieve horribly.

I grieve for the end of eight and a half years and I grieve for so much longer than that, for time I can't even measure, for pain that seems deeper and more than just this.

So the next morning, when my sister calls to check, to ask if I'm sure, if she should send the notes and tell everyone, I am broken when I answer. I am in little pieces.

Twenty-Three Days Later

I close our journal and put it back in the top drawer of our green desk and then suddenly, without planning, I punch the top of it. I punch the top of our desk that isn't ours anymore. The journal isn't ours anymore either. The journal and the green desk. They are only mine.

Slowly then I sink to the floor beside it, beside this desk we bought at the Salvation Army for only thirty dollars so many years ago, and I cry. Uncontrollably, and with one of the old-fashioned metal drawer handles digging into my back, I cry.

I called off our wedding. I searched for an apartment. I signed a lease. I packed all of my things into boxes and bags and suitcases and moved out of the life I thought I had and into this one. I made it through all of that. I made it through every single thing that came before it too, all of the pain and desperation and betrayal and doubt, but now I'm wondering how I will make it through one more night. I don't know how I will make it through just one more night.

I am alone. I am really alone. He let me leave and I left and now I am reaching for the journal again, fumbling in the drawer for it, the drawer that has no track and falls out when you open it. If you're not careful, everything just falls out. It falls out of this drawer and out of your heart and your soul and your whole life too.

Then suddenly I am holding it again, holding the journal against me and crying violently, wondering how this has finally happened and how to live the rest of my life without him. I think that maybe I won't. Maybe I won't ever get up from this spot next to the desk, the desk that is painted green and full of strange markings and loose pieces and imperfections he thought I would not be able to stand, but I did. I accepted the markings and pieces and imperfections, and I loved them. I still do.

I keep crying. I cannot stop. I am like a car skidding on ice even as your foot presses the brake to the floor. I seem to spin out of control and I think that this should be over by now. This dying inside should be over by now, and I look around the room as if searching for answers about how the pain can still be this bad.

I don't find answers though. I just find a room, like all of the other rooms in my new apartment, a room that is completely put together. It is only my second night here and yet it looks beautiful, well lived in, the green desk nestled snuggly against a window that would surely let in light if only I could stand to open the blinds.

Despite the agony, the utter despair, I have still managed to move every piece of furniture, unpack every box, put everything away, because I don't like messes. I don't like broken things. And no amount of pain can stop me from picking up all of the pieces and arranging them. The parts may barely be held together, only wreckage really, but at least they are arranged.

Then, for just a moment, I wonder about this. I wonder what it means about me, if I am more than I know, until I look down at the journal and all of its blank pages that will remain blank, and I see that I am not. I am not more.

Eight And A Half Years Earlier

It was nearly two o'clock in the morning as we approached his driveway and saw a car sitting with its lights out just beyond us.

"Must be someone broke down," I said, but at just that moment the car put its lights on and started inching toward us.

"Who would be here this late?" I asked, and suddenly everything shifted. The night we'd had out, drinking too much and dancing too much and kissing in the parking lot, it all shifted. It moved aside to make room for tension, for a rising panic.

"Go inside, okay? Just go in and let me take care of this."

"What do you mean?" I asked. "Take care of what?"

"Just go. I'll be right there," he told me, his voice filled with an urgency that startled me and pushed me toward the house.

He reached out for me as I passed him, brushed my arm with his hand as if to soothe me and urge me to go at the same time. Worry flooded my belly and I moved more quickly toward the front door, had almost reached it when I heard her scream.

"Who the fuck is that?" she yelled. "Fucking who?"

Blood. It started rushing through my veins at a rate my legs couldn't match, my gut twisting and turning and warning. The door to the house seemed so far away then and I only wanted to get to it, but there was a knowing too. There was a knowing that just getting inside would not get me away from this, and my fear and denial became so tangled inside of me that I almost couldn't breathe.

The door, always unlocked, opened with a stickiness that made me push so hard I almost fell inside, and it was difficult to get my balance as I closed it behind me and heard her scream again.

I turned then, pressed my back against the door just like in the movies when something awful is on the other side and you don't want to be in or out, when you don't know *where* to be. I didn't know where to be, but suddenly a jolt in my heart prompted me to lock the door, and so I turned and reached for it. That's when I heard her scream once more.

She demanded to know who I was, why he was with me, and how the fuck he could do this to her. She demanded to know all sorts of things and every bit of it congealed in my brain, made a big mound of fear and not knowing, and knowing too.

Then, just as suddenly, it got quiet. I could hear his low voice but not his words, and I moved toward the window and peeled back the curtain. That's when I saw her there in the driveway beside his truck, his ex-girlfriend, the girl from our same small town, and somehow I was not at all surprised. Of course. Of course it was her.

They were standing as close together as two people could stand and her back was pressed against his front, her arms pinned to her sides with his large hands. He was holding her there and they were saying things I couldn't hear and it all hit me hard in the stomach and in the heart, like an intimate scene I should not be watching.

And even though I didn't know what I was seeing, I did. I knew.

She screamed again. She screamed and screamed and struggled out of his grip, shoving him and punching him and yelling words I couldn't hear, but I could feel. I could feel every single word.

He grabbed her again then and turned her toward the car, yelling more words I could feel but not hear, and then he shoved her and turned away. He began walking toward the house, toward me, but I knew he wouldn't make it. I knew what she would do even before she did it.

Abruptly she turned from her car and began to run. She ran past him. She ran toward the door. She ran toward me. And I ran too.

I ran until I got to his bedroom door at the end of hall and then I hurried inside and closed it behind me, pressed the back of my body against that door instead. My ears filled with the beating of my own heart, and I tried to quiet the drumming so that I could listen for footsteps, but after a moment there was nothing and I remembered that I'd locked the front door. There was no way she could get in.

Though really, she already had.

More sounds came from outside then and I rushed to the bedroom window, lifted the blinds and peered out. I saw that he had caught her around the waist and was aiming her back to the car, its headlights falling all over me. I didn't want to be seen though, so I dropped the blinds and moved away, the backs of my knees hitting the bed as I heard him yell.

"Fucking go home!" he screamed at her, words so loud and angry I was drawn back to the window. I spread two blinds apart just a little bit with my thumb and pointer finger and saw him as he ushered her to the still running car, pulling and pushing her by the arm. He opened her door and shoved her toward it, the door like a shield between them. She grabbed it by the window and pushed it toward him, tried to push it farther than it was able to go. I heard the hinges creak.

He stepped suddenly away from it then and turned back to the house, where once more I dropped the blinds, not wanting to be seen, not wanting to see either. She continued yelling things at him, things about lies and hate, and I listened for him to say something, to defend himself, but then all of a sudden the door slammed and her car was thrust violently into reverse and I heard it grind way too fast down the gravel drive. Tires shrieked on the road and I heard the engine speeding away right before everything was thrown into silence and darkness and I found myself standing utterly still, quiet and holding my breath.

I looked down then, saw myself for the first time since I'd entered the house, saw that I had not removed my shoes or coat or scarf or gloves, that I'd just been standing trapped in all my clothes, in all my fear. Suddenly the silence and dark became too much and I needed to move. I reached for the purse hanging over my shoulder, but it wasn't there. My purse wasn't there, and in an instant I became frantic.

Hurriedly I began searching the bedroom, the urgency to find my purse becoming unbearable and unreasonable, and then I felt his front door open. I felt the unusual friction between it and its frame as it slightly shook the one-story house, as it shook me.

That was like a switch. I jerked toward the bedroom door and threw it open, stepped out into the hallway and bumped into him. I landed right at his chest, at the same spot where he had been holding her only a few minutes before.

"Hey, hey," he said, soothingly. "Where are you going?"

"Move. I'm going home," I said with surprising sharpness, because I felt so dull, not sharp at all.

"Come on. Don't go. I'm really sorry about that."

His causal words seemed to slap me and anger bubbled up, pushed the anxiety and confusion aside, made room for clarity, for knowing.

"You're sorry?" My voice was soaked in sarcasm but shaking too. I was shaking.

"Yes," he interrupted and started to say more. I didn't let him.

"You're fucking sorry?"

He winced.

"What the hell was that?" I said, screaming his name. "I thought you two broke up."

He started to answer, but I yelled, “You lied to me.” I pushed past him then, searching still for my purse.

“We did,” he said. “I don’t know what’s wrong with her.”

“You don't know what’s wrong with her? That’s your answer to this?”

He reached for me, but I pulled away, still hunting for my purse behind the chair and sofa and on the love seat and end table and all around the floor. I had to look for it, to keep moving.

He tried to follow me, but there wasn’t much space in the small living room so he ended up standing in the middle, covering less ground, seeming just as panicked.

“I told you. She wanted to see other people.”

“Jesus,” I said, then stopped and looked away. I wanted to move, to stay in motion but not to go. There was something keeping me fixed, a pull I did not understand.

“Where the fuck is my purse?” I groaned, and he moved toward me as I backed away.

“Can we please just sit down and talk about this?” he asked. “Then after, if you still want to leave, I won’t stop you. Please just talk to me,” he begged.

I knew I should want to go. I knew I should listen to the betrayal my heart was whispering about, but I felt drawn to this place, to this moment and to him. I stood still, turning my head in different directions, looking for my purse but not really. He moved closer. He took my hand. He pulled me toward him and I pulled away, but not really.

“I can’t talk. I don’t know where my purse is,” I said.

He looked around then, took a few steps toward the kitchen that connected to the living room, and reached in the direction of the table. When he turned back to me he was holding my purse.

“How’d it get there?” I asked with genuine wonder, as if it mattered.

He stepped in closer, held the purse out to me. "I don't know sweetie," he replied.

Don't call me that, I thought. Don't call me anything.

He took my hand then and everything shifted. Just like that, I felt it all shift again, and I let him lead me down the hallway and into his bedroom where slowly I moved to the bed, sat with my feet dangling over the side. He sat down next to me, turned in my direction and bent one leg up on the bed. I kept my body facing forward though, ready to leave, to make it impossible for him to talk me into staying.

He said my name then and I knew this was serious. It's always serious when they say your name.

"I'm really sorry for what just happened. I am." His voice was pleading and the look in his eyes begged of me to believe him and to forgive. Believe what though? Forgive what? I didn't understand, hadn't had enough time to recognize the pulse of my own knowing. And then he reached for me.

"I'm sorry," he repeated.

He sounded distraught, like it was all just a terrible misunderstanding. My heart kept tapping though, whispering that something was wrong.

Tap, tap, tap. Something is wrong.

"I'm sorry," he repeated, his voice louder then, like he was trying to drown out my knowing.

Abruptly I stood, and just as quickly he grabbed my hand, but still I found the courage to say, "I can't do this."

"You can't do what?" he asked urgently, pulling me back to him.

"This. You and me. There's more than you're willing to admit and I can't trust you."

He tugged at me so that I faced him on the bed and then put his leg down, turned his body toward mine and pulled me to stand between his knees. I didn't reach for him, but I didn't pull away. He rested his hands on my hips and I stood completely still while my mind and heart raced. I felt that I was shrinking from shock, from uncertainty and disappointment. It was all too much and I knew.

"Please don't throw away the last month we've had together. It's been the most amazing month of my life. Please," he said.

One month. It seemed so much longer, but he was right. It had been only thirty days. Just thirty days and already I was in love and heartbroken, trying to stay and trying to go.

"There is something really wrong here," I whispered, more to myself than to him.

"No there isn't," he said. "This is the most right thing I've ever had."

"Not for me," I said.

"Do you really believe that?" he asked, his voice twisted with worry and something else.

"Yes," I told him. "I do."

Thirty days, I want to scream now, as I weep on the floor beside what used to be our desk, what is only mine now. Thirty fucking days!

Oh God. I will never forget how he said that. My heart is breaking into a million little pieces and I am glad because maybe I will die and not have to feel this pain, pain from more than three thousand days. That's how long it took for me to leave, for him to let me go. My crying gets harder now, so painful that my throat hurts and my head throbs, that old-fashioned metal handle digging into me again as I let it. I let it dig in, and wonder what I did and why he let me go and what is wrong with me.

But then again I know.

It's this. This is what's wrong with me. It's that I am sitting here on the floor crying and crying with our journal clutched to my heart and my back against the green desk. It's that I am so desperate to be loved that I will stay for years and years, pushing and pulling and waiting.

I know this.

But then again I don't.

The sobs begin to hurt my stomach now and there is tightness in my chest and in a place so deep I don't even know where it is. I think that I must be so horrible and I can't stand to be in my own skin, on the floor of this new apartment, next to our old green desk. I want to go back to that day and change it all, walk away from him after thirty days or make myself somehow better, good enough. I want to find a way to save myself from this heartache, from what I think was the greatest love of my life, all the love I had to give, and not nearly enough.

Eight And A Half Years Earlier
Continued

"Please," he said again. "Give me a chance. I don't want to throw this away."

All at once I felt drained and weak and just then he pulled me close to him, leaned his head into me. My hands went to his shoulders, the back of his neck, in his hair. I didn't seem to put them there. They just went. They betrayed me, same as he did.

We stayed this way for a long time, until he looked up at me and said that he didn't want to lose me. He said that he didn't want to lose me and I knew he wasn't going to, even as I stepped away from him.

"Don't go," he said. But I wasn't going. I was just stepping back, getting some room, space to take off the coat and gloves and shoes I'd been wearing for too long now. While I did, he pulled back the blankets on the bed, the same ones I had pulled up that morning and smoothed neatly before placing the pillows at the head.

Then I made a decision, but I never noticed it.

I climbed inside the covers with my clothes still on. He did too, then pulled the blankets up over us as he rolled onto his side, facing me, and gently stroked my hair. He moved his hand down the side of my face and traced my lips. He kissed my cheek and then said that he loved me. For the first time, he said that he loved me.

And so I could never leave.

It seemed like only minutes, but five hours passed then, five hours since I rested my head on his pillow and fell asleep to his touch, to his love. That was when the door of his bedroom unexpectedly opened and slammed violently against the wall. Then, somewhere between being asleep and waking up, the words fell and I heard them, could feel them even.

"Who is that whore?"

I was on my side, facing away from the door, and I opened my eyes to the harsh early morning light at the same time he rose from the bed, the empty space he left startling me as much as the sudden sounds. I felt exposed and uncertain, so I turned to fill the space with my own body and that's when I saw. I saw him carrying her. He was carrying her away, her back pressed against his front just like the night before, only this time she was flailing. Her arms and legs were kicking wildly as he removed her from the room and she screamed back at me.

"You bitch. Who are you bitch?"

She screamed and screamed as he carried her out of the bedroom, and I watched the backs of them disappear into the hallway, feeling disoriented and confused, but protected too. He was protecting me from her.

And then another thought struggled to creep in, but I wouldn't listen to that. I wouldn't consider that maybe he was just protecting himself.

It seemed like an eternity before I heard him reenter, felt that same friction between the front door and its frame as it shook the one-story house. Again it acted like a switch and I bolted upright in bed, started to crawl for the side of it, when I heard his footsteps move down the hallway as the door of his father's bedroom opened. His father. He had been in the house all this time, since the night before, listening, witnessing.

"Bud, you okay?" I heard his father ask.

"Yeah Dad. Sorry. Go back to bed all right?"

"You know what you're doin' here, kid?" his father asked.

"Yes, Dad," he replied. "I do."

He didn’t though, I think now. He did not know what he was doing and I didn’t either. I didn’t know what he was doing. I never did.

I get up from the floor beside the desk because finally my tears have subsided. I open the journal, the one that’s been clutched to my chest. I turn some pages, look at words. I turn more pages and look at more words and then I start tearing them out, the words and the pages, just tearing and tearing and tearing.

It’s hard. The pages seem sewn into the book by a master seamstress and do not easily come loose. When I try to grab too many at once it is impossible, so I pull only a few at a time, and as they come away from the binding I toss them on the desk, the one that isn’t ours anymore.

After a while only the blank pages are left inside the book, but the ones with our words on them, our life, are torn out.

I set down what is left of the journal and start ripping up the words. I rip and rip until they are tiny bits that make a giant mound on the desk. The rest of the damaged book sits beside them as I leave the room and come back with the garbage can from under the kitchen sink. I place it up against the desk and in one movement swipe all of the torn pages and the destroyed journal into the bin, then leave the room again. I walk back to the kitchen. I open the cabinet under the sink and before I place the garbage can back there, I reach in and push all of the pages and the book way down deep into the trash and stir it up. I mix it with napkins and a banana peel and a mushroom wrapper. The pages and the book become soaked and dirty and finally I don’t even recognize them anymore. Just like I don’t recognize me or this life, I don't recognize those pages either. They are gone. Everything is.

I called it all off.

CHAPTER TWO
Monday Morning

It's Monday, my first Monday morning alone. Somehow I made it through last night, with the desk and the crying and the torn-apart journal. I put some more things away and that helped. It always helps to put things away. I picked out clothes for work. I ironed them. I packed a lunch. I took two sleeping pills too. After trying to read a book, but unable to stop telling my own story, to stop thinking about all I've lost and all I never even had, I finally took two sleeping pills so that I could fall asleep free from the pain of being myself.

Now I'm at work again, dragging this heavy heart into my classroom, but still I am here. I am here and I wonder again. I wonder just for a moment if there is more to me than I know, even though right now I only feel small, like nothing, barely hanging on. But then suddenly the thought is gone. I can never hang onto it for very long.

I unlock the door to my classroom, walk in and flip a switch that illuminates only some of the overhead lights. I can't have too much light. It makes everything too hard to look at.

As I move toward my desk, I find myself breathing just a little easier, and by the time I reach my rolling chair I feel almost ready for this day, for one more day. The room is exactly the same as it was on Friday, as it was before my address changed and before my long, ivory, silk dress was hung in my mother's closet instead of my own. Those truths have not touched this room. It is like a time capsule and I want it to take me back. But to when? To what?

To before he let me go.

It also helps that he is coming over tonight. I called off our wedding just three weeks ago and I live alone now, but he is coming for dinner. I will make our favorite rice and broccoli like

I did when we were together, and we will sit at the same dining set that was leaning in pieces against our wall just days ago. The same dinner at the same table even though nothing is the same and I can't believe I am doing this.

My phone rings then and I see *Dad* on the screen and immediately his name breaks up the flutters of anxiety and self-doubt landing in my belly and all around me.

"Hi Dad," I say.

"Hey babe," he says to me softly. "How are you?"

His voice is just like it was five days ago, after the movers had given me a price and we'd agreed to Saturday and they'd left and my dad had stayed. He'd stayed and assessed all of my things and quietly determined what tools he'd need from his truck so that he could help me take it all apart, help me take my life apart.

He had said then, in that same soft voice, "Don't worry, babe. This'll be easy." And that's when the air had seemed to leave the room and I'd started to cry and instantly he'd known and said that he was so sorry, then wrapped his arms around me as he cried too. We'd both cried, because we both knew that it wasn't going to be easy.

"I'm okay Dad," I say to him now, and I picture us at the two-person kitchen table I left behind, surrounded by boxes and furniture legs and artwork leaning against the walls. I see us eating subs and sipping from large glasses of iced tea and talking about things that didn't matter as we tried to ignore the wreckage all around me. I can still hear the rain that was pounding on the windows that day, as we broke down all of my things into pieces that would fit through the door.

"Well, Mom was wondering if you wanted to come down for dinner tonight," he tells me, and my breath catches and my heart beats faster.

"Oh, thanks Dad," I say, my voice unsteady. "Maybe I can later this week. Tonight I just want to get a few more things settled in the apartment."

I am full of shame then, just dripping in it. How can I do this to them? How can I do it to myself?

My dad is talking to me now, but I can't respond because I am swallowing so much. I am swallowing sorrow and fear and regret, and I am swallowing all of my knowing better.

One Month Earlier

I took it off, put it back in the box from nearly two years before, and set it on the bathroom counter. Then, instead of returning to the bedroom where he was in and out of sleep, I left for work. Without kissing him goodbye or having him hold me for a long time like he always did in the morning, I just left. I went to my classroom where nothing had changed except the ring that had been on my finger for nearly two years.

That was on the bathroom counter in a box.

After work, I raced back home to our apartment and made a frantic dash for the bathroom. I couldn't wait to find the ring still sitting there, sitting with a note telling me to put it back on my finger, that everything was okay.

But it wasn't there. Everything was not okay. My ring was gone, and without thinking I started looking for it, began desperately searching the drawers and cabinets of the bathroom, and when it wasn't there I went to his side of our closet, searched the shelves above the hanging things, searched and searched.

I went to his nightstand next.

I went to his gym bag after that.

Nothing.

Desperate still, I went back to the bathroom and looked again, then out to the kitchen to look in spots that didn't make sense, because nothing made sense, and then I returned to all of the places and searched second and third times, until finally I gave up. I gave up and went back to the bedroom where I sat down on the bed. I just sat, unable to believe what I was doing, that I was looking for my own engagement ring and that this whole thing was such a pitiful mess. I bowed my head and tried to breathe but then suddenly thought, fuck this. Just fuck it. I lifted my head.

I lifted my head and found myself staring at the closed doors of our armoire. I hadn't looked there.

Very quickly I got up. I stepped the two paces to this large structure full of clothes all folded neatly on shelves. I opened the left side, his side. My eyes went to the top shelf. And there it was. It was right there.

The same dark smooth box was there, the one with two tiny hinges in the back. It was just sitting on his shelf in the wardrobe, right out in the open for me to see, to take. Slowly I reached for it, but then stopped, suddenly scared. I didn't know if the ring would be inside, if it was still mine. I wanted to know and I didn't want to know, and finally I reached for it again, wrapped my fingers around the box and held it for just a moment in my palm before slowly pulling open the lid. The tiny hinges acted funny, built to open quickly, not at this slow and fearful pace.

Then it was open and the ring was there. It was just sitting there staring at me as though nothing had happened, as if everything was going to be fine, and I thought then that it would be. He was probably figuring out what to say to me, how to give it back. I would wait. He would bring it to me when he got home a few hours later, and until then at least I could see it and touch it, and that was enough.

But really it wasn't.

That night when he came home I was already in bed, waiting. He slipped into the bedroom quietly and walked over to stand in front of the wardrobe where I'd set my ring back on the shelf just as he'd left it. He opened the door and reached in. I waited silently then, waited for him to get the ring out of the box and kneel at my bedside the way he'd done on my thirtieth birthday.

In the light from the street I could see him pull out a T-shirt and sweatpants, then turn with his clothes hugged to his chest and leave the room. Just like that. He left.

The next morning, numb from crying and hurting and wondering, I got ready for work because I didn't know what else to do and because some seriously wounded piece of me still thought everything would be okay. I still thought he'd put the ring back on my finger and everything would be okay, so before leaving I went to him. I sat on the edge of the bed, and with his eyes still closed he reached out for me, and it was just as it had been for so many mornings, years worth of them. It was exactly the same, yet everything was different and I knew it.

I knew it as I walked away from the bed without my ring and I knew it when I got home at the end of the day and raced into our bedroom to throw open the wardrobe door and find the box. I knew it when the box wasn't there and when I started looking for it again. I knew it after I'd looked everywhere that it would make sense for it to be and I knew it when it wasn't anywhere.

I slumped into a chair at the kitchen table, dizzy with pain and confusion. It was my own engagement ring and he hadn't asked me to take it off and I hadn't said that I would and nobody had said that we were no longer engaged. Nobody had said anything. Not out loud.

I stood up then and went to the wall, my body heavy with a truth I had to speak. I picked up the phone. I dialed. I waited.

"Hey there!" answered my dad.

"Dad?" I mumbled. "Do you have a minute?"

"Oh babe," he said softly. "Of course I do."

I think about the ring now, a month later, as I stand in my classroom with my dad on the phone, telling him that I can't come for dinner because I want to get a few more things settled in the apartment, when really everything is in its place and my dad probably knows that about me. What he doesn't know is that My Ex is coming to my apartment for dinner tonight and that I hate thinking of him that way, as My Ex, and so I don't. Even though I still have no idea where the ring is that I wore for almost two years and even though we are not getting married and even though I moved out of our apartment and now live alone, I won't yet believe that it is over.

I won't yet believe a lot of things, and so at the end of the day I am driving home with fear in my belly, my hands wrapped tightly around the steering wheel because he is coming to my new apartment in two hours. He's bringing some things I left in our old place, only his now, and we're going to have dinner at the same table my dad took apart just last week, and I know that if I don't let go this holding on is going to ruin me. I know, but knowing doesn't make it so.

Moments later, I walk into my living room and take off my shoes. I place them neatly by the door, heels facing the wall. I hang my jacket in the closet with its zipper facing the left like the rest of them. I take my schoolbag into the office and hang it on the hook inside the door and try not to look at our desk, the green desk that is just mine now.

I go into the bedroom, aware of the perfectly made bed with the neatly arranged pillows on top. I try to keep my things in order so that my life will stay in order, but it's not working anymore, and it seems like years in this new place when it has only been two nights. I don't know where we could possibly go from here and I am so disappointed in the choices I'm making. Still, I can't stop making them. I cannot stop.

Tears begin again, drops full of disappointment, regret for not saying no, no fucking way, when he asked if he could come over and bring some things he found and have dinner. I should have said no, no to him and to our old familiar patterns that I know are killing me, like a drug I can't stop taking. I can't stop because I need to numb this awful pain and the only way I can think to do that is to do what I know, to take the same drug that is causing so much of the hurt to begin with.

I walk into the bathroom and turn on the light and when I see the vanity I remember. I go back to the office. I reach into my schoolbag and take out the creamy-colored ceramic snowman with wirelike black arms standing atop a green ceramic block with words on it.

I set it right in the spot where I imagined it would go when I got it last week, then sit down on top of the toilet seat, exhausted and confused, thinking about how a month ago today I set my ring on another bathroom counter and I don't know how I got here. Only a month ago.

I look again at the snowman and remember getting to my classroom the day after the movers had given me a price and my dad had gotten his tools from the truck. A small green gift bag with a white handle had been hanging from my doorknob and I'd carried it inside with me, set it on the classroom counter. I'd taken out a small card, opened the fold, stared at handwriting I had not seen before and read words I couldn't believe. Again and again I'd read them, wanting them to sink into me, to cradle me from the pain, before I set the card down and reached into the bag. Something had poked at me from under the tissue paper, and I'd smiled while unwrapping the wirelike black arms of a snowman.

The card was signed by two colleagues just a few doors down from me, women I didn't know well but who somehow still knew me, who knew pain when they saw it. They'd been watching the day before that, during the rainstorm, when I'd been pacing in the hallway because the buses were late, when I'd needed to get to our apartment and meet the movers and my dad.

"Are you all right?" one had asked.

"I just have an appointment," I'd told her, trying to sound calm.

"Well go," she'd said. "I'll take over your room and dismiss your kids."

"Oh I can't," I'd whispered, almost in tears from the emotion of unexpected kindness.

"Stop it," she'd replied firmly. "There are two of us. Just go. I can tell it's important."

I'm still sitting on the toilet seat now, looking at the snowman as tears flood my eyes the same way they did that day, when I'd turned to gather my things and try to walk to the door without meeting her eyes. Her gaze had pulled on me though, and I'd looked up, seen the knowing in her face as I breathed out a humble thank you and rushed into the storm.

I remember racing to my car with my head down, barely able to see as I'd fumbled with the door handle and finally gotten inside, all at once silent and dark. I remember how I'd sat still a moment and how it had felt like something, like that time almost nine years ago at his house, after she'd stopped screaming outside. It was silent and dark. But more was coming.

I remember three hours later, rain still pounding on the windows, sitting at the two-person kitchen table with my dad eating subs, surrounded by boxes and furniture legs and artwork leaning against the walls. I remember the following morning, walking to my classroom with eyes swollen and red because that's what happens when you pack your whole life into labeled cardboard and sign a lease and take furniture apart and sleep next to the man who will not be your husband.

And these women had known it. They'd known and they'd hung a green gift bag with a white handle from my doorknob, and I get up from the toilet seat now and go to the snowman, pick him up and move him around in my hands, look at the words on the green ceramic block he stands on.

"There's no man like a snowman."

And yet, My Ex will be here in an hour.

I set the snowman back down, and the sound of his base hitting the counter reminds me of my ring. One month ago today, on another Monday morning.

CHAPTER THREE

The Buzzer

The buzzer rings, and I knew it was going to even before I heard it. I'd been watching out the window and saw his truck pull into a parking spot in front of my building. I saw him get out, close the door, lock it and turn toward me. In his hands were a bunch of things, my things. It reminds me of the way he turned from the wardrobe that night, with his clothing hugged to his chest, when he didn't give my ring back and I cried myself to sleep.

My heartbeat speeds up and my face grows warm, the anxious heat that started in my belly moving up. I close the blinds, step away. My hand is on my heart as I go to the wall and push down the lever that unlocks the main entrance. I open the door to my apartment just a little so he will know which one it is, then walk quickly to the kitchen, pretend to be busy, so engrossed in my new life I can't possibly come to the door.

But really I just stand. I stand with one hand on the counter, waiting and scared, busy with nothing but a pounding heart. I hear him. He's at the door but not coming in. He's in the hallway taking his shoes off because we lived together for many years and he knows about this. He knows about clean carpets and well-placed shoes and so many things that don't seem to matter anymore.

Clean carpets don't matter. But then again, they do.

I feel him then. I feel him walk in. He mixes with my pulse, with the beat of my heart, and the fear is overwhelming as hot tears threaten. I want to just die, but instead I step out of the kitchen, and when I see him my grief quickens. I have to swallow it back, almost choke on it.

I move slowly, even though what I want is to run. I want to run away and I want to run toward him. I just want to run, but

I walk, even though it doesn't feel like walking. It feels like being pulled, not like a decision or even an instinct to put one foot in front of the other, but a pull that just happens. It is like that day in his dad's house over eight years ago when I should have moved away, but instead I moved in.

"Hey," he says softly, looking up from his shoes and then standing and stepping toward me as he tries to hide flowers behind his back. My favorite white roses. He has my favorite white roses, and I wonder how he can bring me flowers and still not want to marry me, and I feel like I am in pieces, little pieces.

As I get to him he pulls the flowers out and it's awkward because we don't seem to know for sure what to do or how to place ourselves or where to look, but then suddenly he reaches out for me and it just comes back and I step in. He takes me easily and the grief starts to ease. I'm sinking back into us, sinking. He is like a drug. It is the kind of drug you have to stop taking, but until you are strong enough you need it to keep from hurting. I'm not strong enough. I'm hurting.

I wrap my arms around his neck and he wraps his around my lower back and turns his face into my hair. My lips graze his neck and I go onto my tiptoes, close my eyes and breathe him in. He's breathing me in too. We are like a beautiful puzzle, but with so many pieces missing that we no longer make the picture on the front of the box. We make something else instead and it isn't quite right, so we search and search for those missing parts. We can't find them, but still we search, and we are like this for a while, just sinking into one another and feeling familiar. It is us, even with all of the missing pieces, just holding and breathing and searching.

Then finally there is a sound and one of us pulls away. I pull away or he does or we both do at the same time. It's hard to tell. It's always been so hard to tell.

He looks past me and into the living room then and I am surprised when he tells me how beautiful it is. I wince. I try not to sound broken when I reply.

"It's basically our living room, just in a different place," I tell him.

"No, it's more," he says. "The walls are so white. The carpet too. Everything is so clean and new."

Yup, clean and new. That's my fucking life, I want to tell him, but I don't. If I do he will ask me why it always has to be so difficult with me and then I will cry. I'll tell him he doesn't make it so easy either and he will say he's sorry and I will ask if he's so sorry then why doesn't he do something differently and he will look away and I will just hurt more than I already do.

"It's very clean and new," I agree.

He starts walking through the living room then, looks at things we used to share. He sees our lamps and tables, the couch, the chair, art on the walls. He touches pillows and runs his hand along the top of the TV. He looks at me with a smile then, holds his finger up.

"No dust," he teases.

That's right. There is no dust on my television because I haven't been here long enough to collect any dust and I want him to stop looking and smiling like this is normal, like he is happy for me. I want to scream at him to just fucking stop, but instead I tell him that dinner is ready. I don't really want to eat, not now or not ever, but I don't want him to keep looking and touching and breaking my heart.

He ignores my cues about dinner and says, "This all looks great. You always make everything so nice."

I always make everything so nice, but I couldn't make things nice enough for him to want me, I think. I don't say it though, and I don't cry either. I just turn and pull the pitcher from the refrigerator and fill our glasses that are already on the table, our table. It is the same one my dad took apart and then put back together just days ago, and I hear him walking around before he enters the kitchen, looks at all of the things that used to fill the counters we shared.

"This is really nice, baby. You made it beautiful."

Stop, I want to scream. Please, please just stop!

He walks through the kitchen and across the hallway to the bathroom. He steps inside then turns and comes out smiling.

"There's no man like a snowman, huh?"

I want to fall to the floor.

I tell him again that dinner is ready, but he turns toward the spare room, the room that holds the green desk we bought at the Salvation Army for only thirty dollars so many years ago. I was crying beside that desk yesterday, sobbing my heart out really.

"Wow," he calls to me. "This room looks great too."

I don't say anything because heartbreak is caught in my throat and I cannot speak. I can only think about how I cannot seem to put us together the way I can put a room together and how I hate him for not seeming to notice or for ignoring it maybe. Is he just here to make sure I'm okay so he can feel better about letting go? Fuck that. Fuck that and this stupid dinner and fuck him. I want to die from this pain.

I turn the corner and see him standing in front of our desk, his fingertips brushing its surface. I freeze. He opens the top drawer that used to hold our journal and the drawer starts to fall out like it always did and he laughs and closes it. He doesn't seem to notice that the journal is gone. He doesn't seem to notice a lot of things, and I think then that no matter how much things change, some things stay exactly the same. The green desk is the same. It is exactly the same. That drawer. It falls out every time. Every single time.

"Can I see your bedroom?" he asks all of a sudden, and only then do I realize how much I am not breathing.

"Why don't we eat?" I say, but he walks out of the office toward my open bedroom door.

I turn and follow him and I say again that dinner is ready, but he walks into my bedroom and he is quiet. We both are. I want to ask him what he's thinking, if he regrets it yet, if he wants to change his mind. We are standing so close together and yet there is so much space between us and I know he is afraid I will fill it with words so he speaks.

"Do you want the nightstands back?"

I splinter a little more inside, like that spidery crack across a windshield that fractures more with every bump.

"No. New ones are coming," I say sensibly, thinking of the nightstands I've ordered. They will match the new chocolate-colored armoire and they will try to fill the holes in my heart, in my dreams. I need to fill the holes. I need to fill them with things for this new place, even though I'm afraid I know that this is not really the way. This is not the way.

"I'm not surprised," he responds. "I know how much you love things all put together," and again he is smiling, so happy for me. He is so happy for me that the pain of it becomes overwhelming. It threatens to swallow me up and I fumble to shove it into that deep place inside that stores my despair. It holds it there until later.

He is talking about the new armoire now, about how it has just a single door, not like the one we shared with two doors, and I feel like I have been punched in the gut. I am thinking about my ring behind the door on the left and he is still talking, but all I hear is a low din of hopelessness, the same one that's always there, and I want to scream at him to fuck off, but I should fuck off too. I should fuck off for letting this go on and on and on.

Suddenly he is right beside me and taking me into his arms and asking if I'm okay because he always wants me to be okay. Not for my sake, I think, but for his own. His guilt brought him here today and as I stand folded in his arms I realize this, as if his guilt is seeping through his skin, and it feels sticky and hard and I don't want to be anywhere near him.

I pull away and start walking back to the kitchen. I tell him that we should eat dinner, even though I am not going to eat a thing because my heart is cut wide open. It is slashed with razors, pulsing like the buzzer he rang only moments before, loud and sharp and rough.

After dinner we are on the couch, the same couch we shared in the apartment I left just a few days ago. I'm pressed against his chest the way his ex-girlfriend was all those years before, when she pulled into his driveway and demanded to know who the whore was.

I think of that now. I think of all the things I didn't know then and of all the things I still don't. My stomach is in knots. We have made this so complicated and it needs to be over. He needs to stop being such a coward and so do I. The suffering caused by holding on is finally starting to outweigh the idea of letting go.

And then he talks.

"This is good, isn't it?"

I don't reply and he continues.

"Don't you wish we could get back to this, the way we were before all this marriage stuff?"

What?

My heart seems to drop many inches in my chest, to land somewhere it shouldn't be, and so it has to beat harder. It beats so hard I wonder if he can hear it, feel it. He still doesn't want me, but he doesn't want to let me go either, and I'm afraid that my heart will literally stop beating because it is just not strong enough to hold on this tightly.

"I love you," he says simply, but still I don't speak, my throat tight from choking back tears of goodbye. "I do baby. I love you so much."

I continue to not speak. I can't. I don't know where my ring is and my dress is hanging in my mother's closet and my dad came to my apartment and took the legs off all my furniture and cried at my kitchen table, but he is here telling me that he loves me.

And then suddenly I want to know why. Why can't this be enough? Why can't I just let him love me in his way and not need it to look like something else? Why can't that be a thing? Could it be?

And so I shift. I shift so that I can look at him, but before I can speak he says, "You know what?"

I swallow. I can't even imagine what he is going to say.

"I don't know," I say softly, feeling like I will throw up from so much not knowing.

"I know that I want you to be the mother of my children."

What? What did he just say? Oh my God. What did he just say?

"I know you probably think that sounds crazy right now, but I've been thinking about it. Guys think about things like that, you know? I'm getting older and I think about it more."

Stunned, I do not say a word, and all at once I know that I cannot. I cannot let him love me in his way and I try so hard. I try so hard to be done, to not be so afraid that letting go will be worse than this, worse than the ache of holding on, the anguish that has made a home in my heart and bones and blood, in my smallest cell overflowing with pain.

"Do you think about it too?" he asks me, and I can't answer. I do think about it too, but not like this.

Then I get up. I get up from the space between his legs where my back has been resting on his chest, and I tell him that I'll be right back. I walk toward the bathroom and almost go inside, but then I don't. I go toward the desk, the green desk that is just mine now. I stand beside it and don't know what to do. I take a breath that comes out shaky and shallow and for some reason I look over at the bookshelf and stop suddenly. I see all the stories there, ones I have read over and over, the same words every time. There is a burning lump in my throat now, a lump that goes all the way to the pit of my stomach, to my soul. It is a flaming ball of regret and shame and loss. It is fear and pain and silence and I just want to collapse from the sadness of it all, from the knowing that I have to let this story go, but I don't know who I am without it.

I hear him moving in the living room and it makes me move too. I step away from the desk and walk into the hallway, head toward him with words on my tongue. But when I get there I still cannot speak.

He is standing beside the chair he sat in less than a month ago when he was sobbing and holding me, packed boxes and broken-down furniture all around us. Then, amid all of it, he had let me walk out the door and leave him behind. He'd let me walk out the door, but now he's come back for me and here I am, letting him come back. Over and over I do this. Over and over the same story.

"You all right?" he asks, and I feel his guilt again, or maybe it's love, love I don't recognize. He comes toward me and pulls me into his arms and the pain is so severe I think I will not live. I think I will simply take my last breath because of this lost love, this slashed with razors heart that sounds loud and sharp and rough.

Three Years Earlier

My friend walked into my house and her eyes did not look right. Just like on the phone, she seemed troubled. I was worried about her and I decided not to wait. I asked if she was okay.

"Yeah, I'm fine," she said, but she looked down. "I just need to tell you something."

I looked at her more closely then, and that's when I felt it. I felt something that seemed to reach across the room and grab my heart, and I knew in that instant that I didn't need to be worried about her. I needed to be worried about me.

I leaned against the counter in the kitchen then, seeking its solid support, but just as suddenly it seemed instead like a cage, keeping me too close to this thing that was going to hurt me. I needed to get away.

My friend must have recognized all of this because she didn't waste another minute. She said a girl's name and asked if I knew her. I knew the name, but I couldn't picture the girl, and I didn't want her to be asking me this. I could feel the counter again, wanted to shove it hard and get away from this. My friend started talking again and I leaned more heavily into the counter. She tried to tell me something, but I didn't want to know.

At least a month ago, she said, my boyfriend had become involved with this girl.

I didn't understand, but then again I did. I leaned into the counter as fear filled me up like a swimming pool, deeper and deeper until I thought I was drowning. I tried to swim.

"No," I told her. "That can't be. We've been doing fine again."

She didn't speak.

Several months before he had moved out of the apartment we shared. We had not been doing well for almost a year, and on a Tuesday I had come home from work to find the king-sized bed gone and replaced with the twin from the basement. The space where the television and its stand had been was empty. The closet had been left with only my clothes hanging on the bar, and I'd run my hand along the empty space where his clothes used to be, before falling to the floor beside the bed from the basement.

My friend was saying something more, but I couldn't hear. I was remembering how he had come back to the apartment that Tuesday night several months before, said that he loved me and wanted to be with me and not anyone else, but that he was just not ready for marriage. He had needed me to understand.

"I love you," he'd said. "I don't want to lose you, but I need you to understand."

The next day I'd been too broken to go to work and had stayed in bed until there was a knock on my door. He'd come back, not to change his mind about moving out, but to talk again. He'd begged me not to leave him, to just give him some space and time to think, and I had told him to take all the time he needed and then to get the fuck out of my life. I had slammed the door behind him as he'd left for his new apartment, the one right next door. He had absurdly moved right next door and I had cried myself in and out of sleep for the rest of the day.

After work the following afternoon, unable to bear the blank spaces he'd left behind, I'd gone to buy a new television and a stand to sit it on. I'd pulled into the driveway next to his with my new purchases and struggled to carry the huge box with the unassembled TV stand in it. Finally, when I had gotten it inside, I set it on the kitchen floor in the spot right between me and the friend who was still talking, who had just told me things I could not hear.

I'd gone back outside then, opened the back passenger-side door and stared at the enormous box with the new television in it, realized there was no way I could get it into the house alone. So I'd turned around, started walking to the VFW across the street when I heard him call my name. He had called my name and it had started all over again.

Moments later the television was inside and he was going back to his new apartment next door to get tools to put the stand together and place it in the living room in the same spot the other one had been, the one he'd taken. Four hours later, I'd crawled into bed next to him in his new apartment, in the bed we'd shared just two days before. I had once more decided to just keep suffering, to hang on, to let him love me in his way.

My friend said my name then and I blinked back my memories and heartache and fear, leaned harder against the counter.

"I don't know what the fuck you are telling me," I said calmly. "Involved? What do you mean involved? He's only been gone for two months. That is hardly time to get involved!"

She simply repeated herself then, told me again that she meant involved, and that we both knew the meaning, and I laughed. I laughed at her and I heard my laugh and I didn't recognize it.

With that, I tried to lean back onto the counter even more, but there was nowhere left to go. There was nowhere. With a defensive smirk I asked my friend, "Have you seen this girl? Have you? He would not have something going on with her."

She just stared at me.

"He was just here anyway," I continued. "We're doing fine. He's been talking about getting married. *He* has been talking about it, not just me talking anymore."

My friend looked away from me then. She just looked away.

Three months after he'd moved out of our apartment, moved into the one next door, he'd decided to move even farther. He had moved back to our hometown, forty-five minutes away, to take a job that together we'd decided he should take. It would be a steppingstone in his career and that would be a steppingstone for us. He'd be more ready for our future when his career was more secure.

At least that's what he had told me.

At least that's what I had believed.

The girl my friend was talking about lived there too. She lived there, but that didn't mean anything.

"We're doing fine," I repeated as I looked across the kitchen, past the space where I had set that television stand just months before. "We are doing fine. There is no way this is true."

I stepped away from the counter, leaned toward my friend with squinted eyes and shook my head. I was challenging her, challenging myself. She looked back at me, said she didn't know what else to say but that she believed it, that there was no reason not to. A mutual friend's sister knew this girl well and for two months she had been telling her all about my boyfriend's relationship with her.

For two months.

Abruptly I leaned back into the counter, let it cut into my lower back. I wanted her to stop talking, to stop fucking talking, but she went on as I leaned into the counter with nowhere left to go.

"It was her birthday last week. He gave her presents," my friend told me.

"That's bullshit," I told her.

"They were lotions," she replied. "He gave her lotions from Bath and Body."

Her words came out fast and unrelenting and I cringed, pushed away from the counter. She continued.

"They've been seen out to dinner together more than once. There was also a party at his apartment. A lot of people we know were there." Then, more softly, she added, "She slept over."

"I don't believe any of this," I yelled. "I helped him move everything into that apartment. All of it. There's no way he's bringing some other girl there. No way."

I knew though. In that deep down place where you know things, I knew, and so I didn't tell her I had not been back there since that first weekend over two months before. I didn't tell her because then she'd know too, and I didn't want her to know. Instead, I surprised myself when I said, "I'll call him right now and ask him because I'm sure this is some kind of bullshit."

Immediately I pulled away from that awful counter and picked up the phone and went to the living room at the other end of the apartment. I didn't want to call, but I wanted to move, wanted to get away from my friend and the kitchen and the horrible words she'd let loose in there.

The television was on, the one I bought after he left, when he lived next door before moving forty-five minutes away. I could see the people on the screen and hear their voices, but I couldn't make sense of it. I couldn't make sense of anything.

My friend entered the room as I dialed the phone and I wanted her to leave, but she sat on the couch across the room and looked at me. I looked away.

The phone rang once as I continued to not look at my friend and she continued to watch me. On the second ring he said hello and I didn't waste any time. I wanted to show her.

I did not say hello to him. I just asked if he knew this girl. Just like that I asked him and just like that he hesitated.

"What?" he finally said, and I flooded with heat.

"Did you not hear me?" I replied.

"Yeah, I guess I know her," he replied simply, but not simply enough, and there was something about his voice. It was something I couldn't identify and didn't ever remember hearing before. There was something about his voice, and my insides twisted and turned and begged.

"You guess you know her?" I said.

"Well, she's a dispatcher for the department," he tried to explain.

"So do you have anything going on with her, because I was just told that you do and I want to know if it's true."

I could hear my voice, loud in my own ears, so loud. I could feel it too. I could feel my voice struggling to protect me, fighting to form a dense wall around my heart that would cushion the blows, not let the poison sink in. But the truth was too strong. I could feel it. It was getting in. It started in my heart and now I could feel it in my head, my throat, my chest, wrapping tightly around everything. He was silent.

"Are you listening to me?" I shouted.

"Yes, I'm listening to you. No, there is nothing going on with her," he said, and there was that something in his voice again. What was that?

"So, there is nothing for me to know?" I persisted.

"Listen," he started. "I'm at work. Can I call you right back?"

I was stunned, could not speak.

"It's just been a really busy shift and I haven't had a chance to eat. I was just about to pick up food. I can call you back in a minute."

I could not believe it. I could not fucking believe it, and that's when I knew. I knew then what I had really already known since the moment my friend tossed those words into my kitchen. I knew what the truth was even as I struggled to protect myself from that awful certainty. My sorrow and anger mixed into a ball of fear like I'd never felt before and finally I spoke.

"I just basically accused you of cheating on me and you have to go. You have to go pick up fucking food. Are you kidding me?"

“Jesus,” he said. “I’m just hungry. I’m hungry and tired and you call me and lay this on me and I can’t exactly do this right now. I’ll call you right back.”

“No you fucking won’t. You will talk to me right now.” I could not believe what was happening and I could hear my voice again, loud in my ears, pounding with fear and pain.

“Have you done anything with this girl?” I demanded. “Have you done anything at all? Because I’ve heard that you have a whole relationship going so there must be something. Oh, but you want to call me back, right? You want to fucking call me back!”

He answered quickly. “No. I do not have anything going with her. I haven’t done anything.” Then he paused and I waited. There was more. I knew it and I waited for it. The silence forced him to speak. “I don’t know. I mean I guess she was at my place when I had some people over one weekend after the bars. I think she was.”

He’d had a party. My boyfriend of over five years had hosted a party that I’d known nothing about even though he’d supposedly only moved out of our apartment, not out of my life.

Supposedly.

I was going to die. The knowledge of this alone was enough to kill me, but there was more. There was so much more and it was getting harder and harder to keep it away. Nausea rippled in my gut.

“You think she was there? You don’t know who was at your house?” I started to scream, rage making a useless attempt to cover the heart-wrenching sorrow. “Are you fucking kidding me? You had a party that I don’t even know about and you just *think* she was there?

“Jesus,” he said, and there was that sound in his voice again. That sound.

"When the fuck did you have an after-hours party anyway? You never told me that."

"I don't remember when. I just asked some people to come over and they told some other people. I ended up with people that I didn't really even know."

I didn't understand what I was hearing. There had been people at his house that he didn't even know? Who the fuck was this guy? Who the fuck was I? What the fuck were we doing? The fear was becoming unbearable, threatening to undo me completely, swallow me up.

"You have to be fucking kidding me!" I snapped. "This is bullshit. I cannot believe this is happening. You work so much you don't have time to see me, but you have time for parties at your house that I know nothing about." I was pacing now, moving back and forth across the living room, back and forth and back and forth, my bangs clenched in my fist.

"What have you done with this girl?" I yelled. "Answer me right now and make it the fucking truth!"

"I did answer you," he said. "There is nothing going on. Let me call you right back and we'll talk about this."

There was that sound again. There was that awful sound in his voice.

"Okay, baby? Can I call you back?" he pleaded. "I'll call you right back."

Right there it was. That sound. I knew that sound, could hear it in my own voice too, so loud in my ears and in my heart, in nearly every fiber now. That awful sound.

It was the same sound in his voice, only coming out in different tones.

It was panic.

"You're never going to tell me, are you?" I asked, my voice suddenly steady.

He sighed heavily then, and just as heavily I hung up the phone.

Just like that, I hung up.

My friend moved on the couch and I looked up, saw her where I'd forgotten she had been sitting, watching and listening as everything unraveled, and there was sadness in her eyes as she said softly, "Do you have a phone book?"

I knew right away what she meant, who I had to call.

"Yes," I told her. "I do."

With a jolt I awaken long before my alarm. I'm alone in bed and my pillow is soaked with my loss and I wonder when I started crying.

Years ago, I think. Years ago.

I've been crying for so long and am so exhausted, but still I cannot sleep. I get up and urgently try to shake off this dream I've just had, only it isn't a dream. It is a memory that haunts me still and cuts at my heart.

"I know that I want you to be the mother of my children," he'd said to me last night, and I had choked back heartache and he knew. He knew that I was devastated, but he ignored it and accepted when I said that I was just tired. Maybe he also knew, when I said goodbye moments later, that I was begging myself to let it be the last.

Exhausted by regret and self-doubt, I start to make breakfast, but halfway through my stomach hurts, and I toss the toast in the trash and sit on the couch. I stay there for a half hour, just sitting. I don't turn the television on or lie down or even move. I only stare straight ahead or sometimes turn to gaze out the window. That's all I have in me, just enough to sit and sometimes turn.

Finally I start to realize how paralyzed I am and I get pissed, pissed that I continue letting this happen to me over and over and over again, that still I cannot live without someone I can't live with either.

He cheated on me close to three years ago and yet I said yes when he unlocked my apartment door the following year with the key I never took back, knelt at my bedside and proposed at midnight on my thirtieth birthday.

I still said yes.

And I said yes again when he asked to have dinner last night, even though less than a month ago I put my diamond on the bathroom counter and hired movers and found this new place.

What the fuck, I think. Just what the absolute fuck!

My anger propels me off the couch and toward the green desk. I can see its large bottom drawers and think I'll open them up and take everything out. I'll sort through it all, reorganize it so things fit better, make more sense. I stop at the threshold of the room though, suddenly overwhelmed with grief that I know is not just from this. It is not just from this, but I don't know where it's from.

I move away from the desk and toward my bed, and when I crawl in it reminds me of only weeks ago, after I'd yelled at my sister on the phone, told her to send the notes, tell everyone. Now that canceled wedding is just a month away as I reach for the pillows and then for my cell. I pick it up and call in sick, so sick.

I am sick and hurt, wounded deep down inside of me, in a place nobody ever told me about, a place I have found in my own way, and I can't believe how bottomless and packed it is, like the basement of a house that I have always lived in but haven't really known. Over the years I have shoved many things into that basement, then looked away, never checked on them again, didn't even remember what was down there anymore. I have been living just above all the stuff, not able to go through it, to ever search that deep. Until now.

Now I am finally going down there and finding that everything is a terrible mess. It is such a terrible mess that it is no wonder I have felt so bad. But how did it get like this? How?

My eyelids start to fall then because so much pain makes you weak and tired, and I am only a breath away from sleep when I am startled awake. I'd forgotten to turn off my alarm clock and the sound is awful. It is loud and sharp and rough. It is as I imagine fear and doubt might sound, self-loathing and worthlessness.

Like a buzzer.

CHAPTER FOUR
Bathroom Mirror

Later that morning, I step out of the shower and stand in front of my bathroom mirror, having hoped that the water would wash my sorrow down the drain with the shampoo, but it hasn't. Instead, as I wrap the towel around myself, I still feel exposed, vulnerable, unsure.

I think now about how I'd gotten the phone book out of the bottom drawer of the green desk and called the girl, the one he'd given lotions to on her birthday. She hadn't wanted to talk to me, thought I was a crazy ex-girlfriend who couldn't let go. She didn't know I'd set up that entire apartment she'd been sleeping in. She didn't know he had told me he was on nightshifts and couldn't see me for a while. She didn't know that just a week before she met him he'd said that he wanted to marry me and asked me to wait for him.

She told me that she didn't know any of it and that she didn't understand. I said that I didn't either.

I didn't understand, but he begged me to forgive him and I did, until a year later when nothing about us had changed. Another year had escaped my life when finally I got sick of being devastated all the time and I went to his apartment forty-five minutes away and unloaded a small box of his things and refilled it with a small box of mine. Then I walked out, leaving a note and his key on the kitchen counter, and I did not hear from him and I cried every day.

Until a week later.

On the eve of my thirtieth birthday, he unlocked my apartment door at a few minutes before midnight and snuck into my bedroom, knelt beside my bed. Rubbing the sleep from my eyes, I watched as he got down on one knee with a small box in his hand, that one with the tiny hinges.

I sit up in my new bed now, the bed I had to buy because we don’t share one anymore. I sit up much like I did the night he knelt at my bedside, and I wonder how I could ever have thought we’d be okay. How could I have thought we’d ever be anything other than what we were, what we still are?

Suddenly I feel sick to my stomach and I get out of bed. I walk across the hallway and find myself standing again face to face with an image I don't want to see.

Two And A Half Years Earlier

I was standing in front of his bathroom mirror on the morning of my friend's wedding, the Fourth of July. Only six months had passed and it was still hard to be in his apartment, where he'd had another girl and given her birthday presents and slept beside her.

I wrapped the towel around my hair and put my pajamas back on. I walked out of the bathroom and into his room to rummage through my suitcase and that's when he entered, a sweet grin on his face.

"Don't go to the wedding," he said. "Let's go out on the boat instead." He moved in then, wrapped his arms around me and lifted me off the ground. I clung to him tightly, too tightly.

"Mmm, I wish I could," I whined, then didn't say anything more.

He couldn't go with me to the wedding because he'd not yet asked me to marry him and so he wasn't invited. Only couples were invited. Only real couples.

We let go and he kissed me gently and I walked around him, heading toward the bathroom again. I looked back before I went in though, found him gazing at me with a small smile on his lips, and when our eyes met he told me that he loved me.

And that's why I always stayed. Because I always looked back and because he always said that he loved me.

Entering the bathroom, I shut the door behind me and put my hands on the counter, lowered my head before looking up into my reflection. I stood this way for a long time, my hands framing the sink and my eyes looking back at me, wondering who I was.

Forty-five minutes later, heartache subsided and makeup perfectly applied, I was turning in the mirror and pretending I could not see my panty lines under the formfitting yellow dress that looked better than I'd expected. I walked into the living room.

"You can't see my underwear lines, can you?" I asked as I stood in front of him.

"Yes, you can totally see your underwear lines," he said quickly. "But shit, you look amazing."

"I cannot look amazing with panty lines showing," I said.

"Then just don't wear any," he answered.

"What?"

"I'm serious. Don't wear any," he smiled shrewdly.

I thought for a moment and then started back toward the bedroom. In front of the mirror I reached under my dress, slipped my underwear off, and pulled the dress back into place. I smoothed everything out just as he walked in.

"You look so hot in that dress and you need to get back home already," he teased, then pulled me into him.

I held on. I held on as I looked up over his shoulder and wondered how many things in this room she'd touched. How many?

The doorbell rang then and we let go as he reminded me that I had said I'd be home around ten o'clock and that he would be waiting, waiting to take the dress off. I raised my knee to feign scolding, and as I did so I realized how uncomfortable it felt not to be wearing underwear, more vulnerable and exposed than usual. A sudden sense of dread moved in then, a sense that I couldn't explain. But then again I could.

"I have to put my underwear back on," I said.

"No you don't," he insisted. "I'll get the door. You get your purse and stuff."

"Everyone will know," I worried.

"Nobody will know, baby. You can't tell."

"You really think it's okay?" I asked.

"It's okay," he told me.

Hours later, at the bar just outside the ballroom, I stood with my friends from childhood. One had been in my kitchen just six months before, backing me up against the counter, and the other one knew about that. We didn't talk of it though. We each sipped another glass of wine and talked instead about our hometown and pretended that I was happy and that it didn't bother me to be at our friend's wedding alone.

"God, I love you fucking girls," said one of them, and we all laughed. We hadn't seen her in a couple of years and she'd come on her own from Georgia because her husband had decided not to attend. He'd been invited though. They were a couple, a real one.

On that note, we ordered more drinks and laughed and wrapped our arms around each other as we carried our new glasses into the ballroom. The friend from my kitchen excused herself to rejoin the wedding party, and Georgia and I went to find our table. When we did, we were surprised. Our friend and her husband were there, the two who'd picked me up and were supposed to bring me home later, but the rest of the table was filled with people we didn't know. It was filled with single guys, six of them.

"This'll be fun," Georgia whispered to me as we came upon our seats, so many gazes on us. It got very quiet as we stepped in closer and pulled out the last two chairs.

"Hey," said one of them as he stood and looked me directly in the eyes. He wore a crisp white shirt with a black and purple tie and extended his hand and his name first to my Georgia companion, even though his eyes stayed with me.

He asked our names then and repeated mine, said how nice it was to meet me as his eyes went to my yellow dress, traveled the length of it, the one without panty lines.

Our friend who was married, whose husband had driven us there, slapped my leg then. I jerked out of the moment and looked down at her and laughed before tumbling into my chair and bantering with the two of them while the other singles at the table leaned in, extending hands as we all figured out how we were connected to the bride and groom.

But the guy in the purple and black tie hardly looked away from me, and each time my glance found his he would smile and I'd try not to look back, but I always did. That was my thing. I always looked back.

Georgia exchanged a few words with one of the groom's friends next to her and then swiftly turned to me and asked, "You need another, right?" She eyed my nearly empty glass and before I could answer she grabbed my hand and pulled me into her. We stumbled and laughed and turned toward the door that led to the bar. Then we heard a voice behind us.

"I'll join you," said the guy in the purple and black tie, one of his friends not far behind. The four of us reached the bar together and as I stood there talking to Georgia, I could feel this guy's eyes on me, on my yellow dress.

"It fits you like a glove," my boyfriend had said, only he wasn't there. He hadn't been invited because after six years he had still not asked me to marry him and after six years he'd cheated on me too. Only married couples were invited to this wedding, and probably only people who hadn't cheated.

I felt that familiar lump in my throat and quickly raised my glass to wash it down with my last sip of wine, something sweet and tangy to cover up all of my broken pieces. As the drink slid down my throat, I looked over the rim of the glass and found once again the bright eyes of the groom's friend, another wide smile on his face. He set his drink on the bar and moved past our friends, reached for me. The dread was there again, the discomfort. But there was something else too.

"Dance with me," he said.

"Dance with you? There's no music," I stated.

“We don’t need it,” he told me.

"What the fuck am I supposed to do?" someone whispered.

"Dude, just let 'em sleep."

"I have to wake her up. She's gotta call him."

"I doubt it matters when she calls. The damage is done."

Damage? What damage?

"Sweetie," someone said quietly. "Hey."

Was she talking to me? Where was she? I wanted to find her, but I didn't know where I was and I didn't know why everything was so heavy. It was all so heavy and I didn't understand, except in some part of my brain I did. In some part of my brain I knew something, but it kept slipping away. I couldn't hold on.

I heard more whispering then and I tried to move toward it, but I couldn't feel my body. I could feel nothing except my head full of jagged rocks rolling around, so massive and sharp. My eyelids seemed glued shut, my mouth full of paper. Why couldn't I move?

Then suddenly, oh my God.

A blurry and jumbled memory came, the kind that creeps in slowly and slips away fast. It left something behind though. It left the beginning of panic, a fear that lodged deep in my belly and rose up in waves. I tried to ignore it, to focus on the room, but it had become utterly still and quiet so that the panic had space to shift and bubble, become stronger and more alarming. I struggled in a desperate attempt to lift my heavy eyelids, but they would come only partly open. Even that was too much. My brain had trouble with the slivers of light, so weighted with sleep and pain and with something else too.

Then, like someone wounded, gently I began to lift my head, and that's when I felt for the first time a pillow beneath my face and that's when I saw something. All of a sudden I just saw.

I saw myself stepping into a boat and falling. A guy was reaching for me, helping me up with one hand and holding a beer with another, and then I was on his lap and I was kissing him, a glass of wine dangling at my side. Fireworks were going off, and in their light his features became visible. I could see him. I could see the groom's friend, the one with the purple and black tie who liked my yellow dress and asked me to dance.

Oh. My. God. No!

Terror shot though me, a fear full of knowing and still not knowing. I felt like I was going to throw up and suddenly my eyes just burst open and the light poured into them and the pain was awful. It was in my eyes and my head and my body and soul. With great effort then, my limbs so clumsy and full of weight, I heaved myself so that I went quickly from my stomach to my back and in the process I felt something sickening. It was something so terrible that despair and nausea overwhelmed me and I lost my breath.

Almost choking, I lifted the sheets to find that it was so.

I was completely naked under sheets I didn't remember.

The door opened then. Voices entered, the same ones I'd heard before. I turned my head toward the movement and saw my friend from Georgia. It was her voice I'd been hearing, and the voice of a guy too, maybe the one who was following behind her now. He looked familiar.

"Good morning sleeping beauties," she said, her voice high and strained, searching. With great effort I found a small smile, tried to pretend I wasn't horrified. She smiled back and it looked like mine. Forced. Sorry.

I opened my mouth to say good morning, to sound normal and not destroyed, but suddenly all the air was sucked from my lungs because something next to me moved. There was someone in this bed with me and I hadn't known they were there.

Only really, I had known it all along.

I was still looking toward Georgia as I closed my eyes and felt the weight and size beside me, ached for the forgiveness I knew would never come. I turned in his direction and he reached his arm across my body and quietly pulled me to him and I didn't resist, so dazed and scared, limp with disgust and regret. My friend sat on the bed across from me and said my name. I turned my head to look at her, one slow tear escaping the corner of my eye. She was smiling until she saw it hit the pillow and then she straightened and said my name again.

It is always serious when they say your name, I thought. Always serious.

Scared to death, I turned back toward the person next to me and began to pull myself away, to put enough space between us that I could see his face, unsure what I would find. I didn't know who I was waking up next to or why I was in that hotel room or how I didn't ride home with my friend and her husband. And I didn't know where my yellow dress was either. Where was my yellow dress?

His eyes were closed and I pulled back some more and he opened them and I pulled back some more and then I could see. I could see right into his face and it only took a moment to realize it was him. It was the guy who had surveyed me from head to toe when we first met, the one in the crisp white dress shirt with a black and purple tie who later I had staggered toward the dance floor with. It was the same one I was kissing in the boat with fireworks all around us and another scene appeared then too, a fragmented memory that seemed like maybe just a dream. But it wasn't.

I could see him standing across from me as I sat on the bathroom counter examining a cut on my leg, a half-full glass of wine beside the sink. I could see him helping me get down from the counter and how I'd fallen into him. I could see how I had laughed as he caught me, tried to move away as he kissed me and his hands found the zipper of my yellow dress.

"Oh my God," I said, as I threw my palms to my forehead and inhaled deeply, just trying to breathe. I wanted to sink into the mattress and stay there, hidden and immune, maybe dead. Everything made sense and nothing made sense at all and I was awake with the full grief of it.

"Good morning," he said tentatively, and gave my shoulder a gentle squeeze. I didn't speak. I looked away from him and toward my friend, trying to understand.

"Hey," she said quickly, "do you want these guys to leave so you can get up?"

I swallowed hard, choked down my shame. "Yes," I said. "I do."

The phone rings and wakes me up. I look to the clock and see that it is lunch time in my classroom, but I am not where I'm supposed to be because last night he told me that he wants me to be the mother of his children and so I can't move. I feel as heavy and broken as I did the morning after that wedding, waking up to all sorts of choices I don't even remember.

My phone is still ringing now as I think about how Georgia had gotten the guys out of the room and then brought me a pair of her pajama pants and a T-shirt. I remember how I'd fumbled with the tie on the pants because I couldn't see through my tears and how she'd taken the strings and tied them for me and told me that she was sorry. The last time she'd seen me I had not appeared like someone who would wake up missing hours and hours of the night, naked and suffering.

My phone is still ringing, his name on the screen. I don't answer. Instead I remember. I remember Georgia telling me how he'd shown up at the hotel that night, that he'd looked for me for over an hour, made demands. I remember her telling me about the tears in his eyes when she told him that she'd call as soon as she found me, but she never did.

She never found me.

My phone stops ringing and it is too quiet now as I think about how I'd vomited twice before we'd opened the door of that hotel room I'd woken up in. We turned down the hallway then and that's when the guy I'd spent the night with came around the corner and stopped in front of us, reached out for me and said that he wanted to see me again, asked if he could give me his phone number. I almost threw up once more, could not even look at him as I slowly crumpled into my friend and she told him that I was just having a rough hangover and needed to get home. He had called out to me as she'd ushered us past and asked if he could do anything and if my leg was all right.

My leg, I remember thinking then. What happened to my leg? What happened to me?

My phone starts ringing again now as I think about getting back to Georgia's hotel room that morning, slumping on the side of the bed near the wall and dialing the phone. As soon as he heard my voice he called me a bitch and a slut, and I'd doubled over then, my head to my knees.

He had never called me names before. Never. He might have slept with someone else and lied about it, lied about all sorts of things, but he'd never called me names.

The phone is still ringing now as I think about how he'd hung up on me, and how Georgia had taken the phone and called my mother. My mom had answered before the second ring, expecting the call, and I had waited for her in the lobby. When she pulled up, my friend opened the passenger's door and I stumbled in, still wearing Georgia's clothes and carrying my yellow dress.

The phone is still ringing now and finally I say hello.

"Hey baby," he says. "How's your day going? You at lunch?"

I don't reply because I'm still thinking about that morning after the wedding, driving in pained silence with my mother, both of us hurting. We rounded the corner to enter her street and I saw him, his police car idling in her driveway. She turned to me and told me not to go with him. I could never not go with him though. I could never not go.

"Are you okay?" he asks now, even though he doesn't want to know.

"No," I say. "I'm really not."

He sighs heavily. He doesn't want this burden. I can't say I blame him. I don't want it either, this burden that is me.

The hardest parts should be over by now, I think. But they aren't. The worst is yet to come. Not being his greatest love and not hanging on and hanging on and hanging on. That is still to come. That hurt will be even more than this.

That's why I haven't done it.

The phone is still to my ear and he is saying things as I walk down my short hallway and into the bathroom, stare at my reflection again. I watch my lips move but hardly understand what I am telling him as I begin to cry, my gaze following the tears that drop down my face. He responds to my words and to my crying, but none of it matters. He can't save us and he can't save me. I have to do it.

I have to save myself.

So I hit end on my phone.

I hit end.

Then I just stare into the bathroom mirror.

CHAPTER FIVE
Sixty Days

It was sixty days yesterday. It was sixty days since I hung up that phone, and yet still I am stunned. In my pajamas in the late morning, sitting on my couch with hair a mess and teeth not brushed, I remain stunned.

All day yesterday I thought my phone would ring. I thought there would be a knock at my door. I searched email and checked text messages. I looked out the window into the parking lot.

Nothing then. Nothing now.

I wrap the blanket more tightly around me and think over and over about what I've done, about that morning in November, sixty-one days ago, when I stood in the bathroom mirror and hit end on my phone. I think about how I had been devastated and relieved when he'd called back, told me again how he wasn't ready to give up.

I said that he already had.

Again now, I pick up the phone. I hit the buttons that lead to my list of names and numbers and I see his. I stare at it for a while. Then I hit more buttons and wait as the phone rings. My sister answers almost immediately and I realize I am crying as I say hello.

"Oh," she says, and then my name, because it's serious when they say your name, and this is serious. "I'm so sorry. I know."

I cry and I pace, and then I burrow back into my spot on the couch with my bangs in my fist as I beg her to understand, as I beg myself.

"I've loved him for over eight years of my life," I plead. "I don't know how I can not love him anymore. I just don't know how."

"I know," she says, because what else can she say?

"I can't never talk to him again. I can't," I gulp between painful tears.

"Well, maybe you will," she tries, because she cannot stand my torment. She wants nothing more than to soothe me, even if it means lying a little, softening the jagged edge of what we both know is the truth. She is like my dad, like that day all those months ago when he gathered himself and boldly said that he did not know.

"Honey," he'd said. "I just don't know if I can walk you down the aisle to this man."

And because it was my dad, quiet and calm, not laden with heavy intentions, I broke. The windshield of my life that had been cracking and splintering seemed to shatter all at once as his words sank in and washed away my voice and my breath, made it hard to tell him that I knew he was right. In the pause, he tried to soothe me, to lie a little, but he had already said it. He had already spoken the truth and you can't take back the truth.

My sister listens now. She listens and listens, and then after a half hour I remember that she has a life and a heartache of her own and I hate that I have taken up so much space with mine and I tell her that I am sorry. I am so sorry. She tries to tell me that she's fine and that my burdens are greater, but I hate that I can't be better than this and I tell her that I have to go. I say that I love her, but I have to go.

I hang up.

She calls back.

I don't answer.

It has been two months since I told My Ex what I'd heard on TV, what a relationship expert had said about long-term relationships in crisis, an expert I can no longer name and who I want now to find and kill. I am thinking, "Fuck you relationship expert. Just fuck right off."

The phone is still in my hand long after I hang up with my sister and numbly I start to scroll again through my contacts. I stop. I stare at his name and number and soft tears roll down my cheeks. My stomach is tight and my head hurts. It hurts so badly. It hurts from old pain and new pain and all pain, pain I don't even understand. It is mixed into one cocktail of heartache and it is going to make me call. I don't want to do it, but someone has to. That's what the rule says. After sixty days someone has to call and ask to get back together. Someone has to call.

But there is another option too.

Nobody can call. Nobody can call and it can just end. Finally it can just end.

I double over on the couch and cry.

Time goes by. I don't know how much. It's enough to be able to sit up straight again though, and to look around the room, where suddenly everything seems awful. I toss the phone on the couch and jump up, walk deliberately to the hall closet. I open it up and begin pulling everything out. I pull out neatly folded towels and sheets. I pull out well-placed bins of supplies and perfectly stacked rolls of toilet paper. I put it all on the floor or in the room right next to me, on top of the green desk.

Then I start rearranging. I rearrange everything.

I refold all of the neatly folded towels and sheets. I position them in piles facing different directions than they were before. I replace all of the bottled products so that they are even more strategically aligned according to height, and I restack the toilet paper rolls so that they form a pyramid. It takes me an hour.

I stand back then and I think that it is better, but suddenly I realize that it is not, and so I move the blow dryer and straightening iron to new spots. They are side by side now and it makes more sense. I move a bin of bottled products to a place beside a stack of newly folded towels. I refold the sheets so that they are more compact. I arrange the toilet paper in a new pyramid.

It takes a half hour more.

Finally I start to feel some relief. I make one last adjustment and then close the closet door and go back to the couch. I sit down, but the relief doesn't last. It never does.

Frantically, I reach for my phone again, think of all the messages stored inside, and open the flap with such force that it slips from my hands and hits the floor with a thud that I feel in my head, in my stomach. Everything seems slashed wide open and loose, falling out like the drawer of the green desk.

With the phone in my hands again, I quickly open the flap. I hit the left top key and scroll two clicks to option three. Messages. I scroll down to my inbox. I have to go back pretty far. It has been over two months.

I come upon texts from friends and family on New Year's Eve and the pain of their words is still fresh, less than two months old. They are not wishing me a happy new year but wishing me well on the night that should have been my wedding.

I scroll past. I move quickly. I find them. I find words from him and it is like being visited by a ghost and I have chills as I desperately devour every letter and then scroll back further and find more words and read them just as hungrily, a deep suffering in my bones and in my heart.

I stop on a thread from October sixteenth, almost four months ago, just days before I called off our wedding, more than a month before I packed my things. Physical pain moves through my body as I recall these messages that I did not respond to, the ache of his apologies, so many of them. Reading, I am almost transported back to the hotel room I was in when he sent these, the day after my dad had said those words about not walking me down the aisle, the day after other things too.

Now it's been months and months and I am still here, still scrolling through our old messages and patterns and all of the pain I won't let go of. It has been over sixty days since a relationship expert on television said that if a long-term relationship is in crisis then partners should spend a minimum of sixty days apart, with no contact whatsoever, and on or about the sixtieth day one should contact the other. That's what the rule says. At the end of this time someone calls and they make decisions.

Or nobody calls. And that is a decision too.

Today is the sixty-first day.

As if drugged, I drop my phone on the coffee table and slide onto the floor beside it. It is only Saturday afternoon, and the thought of going through the rest of the weekend without him wanting me back saturates me, soaks me in pain and fear. I feel weak and ashamed and I don't want to pick up that phone. I don't want to need him, but I don't know how to be with just myself either. I don't know how to be.

Suddenly I crawl around to the front of the coffee table and open the middle drawer. I start taking everything out, pouring it all onto the floor, unused candles and candleholders that are already neatly arranged, but that I must sort again.

I know this is useless, but still I cannot stop.

After a short time, I have them all separated into small containers and ready to go back into the drawer, but suddenly I can't do it. I can't do any of this.

I reach for the phone. I open the flap and hit the top right key. I press J. I scroll down and highlight his name, even as I remember that weekend in October just over four months ago, how my dad had said, "Honey, I just don't know if I can walk you down the aisle to this man."

The pain of holding on has become just as terrible as the thought of letting go and yet still I grasp. I grasp and grasp, and then I press call.

Four Months Earlier

I pulled into our driveway at about four o'clock Sunday afternoon and his truck was there. He was home and it didn't make any sense at all. What it made was my stomach hurt.

We're engaged and living together again, I reminded myself, as I positioned my car beside his. Things are different now and not everything has to be a threat. I can be safe.

I pulled the key out of the ignition and grabbed my purse, had barely closed the car door and was halfway to the house when I realized I wasn't breathing and I was running and I had bags in the trunk that I was leaving behind. I needed to slow down, act normal. Not everything out of the ordinary had to be an emergency, I said to myself. The other shoe doesn't always have to drop. Get the bags.

I took deep breaths, turned around and walked to the trunk, tried to convince myself that his changes in plans didn't have to mean anything awful, didn't have to mean I wasn't enough. He was home, but the game he had supposedly gone to see was still in session. So what? There could be reasons that didn't mean anything about me.

Bags in hand, I put the key in the lock and turned it as I pushed the door open and stepped into our kitchen. It was quiet, too quiet.

I shut the door behind me and set the bags on the kitchen floor, then listened for sounds from the living room at the other end of the apartment. I heard nothing but the beat of my own shaky heart.

Our bedroom was right off the kitchen near where I'd entered. The door was closed and I softly crossed the few steps to get to it, then stopped and listened again. This time I could hear something. It was the faint whir of the fan we used when we slept. I placed my left hand on the doorknob and turned it slowly, looked down at my beautiful engagement ring as I gently pushed the door open. The buzz of the fan became louder and I could see the bed. It was not as I had left it, but was completely unmade, the pillows on the floor and the blankets in a heap. Everything was a mess.

Then I saw him, his hand really. I saw his hand and my stomach fluttered.

He was asleep in our bed with his hand sticking out, but he had needed to leave the night before so that he could get up super early to tailgate before this really important game, a game so important that he didn't even stay for it. And that seemed like nothing, but I knew it was something.

I started slowly to back out of the room, thought I'd wait for him to wake up, give myself time to work it out, be careful, think. But I couldn't. With one step backward I felt as though I was sinking, and that if I moved any further out of that room I would drown in deceit and pain and knowing without knowing. I had to kick and struggle my way to the surface so that I could breathe. That's the only way I knew how to be. That's the only way I knew, even though it never really worked. It never fucking worked.

So I continued into the room until I was standing at the side of the bed. His head was turned toward me and I looked directly into his sleeping face, searching for answers, kicking and struggling. Then I whispered his name. His breathing changed a little, but he did not respond. I whispered louder and he turned his head away from me and took in a deep wakening breath, then turned back in my direction.

"Hey baby," he said sluggishly, without looking up.

"Hey," I replied, calm, measured.

"Where were you?" he asked, and finally turned his head toward me.

I wanted to scream. Where was I? Where the fuck were you?

"Shopping," I answered quickly. "Why are you home?"

He paused, always that pause. "We just decided to beat the traffic after the game."

Don't kick, I thought. Don't struggle. It never works.

"But the game is probably just ending right now. You must not have seen even half of it."

He sighed. "They weren't doing well so we decided to leave."

I tried to let that sink in, but it just wouldn't. Instead, I was the one sinking, and the information he was giving seemed to float somewhere above, forcing me downward. I could feel his words hit deep inside of me, the pain like a dull ache on a rainy day. I knew that things were not right. I just knew.

"Did you tailgate at all before the game?

"Not really," he replied.

Don't kick, I thought. Don't struggle.

"I thought that was the whole point of going up last night?" I questioned.

"It was," he said, clearly getting bothered.

"So why didn't you do it?" Maybe kick a little. Struggle some.

"I told you earlier," he said in an even more irritated tone, "because we stayed out too late last night and just didn't get up."

Sinking.

Sinking, sinking, sinking.

"That makes no sense," I said.

He didn't respond and I continued. "So why did that happen? Why did you stay out so late when tailgating this morning was supposed to be so important? What were you doing?"

Here we go. Now for the kicking and struggling. It had been a valiant effort, but when you are sinking what choice do you have?

"Jesus Christ," he said under his breath, then turned his head away before moving onto his side.

It was then that I felt it, with those words and deep breaths and turning away, the beginning of our ending, like a windshield hit with another small pebble, another damaging crack, pain deep inside of me like a dull ache on a rainy day. I felt it mingle with all of the other cracks from all of the other pebbles that had been flying toward me for so long as I'd swerved and changed course and tried not to let the windshield completely shatter in my lap. This time though, I could not swerve fast enough or maybe far enough. That pebble hit and the crack grew, a fracture spreading across all of the glass, across all of my heart.

I wanted to punch him and kick him and make him into a thousand fucking pieces, but instead I turned and left our room, walked the length of our apartment and back again, the length of our apartment and back again.

Back and forth, back and forth. Always back and forth.

It was then that I remembered all of the groceries and other items in the bags I'd carried in, the bags I'd carried along with my fear and pain and self-doubt. I started to pull the new items out, but quickly stopped, opened cupboards and started rearranging what was already in them. I went to the drawers too. I sorted and purged and reorganized and shifted and cried.

Twenty minutes later I was ready to stand back and look, to welcome the familiar relief that comes from putting everything in its place. I waited and waited, but the relief did not come and instead I just felt the crack stretching across the windshield of my life, making a web of sorrow so jagged and loose and exhausting that before I really knew what I was doing I had gone back toward the bedroom door, gently pushed it open.

The buzz of the fan was there again and I could see him lying awake in bed. Then, as if nothing had happened, I pulled off my jeans, put on his oversized sweatpants and wrapped the elastic ankle bands around my feet. I crawled in next to him, put my head on his chest as he wrapped his arm around me and we tried to patch the glass.

Everyone knows you have to replace the entire windshield though. Everyone knows.

He kissed my forehead and I asked, "So, who got the short straw?"

He'd gone to Buffalo with two other police officers and they'd all agreed to draw straws to determine who got a cot because, for the sake of money, they had reserved only one room with two queen-sized beds. The cot would allow them to avoid the awful chance of sleeping with another guy and having toes touch in the middle of the night, but nobody had willingly agreed to take the inferior sleeping arrangement, so I found myself wanting to know who got the short straw.

Really though, I'd wanted to know other things, but decided to start with this.

"Bullfrog," he said lightly, using the nickname I had given one of his friends several months before, even though I had never met him. I had not met any of the guys he'd gone on this football trip with, not one of them.

"Let's take a nap," he said then, kissing my forehead again, quieting me. "Wanna nap with me?"

I didn't want to nap. I wanted to tear this wide open and know every fucking detail, to know what I didn't know, but what maybe I did.

"Yeah," I said. "I do."

The phone continues to ring now and I pray for his voicemail, but suddenly he says hello. Just like that he says hello the way he would to anyone, but I am not anyone. His caller ID should have told him that, unless he has taken me out of his contacts the way he has taken me out of his life. I freeze.

"Hello?" he says again.

"Hi," I say, my voice begging to be steady, my heart too.

"What's up?" he asks casually.

Oh my God.

Oh my God oh my God oh my God. I realize in an instant what I have not realized for the last sixty days, longer really. I realize that I have made a mistake more serious than I first thought, one that will cost me dearly, and I don't know what to do. There's no going back, but now I don't know how to go forward either. My head hurts from the cocktail of heartache I have been stirring and am now chugging down.

"I just wanted to say hello," I try.

There is a pause that it is too long and so I speak again, trying not to let his silence crush me.

"You seem busy," I say uncertainly.

There is another pause, always that pause. "I can talk. Just hang on a sec."

I don't hear anything as I sit on my living room floor beside the coffee table surrounded by newly organized candles and holders. They can't help me now though. Nothing can.

"Sorry," he says after a moment. "I'm out of town so it's hard to talk, but I want to," he adds quickly.

He's out of town right now. Oh God, he's out of town. This statement hurls itself at me again and again, and I have to reposition myself, lean against my oversized chair. People go out of town when they're going on with their lives, when they're doing fine. When they are not doing fine, they sit on the living room floor surrounded by newly organized candle holders, still in pajamas, teeth unbrushed.

"You still there?" he asks.

"Yes. I'm here," I say in a voice that sounds loose because I'm coming undone, shattering like a windshield, just shattering. This is so much worse than I had imagined, nothing at all like what I'd imagined actually. Nothing. It is the most awful pain and it is undoing me, like only a final blow can. It is that last crack before the windshield falls into your lap.

"So, what have you been up to?" he asks.

Oh God. He's out of town and I'm leaning here against my chair still wearing pajamas at one o'clock in the afternoon, staring at candles that I scattered across my living room floor. The candles, I think. I have to put the candles back. I get onto my knees and crawl over to them, holding the phone with one hand and picking up a box with the other. Desperate.

"Um, not too much I guess. I just wanted to say hi, see how you are." I leave him with that as I put the container that now holds only votives back into the drawer.

"I'm good. Work sucks though. I'm workin' a lot of overtime. How's school?"

I pick up another small crate of floating candles and place them in the drawer beside the box I just put in. I'm not breathing.

"It's good," I say, but it comes out as just a whisper because there is not enough air to make the words. I move around the containers that are already in the drawer, make room for the last one. I pick it up.

"Good," he says, and I think that I can't believe this is what we have to talk about. It has been eight and half years and sixty-one days and all the love I had to give and this is what we have to talk about. The pain all over my body is unbearable.

"Well, I'll let you go," I say, and I hear these words and I don't mean them and I feel destroyed. I put the last container in the drawer and place the bigger candles and the holders around them.

"I'm glad you called," he says.

Oh no. Oh no, no, no. He's going to hang up. He's going to let me go. He already has, but this time it's going to be the end, the real end. It's going to be the real end and I will have lost him and it will be over forever and a new kind of suffering will begin and I can't even think.

"Yeah," I say, then start to feel desperate. I stand and walk briskly from the drawer with the newly arranged candles, leaving it open. That final step of closing it seems like too much right now. The final step seems like just too much.

"So," I say. "I guess you're okay then, huh?"

He pauses, barely. "Yeah. I'm okay. I guess you are too, right?"

Oh my God no. No. I'm not okay. This is the real end and I've done everything I can and there is nothing left to do and I feel like I am dying from this pain. I feel like I'm already dead. But I tell him that I'm okay too. I tell him that I am okay even as I think that I never will be again, that maybe I never was.

"So I'll talk to you later," he tells me, and I can hardly hear him over the drum of my heart trying to pound out its final broken goodbye. You won't talk to me later, I want to say. You won't and we both know it, and we both know this is just a closing remark for the sake of being polite and well-intended, and that is fucking bullshit. We deserve more. We met almost nine years ago and you've been my whole life since then, my whole fucking life. It's like there was never a time before and I don't know if there will be a time after and I can't let go. I cannot let go. You don't know what you're doing. Please don't leave me. Please, please don't.

I prepare to tell him all of this, to fight for us again, to kick and struggle and kick and struggle and kick and fucking struggle.

But then, all of a sudden, I don't.

I don't kick. I don't struggle.

I just don't.

"You there?" he asks.

I'm here, I think. I'm right here, but I'm nowhere really.

Goodbye. I've loved you so much. Do you know that I have loved you so much and that I gave you all I knew how to give? I'm sorry it was never the right thing. I'm so sorry. Can you hear my heart with all of its jagged pieces saying how much I will miss you now that you're gone? I'll miss me too. I'll miss us both. This is the worst pain I've ever felt.

Goodbye.

"Bye," he says.

"Bye," I say, and I wait. But there is nothing. It is only quiet and I look at the screen on my phone and it says that the call has ended.

It has ended.

Four Months Earlier
Continued

An hour later I was waking up alone. The sun had gone down and the room was colored with shadows and I wondered when he had left our bed.

I got up and walked slowly out of the room. He was not in the kitchen, so I turned toward the dining room and saw through to the living room in the back of our apartment. I could tell that the television was on and could see his legs stretched out on the couch. I started walking that way, past the coat hooks lining the wall in the little alcove beyond the kitchen, through the dining room and to the threshold of the living room. As I got closer I saw that he was on the phone.

"Okay buddy. Talk to ya later," he said, then closed the phone.

"Who was that?" I asked lightly.

"Bullfrog," he told me, the guy I'd nicknamed even though we'd never met.

I looked at him, waited for more, but there was nothing, and I knew it would do no good to ask my questions so I swallowed them. But the crack in me started to spread like lacework and suddenly I could not stand to be near him.

I turned and walked back toward the kitchen, found myself standing against the counter, the same one that bit into my back the day my friend walked in and told me about that girl more than a year ago. I needed to move. Just like that day, I needed to move, to get away from the quietness that was so deafening.

I walked into our bedroom and was instantly hit with the unmade bed, messy and out of order. I leaned in quickly, grabbed the comforter and threw it back so that I could smooth and flatten the sheets. The pillows that were on top of it flew out as they always do, but this time they hit one of our small wooden nightstands and it tipped over. I heard it hit the floor and I turned to see his watch and some pennies and his wallet scattered all over the carpet. Numbly I knelt down and picked up the pillows, tossed them toward the bed. I set the nightstand back on its feet and picked up the watch and the pennies, put them back on top, the coins stacked neatly. Then I picked up his wallet.

I picked up his wallet, but I did not set it on the table.

I looked at it, clutched it more tightly, turned it over.

I turned it over and over and over.

Then, all at once, I opened it. I opened it like opening the refrigerator when you are so hungry and have no idea what you want to eat or what you will find, but you know it is something. You know you want something and you know you will find it.

Having the wallet open suddenly felt urgent, and I began rummaging through it quickly with no system, passing briskly over his license, the slots for cards and the pocket that held one- and five-dollar bills. Then I came to the next pocket.

This one was filled with small papers of varying shapes and folds. I rifled through them and saw business cards and coupons and receipts, a lot of receipts. There were receipts for Wegmans, Old Navy and CVS. There were gas receipts and a receipt for Subway, for a Verizon payment and for our dinner out last month. I went through them all. Then I went through them again.

I saw them all a second time, all the same ones, but I knew something was missing. I knew, and this time, in the very back of all the others I had just gone through, I saw one I hadn't seen before. I saw a receipt I had not seen the first time.

It was for Motel 6.

Act normal, I told myself. Just act normal. Not everything is an emergency. The other shoe doesn't always have to drop. Someplace deep inside though, in that place with the dull ache, I knew that things were not right and I started to kick and struggle.

I started to kick and struggle even though I knew it never worked. It never fucking worked.

I pulled it out, the receipt from Motel 6, and took it all in with one sweeping glance, frantic and panicking, hardly able to see a thing. I took a deep breath then and steadied my gaze, looked for what I didn't know. My eyes went to the bottom first, and his name was there, signed in that familiar scrawl. I looked at the top next. It read October 15, 2005, the day before. So far, this was everything I knew. Last night he'd stayed at the Motel 6 before a Buffalo Bills game. There were no surprises as my eyes read those things, his signature, the date, the name of the motel. It was always like that, no surprises until suddenly there were.

Somehow, I knew I had not seen it all though, and so I looked again. Toward the bottom there was an amount larger than I had expected. It read $172.80. That was a lot for one night for one room and it stopped me. I had to think, but I couldn't because things seemed to be happening so fast and then again not happening at all.

I looked toward the middle of the receipt at the left. It stated that there was a room charge of $80.00 plus tax. Why was the total more than twice that then? It didn't make sense and I didn't understand, but then again I did.

I calmed down, looked more closely, and my eye caught a number and a word across from the room charge.

A number and a word.

I told myself to hold on. Just hold on, I said to myself, but time seemed to stop as my eyes focused on the middle of the receipt and my breath ceased and maybe the beat of my broken heart too. I thought then that if you could float up and away from your body and look down on your life laid out all flat and rectangular like a map, there might be a thin red line that divides before and after. That's what it felt like in that instant, like I was standing on that thin red line caught between those two times, before and after.

After was about to happen. Before had passed.

A number and a word.

The number was two. The word was rooms.

"2 Rooms."

In moments, I was standing on the threshold of the living room, my gaze fixed on him as he lay outstretched on the couch, a commercial on television. "What's up?" he asked hesitantly.

His indifference hit me hard then, like a slap to the face, but I wouldn't let the pain land. Instead, I welcomed a sudden jolt of anger. I let rage settle in and get comfortable, not let me fuck around with the truth.

"How many rooms did you guys get in Buffalo?"

"What?"

"Oh, you didn't hear me?" I replied quickly.

"How many rooms did we have?" he repeated.

I waited. I was not going to repeat myself. I had become well versed on this tactic. He'd used it in the past, asking me to repeat my words and repeating my words himself. He did that to buy time. He did that to ease his nerves and formulate stories instead of truth. So I just continued to wait until finally he could not stand the silence and he answered.

Quickly he said, "One. Why?"

"You got one room?" Now I was repeating him. "You only got one room at Motel 6?"

"Yes," he said agitatedly as he sat up. He anchored his feet to the floor. Did he wonder how I knew it was a Motel 6?

I took in a deep breath and let it out in one big huff. I looked him right in the eye. I was not entirely sure what he was hiding and maybe he was hiding something stupid and rather innocent. Maybe, best case scenario, he was just hiding how much money he'd spent because he had wanted his own room simply for privacy reasons and not to screw some stripper or whatever other fucked up circumstances my stomach was creating. It didn't really matter why he was lying though. It only mattered that he was. He was lying to me and I had the receipt to prove it. Like last time, would he lie and lie and lie, even when I had the evidence right in my back pocket?

"Tell me the truth," I told him frankly. "Please just tell me the truth. We've been through this bullshit before. How many rooms did you get last night?"

I heard how completely put together I sounded, anger making a home inside of me, but fractures were splintering off too. I didn't know how long I had.

He stood up then and came toward me, walking as if he was going to pass me, and I stepped into his path. He stopped and looked me in the eye, then looked away. There was only one step between us, just one more.

I said his name and then demanded evenly, "Answer me." Just the fact that I was asking such a particular question should have been enough for him to realize that he might as well answer it truthfully, that I already knew. But he was married to lies. He was married to them and not to me.

Immediately he yelled, "One I said!"

Shocked by his fierce commitment to his own stories I yelled back, "Aren't you the least bit concerned that just like another time, I already fucking know?"

I reached into my back pocket then and pulled out the folded receipt. As I opened it I said that I was sorry I went through his wallet and that I knew it was wrong, but so was this.

Immediately he took the receipt from my hand and stared at it.

"Do you still say you got just one room? Do you still say that?" I was ready for him to back up and sit in the chair, put his head in his hands and tell me the truth.

But he didn't.

Instead he shouted, "This is fucking ridiculous."

At first I thought that what he meant by *this*, was what was happening between us, that what was happening between us was ridiculous. Then I fully saw him. I saw him clutching the receipt and staring at it in mock disbelief. He was looking at its parts over and over again as if he was seeing it all for the first time, and I knew that I would not survive these lies.

"We didn't get two rooms. They fucked up. I'll have to call them," he said plainly.

I could not believe it. I could not believe what I was hearing and I said that. I said, "I absolutely cannot believe you are saying this to me," as steady tears of shock streamed down my face. Not again, I thought. I can't do this again.

"Jesus fucking Christ," he said and shifted to push past me, angry and defensive. His sudden movement pulled me from the hole I'd been sinking into and a new fury suddenly gripped me, pulled me back up so that I could kick and struggle, reach for the receipt and snatch it easily from his hands.

When I had it I said, "You want to call them? So call them. Right now."

"I'm not going to call right now," he said, and then said my name. This was serious, as it always is when they say your name.

"Why not? They supposedly overcharged you by more than eighty dollars. Why would you not call right now?"

"Because I'm fuckin' tired, all right? I want to relax. I'll call in the morning."

The windshield was so broken now I could barely see through it.

"You won't call in the morning," I almost screamed. "You won't call in the morning or ever 'cause you are a fucking liar and you know it."

He walked away from me and I followed, fear and doubt forming a tirade behind him, kicking and struggling.

"Why did you have two rooms? So you could fuck the girl you met up there two weeks ago?" I bellowed. "You know, the girl from the strip club you didn't go to."

Some part of me, some fundamental part deep down really did not believe this particular scenario, but I did believe something was wrong and I had to fill in the gaps before they swallowed me. I had to say something since he wasn't saying anything. I couldn't stand the lies and would rather have the truth be awful, unbearable even, than to not know at all. Not knowing was worse than an awful truth. Not knowing was undoing me.

"What the fuck," he said.

"So call then," I said loudly, trying not to yell. "Call so they can fix this mistake they made."

He reached for his keys in the tray on top of the microwave and then turned to walk past me for his jacket hanging in the alcove. He was going to leave, walk out the door and leave me with all of the gaps and the not knowing. I would rather have died. I would absolutely not be fucking left alone again to pick up the pieces he left scattered all around me, and so I thundered over to our phone hanging on the wall and picked it up. I held the receipt in front of me and dialed the number at the top. He stopped and looked at me. His jacket dangled from one hand, keys from the other.

"Fine, give me the phone," he said then.

"Oh no," I said. "You're too tired. Relax. I'll do it. I'll find out for myself."

I walked over and leaned against the counter while the phone rang at Motel 6. Feigning all sorts of bravery and stoicism, I stared at him as the counter bit into my lower back, reminded me.

"Good evening. Motel 6 Buffalo. How can I help you?"

"Uh, hi, yes," I stammered.

I had no plan. I never thought about what I would say. I never thought it would get this far.

"Um, my husband stayed at your hotel last night," I continued. "He only had one room, but it looks like, from the receipt, we've been charged for two," I said dispassionately. "Would you be able to let me know?"

Let me know what? What did I want to know?

"Yes, ma'am. Could you hold a minute?" Everything happened so fast. It always did.

As the music played over the phone, he walked from the refrigerator to the table. He set his keys down on the place mat and hung his jacket over the back of the chair, his movements slow and calculated, like it was taking tremendous effort. He faced me then with his legs shoulder-width apart and his arms crossed just below his chest. He took in a deep breath and looked at me and I thought he looked like a bouncer at the door to a club, calm but waiting for trouble. He was hoping it wouldn't come, ready if it did.

The woman from the motel came back on the line.

"Ma'am?" she asked.

"Yes," I answered.

"You said your husband stayed with us yesterday, October fifteenth?"

"Yes, that's right."

"And his last name please."

I told her his last name, aware that he was not really my husband, probably never would be now, and then I waited. I waited to the sound of her fingers tapping keys and his calm but expectant look.

"Yes, ma'am, that's right. Your husband was charged for two rooms."

"Right. But he's saying he only had one. Can you tell? Did he have one room or two?"

"Um," she said uncomfortably. Surely that last question alerted her to the fact that *my husband* and I were not likely to agree on this. She continued. "His account does show occupancy in two rooms, Ma'am. He asked for and paid for two rooms."

I had known that she would tell me this, that she would tell me the man I loved was married to his lies and that's why he could never marry me. But still, pain seared through my heart, cut like the glass of a cracking windshield.

"It does," I stated coldly, anger coming to my rescue. Then, so he was clear about what she had said, I added, "Your records show that he did in fact have two rooms?"

"That's bullshit!" he yelled, unfolding his arms and stepping toward me. He reached out and told me to give him the phone. So committed was he.

"Are you sure there's not a mistake? I mean, his account shows that he had two rooms, but how do you know he really did?" I asked. So committed was I to proving this awful truth, proving it beyond a reasonable doubt. There was discomfort on the other end again, silence and a strained cough.

Finally she said, "I see the room numbers, ma'am. Room 118 and room 124. He was given these keys at check-in. I see other account information like no charges for the televisions or the phones. The rooms were cleaned this morning at checkout."

He heard the long pause on my end and seemed to become more troubled, unsure. "Let me talk to her," he repeated, but more quietly, with less conviction.

"And it's not possible that he and his friends only stayed in one of those rooms and you accidentally charged him for the other, when really it was someone else's room?"

"Yeah," he interrupted, and I winced. He'd be willing to accept any story, any lie that sounded more reasonable than his own.

"We really don't make that kind of mistake, ma'am, and we briefly go over the receipt with the guest at checkout. So, no."

"What is she saying?" he asked, worried again.

"She's saying you definitely agreed to paying for both rooms and that you used both rooms. So, basically, she's confirming that you are a fucking liar."

"Give me the phone," he demanded.

"Is there anything else, ma'am?" the woman asked, very uncomfortable then.

"Room 118 and 124, right?"

"Yes, that's right," she verified quickly.

To him I said then, "So which room number wasn't yours?"

"I'm sorry?" said the woman at the motel.

"No, I'm sorry," I said. "You see, *my husband* claims he and his two buddies all stayed in one room, but according to his receipt and you, someone had a room of his own."

"Oh," she said with growing discomfort. "Uh, well, can I help you with anything else?"

"No," I said. "Thank you."

"Wait, let me talk to her," he tried again.

"Thank you for calling Motel 6," she said hurriedly.

I hung up the phone.

"Do you know what you've done?" I asked him calmly. "Do you know?"

"Baby, I haven't done anything," he said softly. "You just think I have."

"That's right," I told him. "I do."

I stare now at the screen, at the words under his name. Call ended. The end. The real end.

I close the phone and slowly stand. I can hardly get up. I don't know why I'm standing or where I'm going, but I'm walking without thinking and tears are streaming down my face as I end up in the spare room with the green desk, our green desk.

The phone is still clutched in my hand when it rings and I'm startled by the sound, but suddenly and beautifully filled with hope as I look down to find his name on the screen.

Only I don't. It is not him.

It is not him and I realize again and again that it is over and that he has told me in every way he can. I have known for months. For years even. The gravity of this hits me hard and I slump down onto the floor beside the desk and I just sob. I sob like I have so many times, so many fucking times. I'm holding the phone in both hands between my folded knees, my forehead bent to the cold metal as I cry the same tears I've already cried because I have made the same mistake after the same mistake after the same mistake.

I remember that moment when I got off the phone with Motel 6, how slowly I'd walked to the wall and hung it up, then without a word went into our bedroom and pulled back the comforter and the sheet. I remember how I'd crawled into bed and reached for a pillow to pull under my head, tired and broken. Gentle tears had poured from my heart and I'd curled into a ball on my side, pulled up the bedding and cried myself into a fitful sleep.

The morning after that, I had removed my engagement ring and placed it on the bathroom counter. He'd found it sometime later that day and moved it to a shelf in our bureau and a day after that it was gone from there and he did not mention it to me again, not ever. That was four months ago. Four fucking months ago and still here I am. Still.

I go on like this for many minutes, fifteen maybe, leaning against the desk remembering and crying and shaking, my body searing with the pain of this loss.

Then finally I stop. I just stop. I stand up and go into my bedroom where I pull back the comforter and sheet, let the movement knock the pillows haphazardly about the bed, much like that day I found the receipt for two rooms. I crawl in slowly, still dressed in my pink striped pajama pants and a yellow tank top in the late afternoon. I reach weakly for a misplaced pillow and pull it under my head as I curl into a ball on my side and close my eyes. I am so tired and broken, nothing but little pieces.

I am nothing and everything is over and it will always be over and I am over too. All the love I had to give is over and I remember when it started and every single bit of joy and hurt that happened and I don't know how all of that can be gone and I don't know how I can go through the rest of my days without him, with just me.

Sixty days.

And sixty more.

And sixty more days.

CHAPTER SIX
Take Me With You

Take me with you.

I read these words over and over the next morning, sitting at my green desk looking through old emails from him, from My Ex. I have stopped on one dated Monday, May 23, 2005, and I am trying hard to understand how so much can unravel in just nine months. It is not enough time and yet it is so much.

He wrote that he did not want me to sign a lease and leave him and he wrote that he was tired and sorry. He wrote that he still wanted to marry me, but that he was scared, and he wrote that he loved me so much and didn't understand what had happened to us. Then he said those four words that I cannot stop reading.

"I hope you don't leave," he said, "and if you do, please, take me with you."

I read it over and over and I read ones before that and after that and I spend so long reading about our life together that I start to see things. I start to see things I hadn't noticed about his love and my doubt, things that make my lap wet from all the new tears that fall. They drip off my chin and leave small round spots on my pants, just like another day I'm remembering now. Just like that day.

I get up from the desk then and I walk into my bedroom, and not surprisingly I kneel at my hope chest. I kneel like I am before a grave, and then I lift the lid. I find my dress folded neatly in the bottom of the wooden box. It is still in its packaging. The cathedral-length veil is placed separately in its own bag and rests on top of the gown.

I lift the veil. I set it on the carpet beside me. I reach back in and remove the gown, unfold it as I gently stand and let it fall heavy to the floor.

I bring the dress to my face then and I try to breath in the silky cream color of it, the hint of a train that puddles at my feet now. I run my hand along the angled seam that spreads across the front of the skirt, then stare sadly at the beautifully beaded silk straps that crisscross the back. I turn my attention again to the front that dips low and is polished with the same drops of silver. I touch them one at a time, trying to let go of this dress that arrived a month after my wedding was called off, that my parents paid for and hung in the closet of a spare bedroom until my sister brought it to me and I placed it in this hope chest with my broken heart.

Then, just as suddenly, I can't stand to hold it any longer and quickly I fold it over again and lay it neatly back in the large cedar box, in its coffin. I replace the veil on top, close the lid and stand up. I turn to my bed, crawl toward my pillows just like that day when we called it all off, when it was supposed to be over.

If only it had ever been that easy.

Nine Months Earlier

I stared blankly out the passenger's window and tears streamed over my cheeks as he drove us down the exit ramp toward the apartment we shared once again, after sharing it and then not sharing it. It was long after the birthday gifts he'd bought for that girl, and more than a year and half after he'd knelt at my bed on my thirtieth birthday and asked me to marry him.

"So," he said slowly. "When do you have to order it?"

His words held so much caution, as if just asking would make it happen, and his dread reached for me then. It reached across the seat and put a hand on my heart and I choked back my disappointment, tried not to drown in the grief of it all.

"Now. I have to order it now," I replied vacantly, struggling to keep the pain to just a gentle stream that would trickle down my cheeks and not be enough to wash us both away.

Slowly then, like the swelling of a finger after it has been slammed in the car door, that old familiar alarm started in the pit of my stomach and began to wind its way to my core and through to my heart. It landed solidly on my tongue and words began to pour out as I tried to save us, as I kicked and struggled.

"I really have to decide by the end of the month. At least by then, but even that's pushing it. I don't know if it would be in time. I guess it would be, but just. I have to decide or it's going to be too late."

Then, just as suddenly, I stopped talking. I became full to bursting with the unexpected awareness that there was nothing I had not already said. Nothing. The tears stopped flowing then and my eyes felt laden, heavy and gritty with fatigue. He didn't speak, but I held the weight of him in the driver's seat next to me, all of his love and rejection rolled up into one heavy mound of pain and uncertainty. I swallowed, wiped my wet cheeks. When I turned toward him I spoke more slowly, pushed the panic back down below my heart, into a place where it could wait.

"I can't keep waiting on everything, waiting and doing nothing," I said, as I waited some more, waited for him to speak. He didn't though. He didn't because he was always waiting too.

"Eventually," I continued, "that actually *is* something, you know? Doing nothing. It is something." I waited again, longer this time.

"That actually *is* something!" I repeated more loudly. Kicking and struggling.

"I know," he said softly and then didn't say anything more until finally, like every other time, the waiting made me angry.

"My always waiting and doing nothing is the something you really want me to do though, right? If I just keep waiting and doing nothing then nothing will happen and that's what you want, isn't it?"

My words came out like bullets and they needed to be said, but I regretted them immediately. Like always, I regretted them because I didn't need to say any of it to him. I needed to say it to myself and I needed to fucking listen for a change.

I felt sick.

"Right?" I demanded.

"I don't know, baby. I just really don't know."

Oh God, don't call me that. Don't break my heart and love me all at the same time.

We were quiet the rest of the way home then, except for the occasional soft sound of me wiping tears off my face, begging for courage. Finally he pulled into our driveway, turned off the ignition and leaned his head back against the seat. I took off my seat belt and reached for the door, but he sighed heavily and the truck filled with his breath and held me in the seat, kept the door closed. He turned to look at me then and I didn't look back. I looked away. I could feel him though, feel him still looking and wondering and deciding until finally I relented. I turned to him, ready to accept the verdict.

He shook his head.

"God, I'm so sorry," he said. "God."

Fresh tears started down my face then, retraced the dried paths of the ones that had come before, and at that moment he reached for me. He pulled me across the seat to him and I went. I went to him like I always did and he held me there until finally I spoke.

Into his chest I said, "Just tell me not to. I want you to tell me not to do it, so that I can let go."

I had to let go of him. I knew it.

I just wanted him to tell me.

I waited then, terrified and expectant, motionless under his heap of wanting and not wanting, before he sighed heavily and said, "Babe, look at me."

I sat up and tried to gather myself into a tower of strength, a tower I could feel collapsing. I knew it was all coming down. I knew, but I didn't know.

He stared at me then. He just stared, and there was no sound between us. It was so unbelievably quiet in that truck in our driveway that I could actually hear the tear that dripped off my chin and left a small round spot on my white stretch capris.

"Order it, baby. Do it."

It took me a minute to hear him, to process the words over the drip of more tears falling off my chin and leaving marks on my pants.

He was saying I could order my wedding gown. He was saying he wanted to marry me. He was saying all of that.

But he wasn't.

Tears continued to drip off my chin.

Drip, drip, drip.

I let them fall as I waited for courage, the courage to let him go, to let myself go too. I waited and waited, but it didn't come. It simply did not come.

And so I ordered my gown. I ordered the silky cream-colored wedding dress with an angled seam across the front of the skirt and beautifully beaded straps that traversed the back, elegant and simple, with only a hint of a train and a front that dipped low and was polished with the same infrequent drops of silver that adorned the crisscrossing delicate straps at the back.

And the whole time I spoke to the saleswoman I thought that I should hang up the phone. I thought that I should hang up and never call back, but instead I let her say that the dress would arrive on about November twenty-first, and there was no way of knowing that by this time my wedding would have been called off for a month and my dad would have already taken the legs off my dining room table and the dress would later be placed in a hope chest with the veil resting on top and I would be in a new apartment, crying beside the green desk.

There was no way of knowing.

But then of course there was every way.

Still, when the saleslady asked if I wanted to schedule my first fitting I replied softly.

"Yes. I do."

An hour after placing the dress back in its coffin, I am roused slowly from an aching sleep by my ringing phone, but I know that it is not him so I don't care. I try to roll over, but even that is too difficult, like dragging my heart, actually dragging it across my body. It is painfully heavy, and in my half sleep I sort of dream of it. I dream of my heart, that it is laden with pounds and pounds of ashes and fallen rock and I am trying to scoop them out with a rusty shovel, but there is a hole in it, and so they keep falling through, the ashes and rock, falling back into my heart and weighing me down again.

A few minutes later, when my message indicator sounds and I cannot stop wondering who left a message, even though I know it is not him, I listen.

"Hi dolly. It's me," she says cheerily. "I just wanted to talk to you about our weekend. I can't wait to see you. Get ready, Little! Call me back, love. Bye."

I put the phone down on the nightstand and I feel terrible. I know I never should have agreed to this visit. Visitors have always made me nervous, threatened my precious need for untouched space and control and solitude, and now it will be even worse. Now I have this grief with me that I want to hold in private, carry around, turn over in my hands, over and over.

All over.

Then at once it is the weekend and she will be here soon, My Big, one of my very best friends from our college sorority days. She's already on her plane, flying in from Long Island, and I'm picking her up at the airport in an hour, even though I don't want her to come and I should have told her five days ago, after she left that voicemail. But I didn't, and so she's coming because she too is going through a breakup and our heartache has been the same, even if hers has required lawyers and signatures and the changing of a name.

Names. They always make everything so serious.

Mine never changed though, and I still read our emails again and again and I still see things, things I don't understand, but then again I do. I see things about myself that I understand with increasing alarm and I want to sit with it all for a while, to be alone with this grief, to hold it in a way I can't when others are around. It is sort of like the way you don't linger in a mirror too long when someone else is looking, afraid they may notice your vanity, or worse, how afraid you are, how insecure. Alone though, I might stare, tilt my head, flip my hair, stay longer with my own sorry image.

I'm standing in my jeans and bra now, motionless before my closet. I don't want to reach in and pull out a top, put it on under a winter coat and go to my car, drive to the airport. Instead, I want to change back into my fuzzy leopard pajama bottoms and a black long-sleeved T-shirt. I want to crawl into bed and cover myself up to my head with a thick blanket, nurse my broken heart.

It is too cold. It is just too cold for anything else.

She is counting on me though, and I'm counting on her too, so I reach into my closet, pull out my thick red sweater with an oversized turtleneck, and put it on before I shut the closet door and turn off the lights inside. I leave my bedroom and walk the length of the short hallway to the living room, open the closet by the front door and pull out my heavy winter coat. Too slowly, I put one arm in, then the other. I reach for my scarf and feel tired. I put it on. I reach for my gloves next, and as I do I am suddenly startled by the slow filling of my eyes with tears. I blink them back, struggling not to ruin my makeup, but it is harder than usual. These tears are sudden and stubborn. They torment my lower lashes, threaten to spill over and run down my cheeks, leave lines on my powdered skin.

Blink. Blink.

I want to keep the pain away, but it steals my breath, makes it shallow and shaky, and all at once I don't have any strength and I slide down the closet wall.

I just slide down.

When I get to the floor I sit with my back against the wall and hug my legs to my chest, put my chin on my knees and go still, so still, trying to hold off the sobs that want to run over. I imagine my eyelids pushing them back so that they fall on the inside of my face, drip down into a pool that collects in my heart until it is full with sorrow and fear.

This goes on.

It goes on and on until minutes later, when I can finally almost breathe normally again, and I open my eyes. I stand up suddenly and my head feels too light and I know that My Big's plane will land in only a half hour and I start to panic. I realize that I can't indulge in this grief anymore, but my discomfort is nearly unbearable, so I walk back down the hallway to check that everything hasn't fallen apart since I walked into the closet and slid down the wall.

First I check that the straightening iron has been unplugged, but then decide that it must be put away too. I can't leave it to cool on the counter or when she sees the bathroom it will not look as tidy. For a second time, I realign the three towels on the bar. They still don't seem right though, so quickly I take them off and crease them over again, hang them more perfectly.

I walk out of the bathroom, flick on the hall light and watch it fall into the bedroom. I follow it and notice the bed skirt. It hangs misshapenly and so I go to it and drop to my knees. I fluff it. It falls almost into place, but not quite. I pick it up and let it fall again, but still it is not right. The third time it falls finally into a perfect position, but I don't like odd numbers so I do it once more. It falls right into place again and four is a good number so I can go.

I walk out of the bedroom and turn to my right to survey the spare room where My Big will keep her things. This is the room with the green desk we bought at the Salvation Army so many years ago. The room is perfect the way it is, but I start to imagine it filled with her things, her clothes scattered on the floor and jewelry littering the tabletop. What if she puts things on our desk, my green desk? My stomach flutters and I go to rearrange things that already have precise spots. I move the lamp a little closer to the picture frame, make the edges of the envelopes a bit more aligned in the tray. My movements are not quite enough though, are not relieving me, and I become even more taut with foreboding. I don't want her here. I don't want anyone here. I have to keep all of these things in order or everything will fall apart.

She will want to drink tea, I think. Oh my God. She will want to drink tea and I'll try to sit at the kitchen table, the one my dad put back together for me, but I know she'll want to curl onto my white sofa instead, the warm mug nestled in her hands. I won't be able to say no and I'll constantly ask her to repeat things because I'll be unable to listen, too distracted by the idea of tea spilling from the mug. I will want to control and control and control and I will hate myself for it just as I do now, rushing back into my bedroom to pick up the bed skirt again. I let it fall for the fifth time because five, though odd, seems somehow better than four, and I think more about our life together then, begin to notice more things that I cannot stand.

The time display on my computer suddenly interrupts me, and I realize that I will be late if I keep this up. Being late makes me almost as anxious as messy bed skirts and scattered clothes, so I hurry out of the room, snapping the light switch as I pass and grabbing my purse from its spot beside the couch. Quickly I pull on the gloves that made me start to cry earlier. I open the door to the hallway of my building and step out, then turn to look back, think that when she sees this she will feel welcome and warm and comforted and that is what I want, even though I also don't want her to come. She won't know that I'm scared to death of everything and losing my grasp a little more every day, that I just want to be in sweatpants and a T-shirt, wrapped in a blanket on the couch by myself. I want to be crying and sleeping, with nobody touching my things or making a mess or disrupting my already disrupted life.

And I want so much to be more than this.

But I just don't think I am.

We're going out. That seems to be at the top of the weekend to-do list when you find yourself single again. Maybe I shouldn't dread it. Maybe it will be like therapy, the music and the crowd like medicine. Maybe our low-rise jeans and glittery tops will be healing, the bracelets and long earrings and matching purses making me into something I think I'm not without them.

Standing at the mirror, I apply lip gloss and feel my confidence getting glossy too. Dressing well always does that, gives me a sense of assuredness that I only now suspect is still as false as it was in middle school, entering the auditorium on the first day outfitted in my new JCPenney jeans and jelly shoes, my adolescent friends beside me. When I went home and took off those fancy clothes though, I went right back to not liking myself very much.

"What if they're all dorks who can't get a girl any other way?" My Big yells to me from the other room, the room with my green desk. The one she has made a complete mess of.

"Well, are we dorks who can't get a boy any other way?" I yell back in a voice trying not to be strained.

"No," she says. "We're not." I hear her voice getting closer and now she is standing in my bedroom. "I just think men and women do things like this for different reasons."

In that moment I wonder why we are doing this.

I should have been married less than two months ago.

But I can't think about that the way I want to because suddenly My Big is beside me in the mirror and we are both looking at ourselves until I can't look any longer. I move away, but she doesn't. She lingers with her reflection, twisting and turning and looking back at herself over her shoulder. I do this too. I linger. Just not in front of others.

"Do you know that your mirrors are fat mirrors?" she suddenly calls out.

"What?" I say. "I never noticed that."

“Oh, thanks a lot,” she says, twisting and turning in the mirror, trying to get a better angle, lingering so long again that I have to look away. As I am about to leave the room though, she groans loudly and I stop, look back. She continues to twist and turn and doesn’t seem to care that I am there watching her as she watches herself.

“Why are you looking at me like that?” she asks, and I am not sure how I was looking, but I am at once remorseful because I know what I was thinking. I was thinking that she looks in the mirror for too long and that she shouldn’t, but the fact is, I do it too. I look in the mirror for too long too. I just do it later, by myself, when nobody else can see, and all of a sudden I have this intense desire to be softer and kinder, to others and also to myself. It is the first time I have ever had this thought and it hits me hard and I don’t really recognize it, like a stranger suddenly in the room. I want to sit with this for a while, try to understand, but again it is not the right time and I speak so that I won’t cry.

“You just seem so comfortable in your own skin,” I say honestly. “I’m jealous and confused by it too.”

“Little!” she snaps. “I am not! I do this because I am *not* comfortable in my own skin. If I looked like you, then I would be comfortable.”

I’m surprised. She lingers because she’s not comfortable, because she needs that much time to judge herself. She’s more like me than I think, and I start to argue, to say that she is absurd to want to look like me because I have so many flaws I can hardly stand to travel in this body sometimes, in this mind as well. I start to tell her that I feel trapped, inadequate, broken. I almost tell her to look more closely and she’ll see, but I don’t say it. I don’t say it because I don’t want her to know, to look more closely and realize how flawed I really am.

Finally, we are in the car. It is later than planned and this makes me anxious, but I try to let go of it. We are on our way to pick up the secretary from my school's office, someone who, over the last four months, has been turning into a friend and teaching me something about women that I didn't know.

I didn't know how much I'd need them to get over a man.

We pull up to my new friend's apartment and the door to the building immediately opens. She has been waiting for us and she bounces to the car, opens the door and slips into the backseat with an excited greeting and the signature scent of her cherry almond lotion. I introduce my two friends who have heard so much about each other, and they exchange pleasure over finally meeting, then launch into the logistics of the evening, how the other carload of girls will be meeting us at the Singles Mingle.

The Singles Mingle. We laugh at the sound of this, knowing it's silly, excited at the same time.

I notice that my fog is lifting and I am feeling grateful when my phone rings. I open it to look at the caller ID and it is my friend who is driving the other car. I tell the girls who it is, but they are not concerned. They go on chatting with each other and I am thrilled that they are so easy together.

"Hello," I say, dragging out the word with drama that will cover my worry about being late.

"Hey," she says, then continues talking, but her voice is very low and she is laughing and it is hard to understand her. I interrupt.

"Wait a minute. What? I can't hear you."

She gets control of herself.

"We got here on time, unlike you guys, so we came in. We already ordered drinks so we're finishing them. After that we will meet you somewhere else because we are not staying here. Don't come." There is more laughter and I hear the other girls too.

“Why?” I ask. “What’s going on?” I turn to look at my friends. They are listening now.

“Let me just say that we are the youngest people here, by a lot! These guys are as old as our dads, at least. We are not staying at this thing.”

“Oh God,” I say apologetically.

“Right. So where do you want to meet? Oh, and wherever it is, the first round is on you.”

Immediately I feel defeated. We all agreed to this idea and we all wanted to do it, but it was originally my plan and so I feel to blame. I tell her this and she insists it is not my fault and that they find it hilarious and still want to go out. She just wants me to pick a new place to meet. I make a quick decision and she agrees and my friends in the car are catching on and looking at me as I end the call and give them the story. I try to sound jovial, but really I feel wounded and wish I could just turn around and go home.

They are disappointed that the Singles Mingle didn’t work out as planned, but delighted that we are still going out, and I am lifted a bit by their excitement, even while voices in me still nag. I try to ignore them, but they are so loud, and by the time we pull into a really good parking spot on the street across from the bar, I am exhausted. It takes a lot of effort to battle yourself, to kick and struggle, always kick and struggle.

The three of us agree to take off our jackets and leave them in the back seat even though it is a bitterly cold February night. Since my folly with the Singles Mingle got us here early though, we are close to the entrance and won’t be cold for long. We gather our purses and open the car doors. The crisp winter air hits me and I hear the sounds of downtown and smell the restaurants and the snow and my own shampoo, and I start to relax. I start to think there’s something to be had here and get excited as we run across the street, but I start to worry too, about these constant shifts in my mood. I see something in that, something I hadn't noticed before, and I try not to think of the years with My Ex, things I'm starting to see there too.

When we get to the sidewalk, we stop and dig through our purses for IDs. A middle-aged guy with a ponytail sits at a high round table just inside the door, and even though we are all in our early thirties, he takes each license. One at a time he looks down, looks back up, smiles and nods as he hands the licenses back and we return them to our wallets. When all three of us are ready, we move as a unit toward the bar.

As we make our way I continue to feel oddly invigorated, losing more and more of my angst about the night, quieting that voice that always says I'm not okay, not enough. The sights and sounds and feels of the room come at me quickly and help to fill the emptiness, reshape all of my broken little pieces.

Fortunately, or unfortunately, I have always loved bars, and this one is lifting my spirits with its warmth and its crowd, more people than you might usually find at twenty after eight on a Friday night. The path we walk causes me to brush arms with most of those I pass and the music is loud and people are smiling and holding drinks and leaning in and laughing and laughing. The bartenders are bustling back and forth behind the bar, carrying bottles, taking money, tapping boxes on computer screens and ringing a giant bell when a good tip is left. It feels like a party that we were invited to at the last minute, and I am happy to have accepted as we make our way to a spot just one layer of people beyond the bar. We settle quickly into our little niche and Cherry Almond turns to us with a sly smile and raised eyebrows.

"Oh my God. Did you see the heads turn when we walked in here?"

"Yes," replies My Big, and her response is quick, like she expected the question.

"What?" I ask. "Who looked at us?"

"Oh, Little. You never notice things like that," she says to me.

Cherry Almond tips her head back just a bit, pointing to the group behind us, and says, "When we walked in, that group of guys back there turned one at a time to look at us."

"Really?" I say, only I'm not quite buying it, wondering if they think too highly of us. I'm not harnessing the same self-esteem my friends so openly share.

"Yes, really," says Cherry Almond. "I mean, come on. Look at us."

My friends laugh as I wonder about that, about my five feet seven inches that I think always make me look like a giant and my thick brown hair that would be wavy and unruly if I didn't force it into straight layers. I have brown eyes I think are too big and arms I think are too long, and though I know I fit into a size others say they want, most days I feel fat, like too much and not nearly enough.

"That's right girlies, 'cause we're hot," says Cherry Almond, as she taps a middle finger to her tongue, then touches her rear end and sticks it out dramatically. She makes a sizzling sound as she holds her hand there and winks at us as laughter erupts, but it is not just the three of us who are laughing.

The tallest guy of the group behind us is laughing too as he turns in our direction with raised eyebrows. He looks right at her ass and says, "Is there a fire that needs to be put out over there, ladies?"

With genuine surprise and delight, both of our groups roar with laughter before Cherry Almond grabs my hand and I grab My Big's hand and the three of us move out of our niche and into theirs.

She's leaving, I think. And she's taking me with her.

An hour later our friends in the other car have long since arrived and been introduced to the very large group we've become part of. Three are Rochester firefighters and the other five work in and around the city in various careers. The six of us combined with the eight of them have created a really invigorating group, and I find myself talking exclusively to one of the friends who is not a firefighter. He has been making me laugh since the first thing he said to me, which was, "I know you desperately wanna talk to me and I don't blame you. I'm breathtaking aren't I?"

He'd put out his hand then and I'd laughed more genuinely than I have in a long time, and then laughed again as he gently shook my hand and introduced himself as Guadalupe.

Now we are still talking, harassing each other really, and I realize that for almost thirty minutes I have been completely consumed with his sarcasm and wit, hardly noticing anyone around me as buried remnants of myself begin emerging and I indulge completely in this banter, something I realize I have not practiced with such abandon in a very long time. Too long.

My friends are enjoying themselves too. They come in and out of my conversation and I go in and out of theirs, and every time it is easy and fun, bordering absurd even. It is like having been away for months and months and not knowing how much you missed home until you got back. I feel like I'm home again and hope I can figure out how to stay.

Another hour passes and we are still with these new companions when My Big has to go to the bathroom. I do too, but I don't want to leave Guadalupe, and so it is with reluctance that I agree to go with her. We hold hands as we navigate the crowd and are lucky to find no line when we get there. We are able to go inside and pee quickly, then easily stand in the mirrors afterwards, just like before at my apartment, where we linger too long.

I am not concerned about that anymore though. The lateness and the alcohol and the laughing and the flirting have created a lovely cocktail of confidence as we apply lipstick and twist and turn in our reflections. Then My Big blurts out drunkenly, “So, what the hell is going on with this guy, Little?”

“Who, Guadalupe?” I answer, and we both laugh hysterically.

“You like him, right?” asks My Big, but it is not exactly a question.

“No,” I say. “I mean, I like talking to him, but it’s pretty easy to like talking to someone who calls himself Guadalupe and makes you laugh every two minutes.” I’m suddenly hit with this, that it has been like a show where we are both actors, not playing ourselves, and though it has been really fun, I’m becoming exhausted by it too, ready for a change of pace.

“So try talking to him about work. I mean, what’s he do anyway?”

“He’s an accountant.”

“Good. Ask him something about that, something serious.”

“I tried,” I say, “but somehow it turned into a joke about doing shots with my first graders.”

My Big laughs and asks how that happened and I tell her that I don’t know, but we agree that I’ll try again to guide the conversation to one of just a little more substance. We think that maybe I’m sending mixed signals about my level of interest and he’s nervous, just wants to keep me laughing. I sort of want to keep me laughing too.

We leave the bathroom and gently push our way back through the crowd, angling for our spots near the bar. There is a dance song on and before we are back with the group I see Cherry Almond performing one of her signature dance moves in the middle of everyone. She rubs herself against the backside of one of the firefighters, the one she has been talking to for quite some time and has exchanged phone numbers with. When she has his attention firmly planted, she looks right into his eyes, then shimmies around behind him and undulates down the length of his body, her front pressed tightly against his back. He turns to look over his shoulder at her and a very big grin spreads across his face. The others are looking and laughing. Some are joining in.

My Big and I are still winding through the labyrinth of people when Cherry Almond shimmies over to another firefighter. Her movements with him are similar, provocative and jovial. She loves music. She loves singing with it and dancing with it whenever and wherever, and when we have had a few drinks her moves are increasingly erotic, but fun and harmless. My Big is seeing this for the first time though and she is worried that Cherry Almond is getting out of control. I insist that she is fine, that this is normal and she has not had too much.

"No way," I yell to her over the music. "She's fine. She just gets feisty."

Guadalupe hears me and says, "Feisty is an understatement. Your friend is a wild one."

"She's fine," I repeat.

"I bet the bartenders would agree with that," he replies.

"What do you mean?"

"I just bet they would," he says with a pitch in his voice that provokes me.

"Why are you saying it like that?" I ask.

He raises his eyebrows and points with his beer bottle at Cherry Almond. She's still undulating, snaking her body down to the floor and back up, only now she is in the center of all the firefighters, and when she reaches a standing position again she spreads her legs, but keeps them straight. She bends at the waist like she is going to touch her toes and at first her head doesn't drop with her, but stays flexed so that she is looking up into the eyes of the group. Suddenly though, her head drops and does a half circle to the left as her upper body follows. She then jerks all the way back up, whipping her hair back, and they love it. They cheer and raise their bottles and she moves toward them and still I am not at all concerned.

"I'm sure the bartenders have seen a lot more than this in their days," I say, because I know her and I know that she is fine.

"That's not all she's been showin' though," says Guadalupe.

"Oh really?" I say back, laughing.

"Really," he replies.

He pauses then and seems to be waiting for me to solicit more, but I don't, and so he blurts out that when we were in the bathroom Cherry Almond flashed the bartenders. I think I must have heard him wrong and so I ask him to repeat what he said and he does.

"She did not!" I say flatly.

"She did. Didn't you hear the bell ring? That wasn't for a good tip," he says.

"You're saying that she pulled her shirt up in front of the bartenders?"

"That's right," he says merrily.

"You are so full of shit," I accuse him.

"Fine," he says with that now familiar upswing in his voice.

"What's going on?" asks My Big, who has scooted closer, trying to hear.

Guadalupe answers for me.

"She's upset because your friend over there flashed the bartenders while you two were whispering in the bathroom."

While we were whispering in the bathroom? Immediately I do not like that and I feel something familiar bubble up, something strong and hot and not easy to tamp down, something I had not noticed, until very recently, was such a part of me.

I feel anger.

My Big looks at me and her already large eyes are larger, questioning. Before she can respond though, I turn back to this accountant I have been talking to for a very long time, but whom I hardly know. Then, without missing a beat, I tell him not to be an asshole.

"Woah," he says, a little stunned. "That's harsh. I'm just teasing you."

"Teasing me about whispering in the bathroom or about my friend lifting up her shirt?"

"Oh, about the bathroom," he says. "Your friend definitely has a nice rack."

"We should go," says My Big.

"Hold on," I tell her, and then find a voice completely devoid of sarcasm and full only of genuine concern, not just for Cherry Almond, but for myself too. I need to get this straight. I look him directly in the eyes.

"Look," I begin. "I know you and I have been messing around for quite a while here. I'm not sure if we have said one serious thing all night, but I need you to tell me the truth now. I'm not kidding."

I still look him right in the eyes and I stand tall and I do not smile, and this reminds me of another time.

One of the other guys grabs him then and Guadalupe turns away, seems like he's going to start talking to him, and that strong hot anger bubbles up again. I grab him by the arm and for the first time I am pissed off that I don't even know his real fucking name.

"Hey!" I say, pulling him back and demanding his attention. "I'm not joking!" The grin on his face starts to spread and even though I think he's being a dick, I'm relieved. She didn't really pull her shirt up, I think to myself. Still, I have to ask.

"Seriously. Did she really pull her shirt up?"

He pauses and I am ready for the joke to be over until he says, "Bra and all."

Now I'm really confused. I know Cherry Almond can get wild. I can get wild with her. For her to pull her shirt up though, in the middle of this bar, bra and all, is completely unbelievable. It seems totally impossible. She has never acted like that before and I cannot imagine it, but at the same time I cannot imagine why this guy would continue to lie to me when I have stated very clearly that I want the truth. How many times have I done that? How many times have I stated that I just want the truth? I remember another time, a receipt in my back pocket and pain in my heart. I want to punch this guy in his fucking face.

My Big is convinced he's not lying and begins to whisper in my ear, cautiously watching Cherry Almond as she continues cavorting. Her dancing is absolutely racy, but I see nothing I haven't experienced with her before, and I cannot believe she did what he says. At the same time, I cannot believe he would continue to lie. Just like another time, I cannot believe he would continue to lie.

"I think we should probably go," says My Big.

"I'm not convinced she did that," I retort. "She's never done anything like that before."

"There's a first time for everything," Guadalupe says to me, laughing.

He can't be lying. Can he be lying? I don't know what the fuck to think and then suddenly I snap.

"Look!" I yell at him. "I am seriously not fucking joking. Please don't dick around. Did she honestly just lift her shirt up or not, you fucking asshole?"

I know he is lying. I know it, but I simply will not accept it, will not trust myself. I just never could.

"Jesus," he says, stunned. He turns from me then and I don't wait to see why or where he might be headed. I turn in the other direction. I turn toward my friend who has ceased her dancing and is just swaying slightly as she laughs with some of our new acquaintances. I say her name and gently pull her toward me.

"What up girlie?" she asks gleefully.

As I look at Cherry Almond and hear that familiar high winsome voice, instantly I know. I know that it is not true. I know that it is just not true and I want to scream because he lied to me and because I couldn't just know it. Even with the truth in my back pocket, I have such a hard time believing it, trusting so much in the words of someone else rather than my own, the ones I know without even knowing.

I can practically feel that Motel 6 receipt in my hands as I tell her what Guadalupe has been saying.

"What?" she yells, clearly shocked. "He fucking said that?"

Before I can form new thoughts she is pushing past me, making her way to the culprit. He faces us again and wears that same wide grin, and she says something to him that I don't hear, but immediately he confesses. "Oh chill out," he says. "I was just playin.'"

Cherry Almond then launches into a rebuke so powerful that he actually takes a step away from her and his broad smile wavers. As I watch and listen, I feel strangely protected by her scorn, as if she is not only defending herself, but sticking up for me too.

She turns back in my direction then and vows, "I did not flash anybody. I swear."

"Oh my God," he utters. "I was kidding. Calm down."

"I'm sorry," I say to her. "I knew you didn't."

Then I turn to him. I turn to him and look him right in the eyes and I say, "You know what? Fuck you."

He starts to speak to me, but I don't hear because I have already taken her hand and started leading her back to our larger group of friends. She thanks me for sticking up for her and for not believing him and then she kisses me, fat and wet on my cheek, and I think how I love this new girl in my life and how I might not be getting through this without her, without this medicine. My Big comes up on my other side then, calls me dolly and wraps her arm around my waist as she leans in and asks if I'm okay and I say that I am. With these two girls on either side of me it feels like I am.

We join our larger group and Cherry Almond begins telling them the story, and when she's done we all agree that we should leave, find another place to end the night. As we start to set down our empty bottles and glasses and gather our things, I can't help but sneak a look back at him, at Guadalupe, whose name is not Guadalupe at all. He is looking at me with a gaze of genuine surprise, maybe even regret. He looks as if he wants to say something, but I turn away. I've learned not to listen to apologies.

Finally, we are ready to go. We start walking toward the door and I am compelled to steal anther look, and it is like his eyes never left me. He is staring with that mix of remorse and surprise still on his face, and as we start to pass his group he makes his way to the edge of them. He reaches out to me, but I shift slightly and he comes up short, and I think I hear him say my name, but I don't stop. The bouncer opens the door for us and as I walk out, flanked by Cherry Almond and My Big, I can't help but think of that email.

I hope you don't leave and if you do, please, take me with you.

CHAPTER SEVEN
Shooting Stars

It is exactly two weeks, almost to the hour, since the Singles Mingle that didn't happen, and I'm sitting in a small village coffee shop that I love. I'm forgetting to sip my tea and moving my hands absently around the keyboard of my laptop, straining to hear three girls not far from me, and sneaking glances in their direction.

They are all quiet now and I decide that I should not be eavesdropping anyway, so I turn the volume back up on my iPod just as the band I'm listening to sings about shooting stars and breaking molds, and I wonder about these things.

"It's just," says the girl who sits upright with a thin ballerina shape and long blond hair. But then she trails off, bows her head. One of the girls puts her hand on Ballerina Girl's back. The other two lean in. They wait for her.

My iPod volume is not high enough. I hear her.

"I don't want to go through this," she says softly. "I want to be there already, over it, on the other side."

My belly flips. My heart races. I want to yell to her that I know what she means. And I want to yell that I wonder if all this wanting is causing even more pain.

All this wanting.

I can't look away then. I stare at her because she's beautiful, and I find myself stunned that someone so pretty could be so unhappy. I always think beautiful people must be happy and that I've never really been that happy because I've never thought I was pretty enough, as pretty as I think everyone else is. I wonder about this girl's house then, the house she grew up in. I think people in beautiful homes must be happy too, not homes like the one I came from, one that makes you feel sad and ashamed and angry. Like once you get through the door and take off your pretty JCPenney clothes you are back to your ugly, less-than self. I can't imagine her in a house like that.

But then she is so sad too. Just like me. So do houses make you feel that way or are you already that way and just blame it on the house or not being pretty enough or something else? There are worse things, I think to myself. There are so many worse things than a house that is not beautiful and a body that is not perfect, and I feel so ashamed for not being happier, and I've realized recently that this shame has been with me for a very long time, and is at least partly why I kick and struggle so much.

It's at least partly why he's gone too.

I look back down at the book I've brought and pretend to read. Really though, I'm trying to hear more of Ballerina Girl's story. I'm trying to see how much it's like mine, if maybe she too is always putting everything in nice neat rows and throwing away anything that's broken and scrubbing and dusting and sweeping. I wonder if she has ever sat on the living room floor in her pajamas organizing a candle drawer while the man she was supposed to marry is out of town.

Suddenly though, I can't fake-read another sentence because the door opens and I look up to find my friend shuffling in at a few minutes after seven. She waves as she walks across the room to me and I wave back. When she gets to our table for two she says hello, sets her purse on top and pulls out the chair. She sits and takes a deep breath. My friend is eighteen years older than I am, but it rarely makes a difference. We are timeless together.

"What's up?" I say casually.

"I'm so glad you called," she says. "I wasn't doing anything and I'm just right down the street!"

"Yeah," I say. "That's why I called. Couldn't risk you happening by and seeing my car."

She begins to laugh and I love the sound so I continue. “I thought maybe you’d be busy, but just my luck, you’re not.”

What started tentatively turns into her unmistakable laugh and she pulls her turtleneck up over her mouth so I can hardly hear it, can just see it fill up her eyes. I laugh too.

I laugh.

“You’re such a brat,” she says.

“I know. I’d better be careful or I won’t have a ride tomorrow, which is really why I called you. To confirm my wagon in the morning.”

Dropping the neck of her sweater she says, “That’s right. I’m your Paddy-O-Wagon.”

We both laugh again, and then my friend gets up, tells me she is going for a cup of coffee. I watch her as she walks away and see that she smiles at the girls I’ve been eavesdropping on, not knowing what I know about the pretty blond who doesn’t want to go through what she’s going through, but instead of thinking so much about how pretty she is and how I might not be, I think about something else. I think how I hope this girl will get something from one of her friends like I’ve gotten from this friend of mine, starting several months ago when she hung that small green gift bag on my classroom door. I hope these women who surround her will tell her something profound like mine did. I hope they will say, “There’s no man like a snowman,” and she will be filled with gratitude to have friends who know without knowing.

I feel the lump in my throat that has always come so easily and my eyes start to fill, when I hear my friend’s voice returning, the same friend who watched my students during that storm when I had to meet the movers four months ago. She is carrying a white oversized mug as she sits down across from me and I swallow back tears of gratitude for this new person in my life.

“So, I’m picking you up at ten, right?”

"Yup," I answer. "That's the plan."

"Did you talk to Delicious?" she asks, with another low chuckle. This is one of the nicknames we have for Cherry Almond, the one who works in the office of our school and dances provocatively but does not flash bartenders.

"Yes. I did. We're gonna pick her up at her apartment if that's okay."

She raises her eyebrows at me over her mug as she sips her coffee and gently nods. "Sunny and sixty-five on March eleventh," she says when she's done sipping. "Amazing."

"It is," I tell her. "Now, let's talk color. Green and white, right? Maybe orange? Accessories too. Are you all set with accessories?"

Paddy-O-Wagon begins laughing again and I think I have to string more moments like this together. If I am ever going to survive this loss and whatever else it is that makes me so sad and angry and unsure, I have to string more moments like this together. I have to surround myself with women who love me and bring out my joy and give me things to look forward to, and who look forward to me.

I want someone to look forward to me.

"You've got some big plans, don't you?" she says.

"You know it," I tell her, then look toward Ballerina Girl and think this is the only way to get to the other side.

By going through it.

It's the next morning, the day of the St. Patrick's Day Parade, when Paddy pulls up to where I'm waiting at my building's door. I feel good in my low-rise jeans and what I think is maybe the best shirt I have ever owned. It is a fancy white V-neck T-shirt, smooth as silk and clinging to my body with lace-like material and shiny sequins that line the low dip of the neck. I love this shirt, love it more than I should love a shirt really, but I don't think about that now. Instead, I think about how much I also love the bright green sweater-like zip-up top I wear over it. It has sequins too, green down each arm and across the front, and the unseasonably warm March sun hits them now so that a hundred little spots of light bounce off the windows and all around me.

My earrings dangle with white and green plastic gems and I'm wearing a matching green necklace that hangs to my belly button. The shadow on my eyes is mint green and on my right cheek is strategically placed a glittery green and gold shamrock. My bracelets are green with silver and I'm wearing knee-high green and white socks, shiny green panties and a white bra. I know my underclothes shouldn't really matter, but they make me feel good, and the pain has subsided enough in the last month to actually feel that. I feel a little good.

As I push open my building's door and step out into the bright March sun, something suddenly comes to me though, something with a loud and shocking clarity. I try to push it down but it persists. I've been seeing it in the archive of emails to My Ex and it wants to be known.

A light breeze hits my face and the glow of the day fills me as I put on my sunglasses and step to the car. But this truth will not quiet. This truth keeps tapping, asks me to stop for a moment and notice. Notice, it whispers. Can you see how much of your happiness hinges on things outside of yourself? Do you understand the power you give to lace-like T-shirts and green panties, sunshine and getting married?

Little flutters land in my stomach, but then I open the car door and smell my friend's morning coffee and hear the upbeat music on the radio and I think, fuck that. This is going to be an incredible day and I will be happy.

From the outside in.

"Hello," she says, dragging out the word and smiling hugely, turning the radio down a little. My smile matches hers and I take in her thick green sweater and hanging gold earrings as I tell her she looks beautiful and close the car door.

"Me?" she says. "You look great. A green purse even?"

Dramatically I flip a layer of my hair from one side to the other, knowing that I got it pretty straight today and thinking that, besides the lace T-shirt, it is the best part of my outfit. It feels odd to have so much confidence. It feels fleeting too.

With feigned modesty I reply, "Aw, shucks. I just threw something together."

"Yeah right, like a month ago," she chuckles.

Hardly missing a beat I declare, "Oh, and lucky for you, I have more fancy face stickers." I begin digging in a pocket of my green purse.

"Oh, face stickers. I knew I was missing something." She laughs, lowers the radio some and puts the car in gear. There are still small patches of packed snow on the ground and on some rooftops, but the March sky is cloudless and clear blue. The sun is shining brightly, warming the car enough to put the windows partly down, and as our dangling earrings blow in the wind my friend says something that shocks and saddens me. She says that this weather reminds her of the day her younger brother died, twenty years ago right about now, and I do not know how to respond. She goes on.

She tells me about him and about the accident and I think suddenly about how much I don't know. Our friendship is only months old, since she hung that snowman on my classroom door, and I have not had time to know that her eighteen-year-old brother was killed in a car accident on a day just like this one.

"I'm so sorry," I say to her.

"Thank you," says Paddy. "I'm not telling you this to be sad though. I'm telling you this because I'm glad to be making new memories with you today. This is good."

"Yes," I tell her. "This is so good."

"Now," she says. "Let's talk about something else."

But for a moment we don't say anything because it's hard to know what to say about how life goes on no matter what kind of grief you carry around.

Shortly, we pull into the parking lot of our friend's building, the same one I pulled into less than a month ago for the Singles Mingle. Like then, she is waiting for us, standing right outside in the morning sun and, as promised, adorned in similar St. Patrick's Day regalia. Paddy hadn't wanted to dwell on the memories of her brother's death, but I haven't been able to stop feeling it in the car with us, as Cherry Almond shimmies our way and Paddy's slow easy laugh begins to bubble up. I find it incredible how something so important as the death of a sibling can exist right alongside St. Patrick's Day. That's how it all works, I guess. Love and pain. They ebb and flow and get all tangled up in each other from one minute to the next and you have to do a lot of letting go and holding on and pushing back and leaning in. You have to keep all of the little pieces together, not let the windshield fall in your lap.

I want to stop and think more about this, but our dancing friend approaches the car, her blond hair pulled into a ponytail by a fat green elastic band, and her green post earrings shining in the sunlight. She has a beaded necklace and a bright green T-shirt with bold white letters across the chest, and as she gets to my window she pulls the shirt taut against her so that we can read the words.

"I'm a *little* Irish, but kiss me a *lot*."

The smile on her face is absolutely delighted as Paddy and I laugh and motion for her to get into the car where we are greeted with the scent of cherry almond lotion and her characteristic hoots and hollers of excitement. It feels like game day, like I have been picked up by my fellow cheerleaders and we are hurrying to make it in time for kickoff. Still, I think of Paddy's brother and I think of letting go, of not kicking and struggling so much.

"Oh my God you guys," giggles Cherry Almond. "I'm so excited. Can you believe this weather?"

"I know," Paddy and I say together.

"This day is going to be so awesome!"

"Yeah," says Paddy, "but I'm afraid because the weather is so nice we won't be able to see the parade. Too many people."

She is hardly done speaking when I take in a deep dramatic breath and swing my head toward her in mock horror. Before I speak my two friends are already laughing.

"How many times do we have to tell you? How many?" I say with pretend disdain as I position my entire body to face her in the driver's seat. I pause and just stare at her for dramatic effect and their giggles grow into more wild laughter. "We are not going to the parade to watch the parade!" I yell.

Cherry Almond's high-pitched laugh resonates from the back seat while Paddy laughs and whines to me as she pulls her sweater up to her mouth, that characteristic move. "I know, but I really want to see it."

"Oh God," I say, perfecting my disgust. "Let me guess. You brought a chair, didn't you? Tell me you did not bring a chair." Both friends are hysterical now and I'm encouraged. "I swear, if there is a chair in that trunk you are on your own."

Paddy and Cherry Almond are laughing so hard now and I love the sound. I love what it means about them and what it means about me, that I am becoming more like myself, more than I have been in a very long time, maybe ever.

This is me, I think.

Is this me?

Then all of a sudden I get scared too. I get scared because it has been such a long while since I felt this joyful and I wonder how to make it last. That's the part I can never get right, making it last, like there is a sadness always waiting for me to return to it.

I blink my eyes then, take in a deep breath that I let out long and slow, like I'm letting out that thought too, because there is some knowing deep within me that is starting to speak up. It whispers to me that what I think about things contributes to my misery as much as the things themselves. Something whispers that it's not all coming from outside, from the loss of this love. It's coming from inside too, a sorrow that has always been there, is just now trying to name itself.

Soon we are pulling onto Main Street and looking for the Rent-A-Car sign that marks the entrance before the private lot we have been told to park in. Another friend from school, the one who was part of helping me on that day in the storm when the buses were late, should be waiting there with her husband and very Irish siblings. We barely complete the turn onto Main Street when we see them, our friend in her tall brown and tan Guinness hat towering above the heads around her. She is at the edge of the lot, almost in the road, and she is waving wildly to us. We all see her at once and start laughing at her not-so-private private parking lot.

We slide into a spot right beside Guinness's vehicle and before the engine is even quiet we are gathering our purses and sweaters and sunglasses and opening the doors. Our feet hit the pavement as Guinness saunters over, carrying with her a beer and a wide smile.

"Hey there! Want one?" she says to me, as I hug tightly this new friend of mine, another new friend.

She reveals an unopened bottle and I squeal with surprise, take the beer and hand her a face sticker covered in glitter.

"All that glitters is gold," I tell her.

Two hours later I'm walking away from the street. I've just left Paddy, who despite our protests has decided to watch the firefighters and baton twirlers march, while everyone behind her drinks and hollers, crowds the sidewalk and lawn and patio at the bar on the corner. I see my other playmates, Cherry Almond and Guinness. They are exiting the bar and walking toward me as I get through the crowd and stand in a clearing to wait for them. When they enter it, I see that Cherry Almond is carrying drinks and quickly extends one to me. It is my signature mix, Captain Morgan and Diet Coke.

"I love dating you," I say to her, as we laugh and form a circle at this spot on the path.

Two guys we've been talking to have found their way back into our circle as well, and everyone is smiles and laughter and music and sun as Cherry Almond begins telling a clever story of their harried trip inside to retrieve these drinks, speaking with intense animation after several vodka and cranberries. As I listen, I think that we are drinking more than just alcohol. We are drinking new friendships and letting go.

Cherry Almond is still going on about the crowd inside while the warm sun kisses my cheeks, and it feels like I already have a mild sunburn. I decide to remove my green jacket, slinging it over my arm and feeling thinner than usual in my low-rise jeans and glittering white T-shirt that I love too much. I look up at the sky, soak it into me, then back down at my shirt again, and suddenly I think something. I'm a little drunk so I think that it reminds me of the top of a wedding gown with its lace-like neckline full of sparkle. It reminds me of the wedding gown I never got to wear, and quickly I feel this thought pulling me down.

Just as quickly though, I tell myself that I am okay. I have the prettiest shirt and a strong buzz and my new friends and music and sun. I know that I am fueling my contentment with things outside of myself, and I've heard how fragile that is, but I don't know if I believe it. I think maybe it will work for now and I can find that inner happiness thing later. Just a little later.

Cherry Almond is still talking and I hear her and she's funny, but I'm becoming distracted by the constant battle in my thoughts, a tug of war between joy and fear. As my friend continues, I try to focus on her, arms and hands flailing in a dramatic performance about her trip to the bathroom. I look into her bright blue eyes and smile, feel the warm sun continue to feed my soul as I turn my gaze back to the blue sky. I think that everything is right and that even when it isn't I can still be okay, and I bring my attention back to Cherry Almond, to her hands moving in many directions.

Just then, her arms wave over toward me and I take a tiny step back, the tiniest step that should have been far enough, but it was just a beat too late, just a beat. In an instant that I saw coming and that I didn't see at all, my delicate veneer is soiled. Literally, it is soiled.

Cherry Almond had thrusted her arm into the air to demonstrate the amount of space between her shoes and a stream of pee on the floor in the bathroom, and she'd hit Guinness's cup of dark brew. That cup had made a short leap out of her hand, rim first, onto the front of me, the front of my glittery white T-shirt that reminds me of my wedding gown.

But it is not glittery now. It is soaked and brown. And I am too. I am soaked and brown, the dark liquid seeping into my white shirt and pasting it against me. It seems like minutes, but it is less than seconds, as the piercing cold beer plasters the shirt to my frame and my white bra shows through the bronze-colored breast of my previously white T-shirt. My belly button shows too. Looking down I see it, flat and round and sunken.

"Oh my God. Oh sweetie. I'm so sorry," says Cherry Almond. She covers her mouth with one hand and bends to set her own drink down on the sidewalk. I don't say anything at first, but I am already thinking how without this shirt I won't look good anymore and since so much of my happiness is wrapped up in looking good, I can't possibly be happy, not anymore today. That's it right there, the problem with happiness hinging on things outside of yourself. It ends when they end and it is swift, without warning.

"Sweetie," my friend says again. "I'm sorry," and she is blotting my shirt with something and I don't know what to say because I know I am about to make this much bigger than it should be. I know this, but I can't stop myself, even though I try so hard.

I stammer that it's fine, but I know at once that you cannot be fine when your well-being hangs on a lace-like glittery shirt. Just like the JCPenney clothes. Now that they are gone I'm back to being me and that's not enough.

I don't want my friend to know this though. I don't want her to know this about me, but then suddenly I think she already does. I think she knows it about me and she knows it about herself too. I begin to see her own fragile joy reflected in mine as she panics, her eyes and voice and quick actions betraying her. She is trying to find something to dry me off and she seems to be experiencing such regret that it starts to break my heart. It breaks my heart that I can be this unhappy over something so small and that I can force that onto her too. I can't bear to cause her more suffering, so I form a smile. I tell her it's all right.

"It's not," she says, her eyes now filling with her classic easy tears. "You love this shirt."

I pull the fabric away from my skin and jerk it back and forth, fruitlessly hoping to shake off the brown beer that makes it cling to my body. Then I let go, and once more it falls heavy against me, resuming its soaked position. I let go of my joy too, let it float away on the breeze so that worry falls as heavily against me as the shirt just did. Still, I try to be playful.

"It's a wet T-shirt contest," I say.

That's when I notice that Guinness carefully watches us. She is not so fragile as Cherry Almond and me and seems to notice the sudden sucking away of our glee, so that she starts a cautious laugh and reaches out to touch the front of me. "Yeah," she says. "And I think we know who the winner is!"

"Not me," I reply, "I'm the only contestant, and I still lose."

I realize I am making it worse. Cherry Almond is not laughing and her eyes are filling with tears and I am already forming a plan about how to go home because my perfect white shirt is ruined and I don't really know how to be happy without it. This truth itself makes me even more miserable. I feel pathetic and selfish and so sorry. Still, what's true is true. My fragile happiness has been drowned in a cup of beer because it wasn't pure to begin with. It wasn't pure happiness, and I think my friend is so upset because she understands this about me, understands it about herself too.

"I'm just so sorry," says Cherry Almond, and I want to comfort her, want to comfort myself.

"I know," I say. "It was an accident." I reach out and touch her arm, but all I can see is going home and getting into my pajamas and curling up on the couch.

I look down at myself again, at the sight of my once soft white shirt with its glittering low neckline, and I try to smile, but without warning I am assaulted with another image flooding my supple mind. I take a quick breath in through my mouth, then swallow hard as I see it. I see it folded neatly in the hope chest at the foot of my bed, still wrapped in its plastic packaging, long and silky and cream-colored. Cherry Almond is still looking at me as I imagine the cathedral-length veil packaged separately in its own bag, and when she says my name I look up, but quickly back down again, able to see how much sorrow comes from not letting go of what is gone.

Our friend Guinness has been mostly quiet since the beer spilled, but now she says, “Why don’t you just go into the bathroom and see if you can get it out?”

I don't speak, but Cherry Almond becomes suddenly animated as she says, “Yeah yeah. We can try at least. We can wash it in the sink. Ooh, and dry it with the electric hand dryers.”

She sounds so desperate to make this right, excited by this new plan, and I start to think that maybe at least for her sake I can let it go, but then I look down at my shirt again. I see it plastered to my stomach and soaking my bra too. I think it’s just not worth it.

As if she is reading my mind, Cherry Almond says, “We’ll wash the bra too and you can just zip up your sweater until they both dry and they’ll be dry in like ten minutes I bet.” She looks at me, hoping.

I don’t want to though. I don’t want to wash my glittery shirt and silk bra in the filthy sink of a bar bathroom and then zip my green sequin sweater up to my chin. That is not the perfect outfit I’ve had planned for the last month. I only know how to be happy when I think everything is right, when it has gone as I’d imagined, and as much as I hate this about myself it doesn’t change its truth, and doesn't change that I will likely not make it through the day like this. Maybe I will not even make it through this life either.

Suddenly I am so tired. I look down again at all the brown and wet and cold plastered to my chest and stomach and feel nothing but defeat. I’m poised to say that I’m going to find Paddy and have her take me home, but before I can speak I look up again and my eyes lock with Cherry Almond and I see her there. I really see her.

I see her pleading. She is pleading with me to hold it together so that she can hold it together too, and it is not just about the beer all over my shirt. It is about so much more than this and that's why we are here together in the first place. That's how we found each other. We both need things. We need things, and she is pleading with me not to let that go.

"I don't know," I say, stalling for time.

"I know," she interjects sadly. "I'm sorry."

In that instant, my friend's agony over this overwhelms me, and in the next instant her distress transcends my own and I am agreeing to wash my garments in the bathroom sink. I don't even know what I am saying as I begin speaking because somewhere deep inside, in a place I can't often get to, I know that this is not a big deal. It feels so big because I am not well. I am just not well. Really though, it is small. It is small and I need to get well. I need to know that my friendship is big, bigger than this. It is bigger than me.

I am the one pleading now. I am pleading with myself to just be okay. I want to just be okay and agree to wash my shirt and bra in the filthy bathroom sink, then zip my green sweater up to my chin. I want to not have to be perfect, to not have to put every single thing in its place.

I want to be more than I think I am.

A minute later, our chugged and empty drinks are on the sidewalk beside us and we are fighting through the line of girls outside the bathroom door. My friend is reassuring them, insisting that we don't have to pee, that we only need to use the sink. She points to my shirt as she excuses us over and over, saying that we just need water and the hand dryer, and eventually we get to the sink. I begin gingerly removing my bra first and then my shirt, and it is not easy because at the same time I am hiding inside my green sweater, trying to maintain privacy and keep my clothing from touching anything in this dirty bathroom.

I am thinking about that too, thinking too much about things that are dirty and messy, but then my friend punches the hand dryer and my attention is drawn back to her.

"Why are you hitting the dryer already? I don't even have the shirt off!" I say.

"Well, lucky for you, I'm thinking ahead. What if we'd soaked your clothes under the faucet and the fucking hand dryer didn't even work?"

"Oh, right," I tell her. "That's smart."

"You know it baby. We ain't no idiots."

I try to laugh. I try to be all right. I can feel the joy asking me to let it in. "Let me in," it is saying. But pain has made such a home in me it is hard to find room.

The music coming from the bar and from the street is loud. It is so loud, and the girls in the bathroom are singing and yelling and laughing and my friend has to raise her voice above all of that to tell me to give her my shirt and that I should deal with the bra. I hand the shirt to her, then make sure my green glittery sweater is zipped up before I lean toward the sink and start running the bra under water.

"Take my heartache with you," I whisper to the water. Please. I can't be this sad over something this small.

We go on like this for a minute, and it's as if I am in a mournful trance until all of a sudden I happen to look up. I simply look up into the mirror and I see us, Cherry Almond with my shirt under one faucet and me with my bra under another. I see us, really see us, and something happens. It just happens. I feel a bit of hysterics start to creep in. I feel out of sorts, but not the kind made of sorrow, and I don't want to cry. I want to laugh. I want to laugh so hard and I try to hold it back, but it doesn't work. I turn and look at her and she looks back at me and all of a sudden we are both laughing. We are laughing and laughing and laughing, and if our hands were not so full of my wet clothes, we might throw our arms around each other and hug and jump up and down, and I love her right then. I really love her.

We are shootings stars, I think. Only shooting stars.

CHAPTER EIGHT
Big Mistake

"Oh Christ," I say with feigned disgust. "This was a big mistake. You guys are going to smell like onions and nobody will come near us."

"Ketchup and mustard," says Paddy to the vendor as she starts laughing and shoves me. I'm not so steady on my feet and I stumble backwards as we all laugh.

"Just ketchup, please," says Cherry Almond, who vamped our way into the men's bathroom two hours ago when, despite her testing, the hand dryer in the women's room suddenly stopped working. My shirt is in the car drying and I'm wearing my still-wet bra under my green zipped-up sweater, but I don't care. Guinness brought shots to us while we were at the sinks trying to save my outfit, and after that one, and then the next, my perfect glittery shirt didn't seem so important anymore. I had slapped my soaked bra back on my chest, zipped up my green sequin sweater, took Cherry Almond's hand and headed into the crowd.

My friends reach to take their food from the vendor now, and Cherry Almond bites dramatically into hers before looking at me with her mouth wide open. I scream and look away, start walking ahead and laughing as I yell at them to keep moving and they yell at me to stop rushing them. We have about six more doors to pass before reaching the bar on the corner, and even though we can see that the line to get in is surprisingly short, the gang behind us is getting closer and I'm worried they'll get ahead of us and there won't be a good spot left.

"Hurry up you freakin' pig faces!" I yell.

They start laughing and Cherry Almond calls back, "Oh shut up you little bitch!"

Paddy almost chokes on her food and we all laugh loudly and I tell them to eat faster and they tell me to shut the fuck up, and we can hardly walk with our hysteria.

A moment later, doubled over in laughter, we are outside the bar and still ahead of the mob. I again rush them as they lick the last of the condiments from their fingers and finally we walk into the sun-filled room. "Ooh, ladies," I say, eyes wide and a huge smile on my face. "Lookie, lookie."

I point to the stairs of the usually closed second floor and then take them two at a time, calling to my friends over my shoulder, but as I get close to the top I turn to see that they are not with me. They have stopped to talk to Paddy's son and his girlfriend who unknowingly entered behind us, and I smile and call out delighted hellos as if we were not just with them a half hour ago, dancing with bagpipe players. We continue greeting each other as they all try to reach me at the top of the stairs, and we are using the merriest voices, and it is absurd and glorious, and I am so glad that I dug down deep enough not to let all of this go over some spilled beer and a soaked shirt.

"Move it lady," yells Paddy's son as he lifts me up and carries me the final steps, and everyone laughs because this is how it is at three o'clock on St. Patrick's Day when you have been drinking for almost five hours. This is how it is when your shirt was soaked with beer and you had to remove it in a crowded bathroom, clean it in a dirty sink, then try to dry it with a wall-mounted hand dryer in the men's room. This is how it is when that shirt is hanging over the seat of your friend's car and your sweater is zipped up to your chin and you've told your story to a dozen drunken strangers. This is how it is when nothing has turned out how you wanted it to, not today and not in a very long time. This is how it is when you're making the best of it, the best of how things have turned out. This is how it is when beautiful new friends are helping with that.

I yell at him through hysterical laughter and he finally sets me down as everyone enters the second floor and we notice a small group of colleagues from our school building, a group we saw earlier that has now congregated here as well. It appears that they are intermixed with several people we are not familiar with, and my friend gently shoves past me calling out to them.

"She's goin' in for the kill," I say to Paddy. "Which oughta be especially bloody since we've been drinking for more than half a workday now."

My friend begins her hearty laugh then, and we delight in our memories of the last several hours as we follow behind Cherry Almond. She enters this large mass of people we know and people we don't know, and more boisterous hellos are exchanged. My senses overflow as I experience the palpable spirit of this new group and the smell of food from the street and the music we yell over to be heard. It is at just this moment, when I am burning with energy, full from this merriment, that a tall slim guy emerges from the bunch and heads right for me. Our eyes lock and a playful grin spreads across his thin face, and in that second I recognize him and react, move quickly in his direction as I call out his name. He bends low to reach me and we embrace dramatically, exchange loud greetings over each other's shoulders before he steps back and takes my hands at the fingertips, spreads our arms out wide and says, "Damn, girl."

With fondness I remember the quick banter we used to share, and it comes back easily as I smile at his raised eyebrows and that playful grin. "Yeah, well, I looked better before," I retort. "I sort of had a Guinness and white T-shirt problem, hence this zip-up look I'm sportin' now."

I sound light and funny, but really my explanation is an effort to hide how self-conscious I am about this imperfect outfit, like if I point out my inadequacy, maybe others won't judge me for it.

It is something I do. Not just today.

We are both about to say more, but our words are interrupted as a presence begins to take shape next to us and I am drawn all at once to my right, where a guy even taller than my six-foot-two old college friend is suddenly standing. He just seems to appear beside us, facing me and taking up so much space, so much air. So much.

And I had not seen him coming.

The suddenness of his approach and his size overwhelm me and probably would have anyway, but after hours of festive drinking my power is dimmed more than usual and enough to make him very imposing, distracting. He has my full attention. I can't seem to focus on anything else and I suspect right away that he knows it, though I don't want him to. I really do not.

"What's up, bro? You gonna keep this pretty girl all to yourself over here? That's not right."

The college friend I've just reunited with steps toward me, laughing. He puts his hand at my back and introduces us. I reach out to shake the hand this new guy warmly extends, and as my fingers slip into his I am instantly struck by how large his hand is and by the unmistakable energy that seems to move from him to me and back again. He has all of my awareness. All of it.

"Beautiful name," he says to me. "Very fitting."

For various reasons, I bristle.

"I bet you say that to all the girls," I challenge. He puts his left hand across his chest and says he is deeply hurt that I would suggest such a thing.

"You can't be that hurt," I say. "Your heart's on the other side."

He drops his head to look down at his chest and both guys start laughing as this new guy turns to College and says, "Dude, this girl doesn't mess around."

"No, she doesn't," College responds.

"So, what're you drinking?" he asks me.

"Nothing at the moment," I say, lifting my arms, empty palms facing up. He looks at our mutual friend with feigned disbelief and asks for his help.

"What can I tell ya, buddy?" says College.

I like this. I like it a lot. It feels like power and control and I need that. I need to shake off some of the self-doubt and fear, and this will do for now.

My college friend puts his arm around me and tells me to let his friend buy me a drink because then he'll probably buy him one too and he could really use another. In response, this new guy immediately takes his wallet from the back pocket of his khaki shorts and asks College what he wants to drink, then turns and asks me.

"Captain and Diet," I say graciously.

"Captain and Diet," he repeats.

He then faces the group behind us and asks loudly if anyone would like a drink and I am instinctually impressed by this, but I don't want to be, and so I focus on College, who is excusing himself to go to the bathroom. That's when this new guy and I are left suddenly alone in the spot where we have only just met, and I become even more aware of a pull that seems to draw me to him, a feeling not necessarily sexual or even physical, but touching some other level I can't name. I have felt it before. It did not turn out well.

He is facing the bar directly behind me and he swings his right arm toward it as he tips his head just slightly in that direction, indicating for me to lead. I take the few paces to the bar, then lean on it. My elbows splay out to the left and right and I lift one boot to rest on a ledge underneath. He comes up on my right side and leans in too, the front of his body against the bar, his elbows also splaying out. His left one touches my right, gently and hardly at all, but I feel it and I want to pull away.

He draws me in though. He draws me in with something I can't name and then he is ordering our drinks and tossing a twenty onto the bar and I am in too deep already. I am in so deep.

The bartender walks away then and we watch in silence as he retrieves two beers, removes the caps, sets them on the bar and turns to prepare my mixed drink. My new companion picks up his bottle and I watch with my peripheral vision as he brings it to his mouth, tilts his head back and swigs. He sets the beer back on the bar as College returns and reaches between us to grab the neck of the other bottle.

"I'll just be over here," he says, pointing to the group of our intermingled friends behind us. I look for Paddy and Cherry Almond and find them laughing among a mix of people we know and people we don't know. College puts his arm around his friend's high shoulders and turns to me.

"If this guy gives you a hard time, come let me know."

"I think you'd better worry about him, not me," I retort, sounding light and funny again, hiding self-consciousness, layers of inadequacy.

Both guys laugh loudly and then College moves in and hugs me, says how good it is to see me again and that I'd better not go anywhere with this jerk or he will find me. He moves back to the group and this new guy turns to face me, rests his right side against the bar. I turn to face him too, and that is when I see it. I see it and I cannot believe I didn't notice before.

I cannot believe the things I just don't notice.

Four Months Earlier

It was twenty minutes before eleven at night when I heard the apartment door open and the sounds of him entering. I'd been lying in bed, trying to sleep, waiting for him to get home, troubled by the presence of the packed boxes lining the opposite wall.

I didn't breathe. I just listened.

I heard his keys jingle lightly, but not into the key holder by the door. That had been loaded into a crate that was stacked under the kitchen window, the one I would no longer look out of every morning as I drank my coffee. It was packed next to the mail organizer and a little wooden bin that once held our assorted items.

So I wondered where he'd put his keys.

And then I began to wonder so much I could feel the blood start to pound in my head.

But not about the keys.

I heard his footsteps then and willed him into our room, the room I would spend only two more nights in. I strained to listen. I breathed less and finally heard the sound of his feet again, heard them moving farther and farther away. Until it was quiet.

I listened and listened, but it stayed quiet and stayed quiet. Minutes went by and finally I was unable to stand it any longer. I got up and turned off the fan, strained to hear again. Still there was nothing, and the lack of sound was too much. It filled my head with its own noises, with the sound of pain and loss and regret. It was deafening. I crawled back into bed, pulled the covers over my face and tried to manage the weight of so much sorrow and fear. A heat rippled through me then, seemed to land in my head and all around so that I could hear it. I could hear my hurt like a real thing in the bed with me, like a windshield shattering.

Still, on the other side of the bedroom door, the quiet continued. Except for the sound of my pain, there was nothing but the persistent ticking of the clock on the bedside table, the clock that would in two more mornings be put into a box with a small lamp and some books.

Then, all at once, it became too much to bear. It became just too much.

I pushed off the covers and sat up. I swung my feet to the floor and started walking toward the door, thinking with each step that I might die of heartache and fear, that I could not get enough air. In then out, I thought. Just in then out. The simple acts of breathing and walking so difficult, so uncertain.

Like my entire life, shaky with worry and doubt.

Finally I reached the door. I put my hand on the knob and turned. I pulled it open. I stepped out of the bedroom where his things were still hanging in the closet and folded in drawers, but where mine had been piled into boxes and bags. I entered the kitchen and stopped at his keys on top of the table, the kitchen table that had both leaves dropped down and had hours ago been pushed against the wall under the window, boxes piled on and around it. My dad and I had eaten subs on that table just four hours before. He'd been seated across from me and we'd eaten slowly and talked cautiously, our eyes all the time filled with tears.

I reached for the light switch so that I could make it all black. I didn't want to see. I turned toward the dining room then and looked past it to the living room at the end of the apartment. I saw that a light had been turned on but not the television, and there was no movement. Waves of uncertainty washed me down, threatened to stop me. Still, I moved forward, propelled by the familiar flutter in my belly. It was fear. It was sorrow. It was needing to know.

I walked into the short narrow hallway that connected the kitchen and dining room, my attention surprisingly drawn to the coat hooks along its one longer wall, and I stopped to stare.

There was only one now, one jacket hanging alone among all of the other empty hooks. It was his. Mine had been packed into boxes and placed in the other room. Only his remained, and I just stopped and stared at it, at his one coat alone on a hook.

A coat hanging all by itself can do that. It can stop you.

I moved then. I entered the dining room, moving toward the living room beyond, and I tried not to look. I tried not to look at the dining table my dad had helped me take apart earlier, stacked in parts against one wall, the bottom of it facing out. I looked away, saw the six chairs with their backs against another wall and the four table legs piled beside them, and I noticed that my heart was there too. It was on the floor beside the table legs, taken completely apart.

I continued walking toward the light in the living room and finally came to the threshold, stood just before it and froze, froze at a sound I could feel more than I could hear. I could feel it, the shaking and the asking and the heartache and the fear. I could feel it and I was stunned. I didn't know. I just did not know.

I stepped forward then and turned. I turned to see him sitting in the chair that less than a month before I had been sitting in when I'd yelled at my sister on the phone.

"Call it off. Just call it fucking off."

He was sitting in the same chair, his legs shoulder-width apart and an elbow on each knee. His face was in his hands. His face was in his hands and the sight of him was like a blow to the chest, so startling and painful it was hard to move.

Tentatively though, I took a few steps toward where he was seated, and that's when I saw. I saw his large shoulders pulsing almost imperceptibly, and I stopped again. I stopped moving and I stopped breathing and it was utterly silent except for one unfamiliar sound, something other than the sound of my own broken heartbeat. I heard a sound that filled the space between us and deepened the ache flowing through me.

I heard him crying.

Softly I said his name and took the remaining steps between us, bent my wobbly legs as I lowered myself to the carpet before him. I put my palms on his knees and didn't speak. He didn't speak either and he didn't shift. He just stayed with his legs shoulder-width apart, an elbow on each knee and his face in his hands. Nothing moved but his shoulders, pulsing to the rhythm of his tears.

I waited several seconds, stunned and broken. I waited before finally he lifted his head from his hands and gazed at me. His face was red and wet and swollen, and his eyes held the kind of anguish I felt behind my own lids. I could not speak as he stared at me and then moved his gaze over my entire face before stopping again on my eyes. He began to shake his head and his hands came down and covered mine when he spoke and I felt destroyed.

"How am I supposed to live without you?" he asked. He swallowed hard then. "How?"

I winced, and my voice stuck in my throat. I sat pained and silent, devastated. His red, wet, swollen eyes stared right into mine and he asked again. He almost yelled.

"How?"

I rocked back on my heels.

"I don't know how. I don't know how to live without you," he repeated, and his suffering was the kind I could almost reach out and touch, and then the room seemed to be bursting with it, with his sadness and with mine too, and I thought that I could almost hold it, carry the pain around the way you would a load of laundry. His heartbreak seemed finally to match my own, finally to look and sound and feel like mine. Where had it been all this time? Had he not understood that it would come to this, boxes piled high, the dining table in pieces, only one coat left on the hooks? Had he not understood?

He looked around then, as if reading my mind, and raised his eyebrows in question. He spread his arms, palms up, shrugged his weary shoulders.

"Look at this," he said through a choked sob. "Look at it!" I started to look around too, at our broken-down boxed-up life. But it hurt too badly. I couldn't stand to see it, and quickly I turned back to him.

"You're leaving. You're really leaving?" It was a statement that he repeated as a question and quickly I questioned too. I wondered. I wondered if the time for this had really passed, the time for him to ask me not to go. Then I wondered how I could even be wondering that.

Fuck, I have to go. No matter what he says, I have to. Please don't make me stay. Like that day in your bedroom over eight years ago, I thought. Please don't.

"What did you want me to do?" I asked, my voice barely audible.

"I don't know," he whispered back. "I don't know, but I didn't know it would look like this. I didn't know."

I had waited so long for him to know. I had waited and waited and waited.

"I only know you," he said. "You and me," and then he started to cry harder. "How did this happen?" he choked.

Without restraint then he reached for me, raised me up from sitting back on my feet and pulled me into the space he made between his legs. He gathered me at his chest and wrapped both of his arms completely around me and buried his head in my hair and I felt consumed, utterly consumed, and it was what I wanted. It was what I'd always wanted, to be consumed by him.

We fit perfectly into each other then. We fit so perfectly, and yet we did not at all, and I felt more pieces inside of me seem to shatter then, and I felt full of them. I felt full of millions of tiny pieces that created a pain so deep it felt like I would simply not survive.

He continued to cry and cry and I came completely undone, devastated by the loss of this love. I held tightly around his neck and put my cheek on his shoulder and my tears dripped sideways over my nose and across my top lip, landing sometimes in my ear and other times on his shoulder and I could feel all of it. Every single thing.

Then I wondered again. Could I come this far and still go back? Could we unpack those boxes and stay, love each other, get married? He always told me that this time it would be different. This time. This time. This time.

Maybe this time.

Our tears continued to drop while he held me as tightly as I could ever remember and cried without restraint. He cried and cried and cried, his head buried in my hair, and he held onto me so that I felt like a winter coat on the coldest, windiest day. I felt like a winter coat he had not figured out how to button, but instead just pulled tightly around him. Our pain and sorrow and regret were like the piercing wind hitting his body so that he had to hold the coat even closer, try not to let it fly open. He pulled me into him, the coat, fastening our love to his chest even as so much hurt whirled around us.

Quickly though, a thought came to my mind, the beginning of something deep and dark and too much to bear. It was about how you can't hold on to the jacket forever, this coat that just will not button up. Eventually you will let go. You will need your hands for something else and the piercing wind will grab hold, pull it away. That will happen to me too. Our pain and sorrow and regret will grab hold of me as soon as he shifts. It will pull me away like the winter wind grabs at an unbuttoned jacket, and in that moment I knew. I knew his tears were not the ones of someone who was holding on. His tears were the ones of someone letting go.

Oh my God.

Oh my God, my heart. He wasn't going to unpack those boxes. He wasn't going to put the table back together. He wasn't going to rehang my coat on the hook beside his. He wasn't going to ask me to stay. He was going to let me go.

As I knelt on the floor between his legs, his arms wrapped tightly around me and his sobs buried in my hair, he was letting me go. He was letting me go and I felt sick to my stomach.

It was like that to be let go. It was sickening.

So I pulled away. I pulled away and looked at him and he looked back at me, still sobbing, as silently I begged him. One last time I begged him. Please, I cried silently. Please don't let me go.

He pulled me back in then. He held me so tightly. He held me the way you hold a winter coat that just won't button, the way you hold a winter coat right before you have to let go.

And then he did. He let go.

"I'll never stop loving you," he whispered to me. "Never. No matter what I do."

I see it and cannot believe I didn't notice before. He is saying something to me, but I don't hear. I am picking up my Captain and Diet from the bar and preparing to walk away. Before I turn though, I figure I will let him know what an asshole I think he is. So, with my voice full of thinly veiled indignation, I say, "Nice shirt."

He looks down at the cartoon likeness of a stubby bride in her gown and veil with an equally stout groom in his tuxedo. The two are facing forward as if walking down the aisle, holding hands and a bouquet of flowers. Printed boldly underneath their figures, big white letters against the green background of the shirt, it reads "Big Mistake."

His face forms an innocent smile and he shrugs his shoulders.

"No comment?" I ask curtly.

"My friends got me this shirt," says Big Mistake.

"Oh?" I ask with mock wonder. "I've never met a grown man who lets his friends choose his clothes, especially ones with such poor taste."

He laughs. I don't.

He swigs from his beer, then sets it down on the bar. He looks at me again and his face shows growing concern as I stand there still as a statue, kicking and struggling, always kicking and struggling.

He leans closer to me as I face him, still keenly aware of his presence and confused by the lack of urge to draw back even though I think I should. Instead, I want to move toward him and I can't believe it. Have I learned nothing?

"Do you want to hear a story?" he asks.

"A story?" I repeat. "I've heard lots of those."

What I really want to do is cry. That's why I'm playing the tough guy routine, because I want to cry. I should have been married for two and a half months by now, but instead I am standing here in this bar and I'm drunk, looking at another big mistake.

All at once I am again uncomfortable in my damp bra and zipped-up green sweater. I stand there looking at him, feeling inadequate and exposed and wishing I had my beautiful white T-shirt and wishing I had a lot of things. Now there is a lump forming in my throat and painful drunken tears pressing against the backs of my eyes, and suddenly everything about his face changes and I have the distinct impression that he can tell I'm not doing well, and suddenly he says, "I just got divorced."

His words pull me sharply from my reverie and I look at him, seeing him again for the first time in several moments and feeling dazed. I am dazed.

"I've been really down about it," he says. "I didn't want to get divorced. So my friends got me this shirt. They thought it would be funny, make me feel better."

I don't know what to say. I did not expect this. He's divorced. He was married. Hesitantly he sips his beer, looking at me over the bottom of the bottle as he tips it up, his eyes searching for a response. I look back at him, humbled all of a sudden.

He lowers his beer bottle and says softly, "I'm sorry you're offended by it."

For a moment I don't know what to say. I just look at him and then look away and then look back. "No, I'm sorry," I say, swallowing and trying to breathe deeply. "I didn't expect you to say that." I smile then and lean into the bar. I tilt my head, softening the outrage I felt only an instant before. From the outside in. That's how I roll. Always from the outside in.

"I guess I can forgive you," I tease.

Gently he sets his beer back on the bar and his eyes relax, a smile forming on his full lips. It widens. "You mean because I'm divorced it's now acceptable for me to wear this shirt."

"Yes," I say frankly. "You earned it."

"Oh," says Big Mistake, laughing. "You're divorced too?"

I reach for my drink and take a long sip. "No," I say with something like sorrow.

We are quiet for a moment before he says, "You wanna tell me about it?"

I put my drink down. I look at his shirt. I look at him.

"I'm not divorced because two months before the wedding, I called it off. That was in October. So, *I'm* really down about *that*."

He looks away and lets out a deep breath. Then he looks back at me and says deliberately, "I'm really sorry." He holds onto my eyes and I can't look away.

"So, we're in similar situations, just different," I tell him. We both pause, sip our drinks. "At least you have a shirt for it though. I don't have a shirt," I say, then think about what I just said and add, "Literally."

We both laugh out loud and his laugh is thick and raspy. I'm drawn in even more.

"Do you want to sit down?" he asks.

"Sure," I answer.

He motions for me to follow him and starts to lead us through what has become a dense crowd. I'm following closely at first, but then someone steps between us, and then another and another, and quickly he is way ahead of me.

Until he turns back.

He turns back and he stops and he reaches for me, and an indescribable energy moves between us and has a power I cannot name. I cannot name it, but I recognize it. As I put my hand out, I recognize this energy and it scares me, like that day in My Ex's house, looking for my purse, moving but not leaving. Still, I reach out my hand and he takes it and gently he pulls me toward him, pulls me through a particularly tight spot.

Maybe that's what he's doing, I think. Maybe he's pulling me through a particularly tight spot. Can I let it just be that? Can I let it just be?

Within seconds we are at a high table for two and he stops, sets his bottle down and turns to me. I blink back tears and hope he doesn't notice and he looks away, either because he did, or because he didn't.

Our friends are all around us and yet I feel totally alone with him, this stranger who suddenly seems not like a stranger, and it worries me and comforts me at the same time. I want to move toward him, but I want to move away, and I always choose toward. That's what I always choose.

"Let's sit," he says, and then he is pulling out a chair for me and I am disoriented, trying to recall any other guy ever doing this before, ever. It has not happened. As I sit down, I realize that nobody has ever pulled out my chair before and I realize too that I let little things mean big things and that this is part of my problem. Still, knowing that something is a problem doesn't fix it, and my heart begins to race with the intensity of this guy and the first time a chair has ever been pulled out for me.

"Hey you. There you are," comes Paddy's voice as she approaches us from behind. "I was looking for you." She looks at Big Mistake and smiles, then looks to me with raised eyebrows. "And who is this?" she continues.

And who is this?

Oh shit. Oh fuck. Oh fuck, fuck, fuck. I cannot believe this. I cannot believe it. I have forgotten his name. I only heard it once and that was so many minutes ago and alcohol is the primary thing fueling my blood and my brain and so his name has been erased from my thoughts. I no longer know his name. This guy who has filled my senses so quickly and completely has no name other than Big Mistake.

To my great relief though, I pause just long enough for him to naturally fill in the space. He turns to Paddy, extends his hand and introduces himself.

"Well, looks like you're doing fine," says Paddy with a sly smirk. "Our other little leprechaun is doing fine too, so this old-timer is gonna get going."

Before acknowledging the fact that she is planning to leave I strain my neck, scanning the crowd for Cherry Almond. As I do, Big Mistake does the same, though he doesn't know who she is. I search for her blond hair or the tall green hat she's wearing, the one we found on the street an hour ago. After a moment I spot her.

"Oh my God!" I yell. "Look at her!" Paddy looks as I point and immediately she sees her too. She bursts into laughter, covering her mouth with the neck of her sweater.

"She's kissing that guy," I say. "That guy we were talking to earlier."

"She's kissing a guy? A guy you know?" asks Big Mistake.

"If meeting someone an hour ago counts as knowing him," I say with gaiety.

Laughing and settling back into his chair he says, "That's freakin' awesome."

"Oh, you would say that," I tease, as Paddy and I laugh and stare at Cherry Almond. "How can you leave at a time like this?" I ask Paddy with mock horror.

"I know," she says. "This has been so much fun, the best day ever, but don't forget I'm much older than you girls."

"Oh stop!" I say.

"So listen. I've left a few of the more responsible crew members in charge of lookin' out for you two and I expect you to stay together and call if you need anything, especially a ride home."

"Wow, you're awesome!" exclaims Big Mistake.

"Thank you," she replies with a laugh.

"And if you don't mind," he continues, "I'll watch out for her too."

My heart catches.

"I think that would be great," she says to him, and Paddy and I exchange glances that say everything we are not saying, and then he interrupts. He asks where her car is, and when she tells him he says that she shouldn't walk there alone. He says that he should walk with her. Then he is standing up and going to get his coat and my friend is moving in close to me and I can't believe any of this.

"Jesus, who is this guy?" Paddy asks.

"I just met him," I say, which is not really an answer.

"Well, he seems really great. I can't believe he's going to walk me to my car."

"I can't either. I'm trying to hook up here and you're movin' in on my territory."

My friend is laughing audibly when Big Mistake returns with his coat and, to our surprise, trailing right behind is Cherry Almond and the guy she was kissing.

"Oh my God," I say to Paddy. "Here she comes with The Kisser!" We both start to laugh.

"Ladies," says Big Mistake. "I brought a buddy to walk with us."

Paddy and I realize that he is talking about The Kisser, and we realize this at just about the time Cherry Almond looks around him and sees us and absolutely shrieks.

"There you are!"

This is when we realize that The Kisser and Big Mistake know each other and we all laugh out loud, just as College, my old grad school comrade, walks over and joins our group. It turns out that the three of them used to live together until Big Mistake moved away to get married, but he is moving back now, and I am looking at my two girlfriends and all of these guys and the rest of the group now moving closer, and I am in awe.

There is so much laughter and embracing and music and warmth and sunlight streaming through the windows, and it all combines to create a beautiful elixir that lures me into this world I know we will never have again. Ever. We can never recreate this. It is one moment in all of time, and I am sure that I need to feel every bit of it right now. I need to feel every last bit and I do, and I know it is from the outside in, but it is filling me up and I am so grateful. I am grateful to be buying some time from the outside until I am better from within.

Cherry Almond is embracing me now and College is leaving to get more drinks and The Kisser is debating with Paddy about being responsible enough to get us home later, and I feel a gaze on me. I turn toward it and see him staring. He is looking at me with an intensity I think he didn't mean for me to see, and quickly it leaves his face as he smiles softly and winks so that a new warmth spreads through me.

He turns back to his buddies then and I can't see the writing across his shirt anymore. I can't see the big mistake.

CHAPTER NINE
Waking Up

It is the next morning and I am just waking up, cautiously opening my eyes to a cloudy sky that fills the panes of a sliding glass door in the dining room of Cherry Almond's apartment. I see this over the top of his body lying on the floor next to me, so big I can't see the front of his T-shirt now and don't have to think about any mistakes, like that time in the hotel room after my friend's wedding. This is not like that.

But then again, it is.

This time though, I am fully dressed. I am fully dressed and lying on the floor with the blanket he placed over me four hours earlier, at three o'clock in the morning. My head is resting on the pillow he put on the carpet for me, after drinking and laughing and singing and dancing for fourteen straight hours. Unlike the time after the wedding, I am certain of who he is and what we've done.

But then again, really, I have no idea.

As I become more awake, a bit of dread starts to seep in, the kind made of the purest self-doubt and deep-rooted anxiety. It starts now to completely fill my veins, and even though I know every important detail of last night and into the earliest hours of this morning, even though I know I have nothing to be ashamed of, somehow still I am.

I rise to a seated position on the floor next to him and reach for my socks sitting beside me. Starting to pull the first one on, I realize that I don't recall exactly when or why I took them off and another jolt of panic moves though me. All at once my motions become erratic and he stirs, as if he feels it. I try to settle, but then his hand is at my back and I turn to see that he has shifted onto his side. He has propped himself onto one elbow, his other palm now gliding back and forth over my spine like a leaf in a breeze. So gently he whispers good morning, as though he knows I can't handle anything more than that. Only a whisper.

He tugs the bottom of my T-shirt then, the white one that finally dried while hanging over the passenger's seat of Paddy's car yesterday. There is not even a trace of the beer that soiled it, as if it never happened, as if none of this did. I know it did though. I know that so many things happened and I want to believe they were real. I want to believe that I am.

He gives my shirt another tug, and when I turn toward him he motions for me to come onto my back on the floor beside him, and I move there as if pulled by a force that is not my own. He leans over me then, softly kisses my forehead, and I cannot help closing my eyes. When he pulls back I open them and he looks at me and tells me he can't believe how beautiful I look first thing in the morning, and I almost fall for it. I almost do, but then I see it again.

I see his shirt and read the words and I am so quiet that he says my name. And it is always really serious when they say your name.

Four Years Earlier

The oatmeal was hot when I sat down next to it, but that was a while ago, and as the bedroom door opened behind me I took hold of the spoon again, pushed it around some more. My mother walked to the other side of the table. She looked at the bowl and then back at me. "You have to eat, honey," she said. "You'll make yourself sick."

I already am, I thought. I'm so sick.

I didn't say it though. Instead I just pushed my spoon into the food, scooped up a helping and brought it toward me as nausea once again threatened to jump off its end of the seesaw, send me crashing down. I dropped the spoon back in the bowl, put my hands in my lap. "I can't do this," I told her.

"I know it's hard," she said. "But you haven't had one thing since I got here."

She'd come the day before, only an hour after I'd called her, when the pain was so bad I couldn't stay at work. She'd picked up on the first ring but hadn't said hello. Rather, she'd answered, "What's wrong?"

Through choking sobs I had told her what my friend had told me the day before, when I'd been standing in my kitchen pressed against the counter, and how it was true, how I'd found the phone book in the bottom drawer of the green desk and how I'd called the girl and how she'd told me.

"I'm leaving now," my mother had said to me the day before. "Right this minute."

When she'd arrived about an hour later, at just after eleven in the morning, I'd clung to her and told her I couldn't talk about it, but then told her everything. After that, I went to bed and did not rise again until close to nine at night, when I'd tiptoed out to her on the couch, my face soaked in tears and heartache. She'd been asleep, but as soon as I'd stepped across the threshold of the living room she'd bolted upright and reached out to me, like she'd been waiting.

"I just don't know what to do," I'd said.

She stood then, left her Diet Pepsi on the coffee table and put her arm around my shoulders, turned me back toward the bedroom. We crawled into my king-sized bed and I moved right up against her, right up close to my mother. I was almost twenty-eight years old, but I was nestled beside my mom, her arm around me, stroking my hair as I thought how the day before I could never have imagined being this close to her. I would have wanted a safer distance then, but that was before. That was when there were safe distances.

"Thank you Mom," I had said, before mercifully falling asleep.

The next morning, staring at that bowl of oatmeal the way you might stare at medicine you don't want but know you need, I put my face in my hands and told her again that I just couldn't. I could not.

She didn't speak. Instead, she reached for the phone resting on the table beside my cold bowl of food and went to the faculty phone chain hanging on the wall. She dialed the number of my school building and waited. Eventually she said, "Hi, I'm calling for my daughter."

Then I heard her say that I was sick and would need another day off, and before she was even done talking I got up. I walked into the bedroom and took off my boots. I let them fall to the floor near the bed, a place where I would normally never leave my boots. This was not a normal time though. This was just not normal.

I reached for the unmade covers and then, fully clothed, I climbed in. My skirt and sweater folded around me and I burrowed in on my side. I pulled the blankets up to my chin and closed my eyes, unable to look at the bedroom I used to share with him. I used to share it with him until he moved out because he didn't want to get married and then moved an hour away so he could take a job that he said would be good for our future, would give us the security he needed to be a husband. All it had given us though was his opportunity to sleep with someone else without me knowing and to take her out for dinner, buy her birthday gifts and meet her mother. I could not eat or sleep with that knowing. I could not even breathe.

I heard the phone ring and wondered if it was him calling again, the way he had called and called and called yesterday and we had not answered until one time when my mom finally did. Finally she had picked up the phone and told him to go fuck himself.

"It's over," she had said to me after that. "It's over."

I thought it was too. I thought it was over, but then again I knew in some deep and desperate place that maybe it wasn't. As broken and terrified as I was, somehow I thought that it might not be over and that parts of the pain might have been from that. Parts of the pain might have been from knowing that it still wasn't even the end.

My mother peeked in then. "Honey, do you need anything?"

Tears streamed down my face. I wiped them away. I turned to look outside, found a cloudy sky filling the panes of the bedroom window that used to be ours.

"No," I choked out. "I don't."

But as she closed the door, I knew that wasn't true at all.

I need things, I thought. I do.

“Come here,” he says now, and pulls me to him. He shifts onto his back and puts his arm out to encircle me as I turn onto my side and put my head in that place that is not quite his shoulder, not quite his chest either. I cannot believe I am here, and I think back to that day four years ago on my bed, wrapped in my skirt and sweater and staring at a cloudy sky much like this one at my friend’s apartment.

Four years ago, and yet I did not leave until four months ago. It can take such a long, long time to leave.

“You doin’ okay?” he asks.

“Yeah,” I say softly.

“Really? Because you seem like something is wrong. Is something wrong?”

His gentle words cause a shift in the unease that was making a home in my heart and my belly. Quickly they start to dissipate and I know that it is happening again. From the outside in. I’ve been reading the messages between me and My Ex and I’ve been seeing it there too. The outside in. Always from the outside in.

Still, I feel some relief and I appreciate it and I tell him that nothing is wrong. I say that I’m simply tired because I didn’t get much sleep. I say that someone kept me up all night. He laughs a low deep laugh that I instantly remember. Through the filters of sobriety though, the sound is even more rich, and it draws me closer. He feels it too and puts his closed lips to the top of my head, takes a deep breath in and lets it out slowly, so slowly, and I feel close to him, too close, like we’ve known each other for so much longer than just sixteen hours. Then I start to think about how dangerous this is, a knowing that creeps in and starts gently to whisper, but suddenly Cherry Almond’s bedroom door opens and I am grateful not to have to think about dangerous things.

I peek up over Big Mistake's body as my friend emerges and bounds gleefully down the few steps that lead to the living room we are in. She calls out, "Rise and shine!"

Big Mistake and I both moan at her and she laughs and says, "If you two, well, three," she corrects, tossing her head toward The Kisser in her bedroom, "want a ride home, get your tails in gear."

"We're coming," I call back in a whiny voice, and she laughs the softer morning version of her laugh, then turns away, leaving us in a vapor of sweet cherry and almond lotion.

"Guess we'd better get up," he says.

I inhale deeply and say that we should, then make it to my feet and reach for my purse on the chair as he rolls over and grabs my ankle. I laugh, shaking free of his light hold, then walk up the few stairs to the second level. As I get to the top I hear a sound that I can't quite make out. I turn to look at him.

"What?" I ask, lured by the look in his eyes.

"You just look so damn good, girl." I smile at him as he asks, "Even first thing in the morning? Shit."

My smile widens and our eyes lock, but quickly I look away, that dangerous knowing creeping in again as I turn toward the bathroom. Once inside, I find myself filled with an unfamiliar confidence as I glance at my reflection in the mirror and am surprised to think that I look better than I'd expected, that maybe he's right, and that maybe I should know that without anyone having to tell me.

But I don't.

I rinse my mouth with warm water and rummage through my purse for a piece of gum. I find one, half out of its wrapper and smushed to a wet nickel underneath my wallet, and I wonder why my things are wet as I begin to laugh out loud.

I finish unwrapping the soggy gum, pop it in my mouth and open the door. The Kisser is emerging from Cherry

Almond's bedroom and looks miserable. Sweetly I say hi to him and he nods but does not respond. He walks down the few steps to the living room. I follow him and find Big Mistake right in my face, and once more I hate that T-shirt and hope that after this I never see it again. I wonder if I want to see *him* again though. I think I do, but I'm scared and think it's too soon, and then he smiles at me and reaches for my hand and says he doesn't know if he is even sober enough yet to tie his shoes, and we all laugh as he just holds my hand.

"Why are we up so early anyway?" moans The Kisser, and Cherry Almond reminds all of us that she cleans offices every Sunday morning so she has to take us home now. Big Mistake says that he truly appreciates the ride and I look at him and he winks at me and I pull gently away, reach for my jacket and start for the door. Within seconds the four of us are heading down the stairs to the lobby and out into the parking lot. The day is not like yesterday. Instead it is cloudy and cold and I feel a small leak in the air of confidence I've been floating on. I think I must look terrible in this gray light and he will notice and never want to see me again. My heart begins to pound.

There are much prettier girls, I think. There are much nicer houses.

My friend unlocks her car door and gets in. She reaches across to unlock the passenger's door and Big Mistake opens it, pushes the seat forward and motions for me to step in first, then struggles to follow me into the back, trying desperately to fold his very large self into this space that is too small for him. We grin at each other as my friend starts the car and eventually he is securely stuffed inside. The Kisser gets into the passenger's seat and we pull out of the parking space and we are all very quiet, too quiet. The silence makes me edgy and I realize how different this ride is from the ride to Cherry Almond's last night, after midnight, when we'd called Paddy to get out of her bed and her pajamas to come back downtown and get us. She was shocked and thrilled and absolutely baffled by the addition of these two guys who were friends with each other when we met them separately.

That entire ride to Cherry Almond's was filled with raucous voices and screeching laughter and silly voicemails left for friends who were not with us. It wasn't at all like this eerily silent ride now, where I wonder what everyone is thinking and what I am thinking too. I wonder what the fuck I am thinking with this stranger sitting next to me, my knee unintentionally resting against his leg. It feels odd, like I should move it, even though last night we touched much more than that and I didn't feel odd at all.

I want someone to say something and I am possibly just about to scream from the quiet that has become too loud, when Cherry Almond suddenly turns on the radio. Country music breaks the silence that was filling my head with its own painful noise, and that is when he seems to come awake too, to realize my knee is resting against his leg. He looks at this spot where we are touching and then glances at me, holds my gaze and smiles as he puts his hand on my leg, just lets it rest there while my stomach jumps.

Before I can fully form my smile back he looks away, looks out the window on his side of the car. Unease snuggles safely into my heart and belly now and my pulse quickens with its unspoken questions, with not knowing. I want to tear this all open, see exactly what is inside, every detail. I am no good at just letting things unfold. I am just no good.

Finally, we are pulling into the entrance of my large apartment complex and this guy who put a pillow down for me last night and draped a blanket over me too, turns and asks for my phone. I wonder why he wants it, but I'm not thinking clearly enough to ask, so I just dig it out of my purse and hand it to him.

He flips it open and begins dialing a number with one hand as he reaches into his coat pocket with the other. A moment later another phone rings. It is his own phone in his hand.

"Now you have my number," he says in a low tone.

"Okay," I say, and inside of me the familiar gift of confidence begins its ascent. I start feeling sure and strong, but then it quickly mixes with a swift and sudden frustration too. Just seconds ago I was worried and weak, and now, because of his approval, I feel buoyed. I couldn't summon that strength myself. I needed this guy to give it to me. I need the attention of a guy I hardly know to give me my worth and I don't want that. I do not want that, but it seems to be who I am.

"You all right?" he asks for the third time this morning, because the struggle in me is maybe not as private as I think. It seeps out. It seeps through my eyes and my heart and my skin. I wonder if people have always noticed it as often as he does. I wonder where it comes from too. But I also think I know.

"I'm just tired," I say softly.

My friend pulls up to the entrance of my apartment building and The Kisser opens the door. He gets out and pulls the seat forward so that Big Mistake can excavate himself from the back seat where he does not fit. I am alone in the car for just an instant with Cherry Almond and I look at her and she gazes back at me, both of us with wide eyes and barely contained smiles of wonder and a million questions.

"Thank you," I say to her. "I'll call you later."

"Oh you better, Chicky!" she says.

I step out of the car and The Kisser gets back in, keeping the seat pulled forward so Big Mistake can reenter. He turns to me and smiles.

"Call me," he says, and I think that those are famous last words, but I smile and nod my head. He touches my hand and there is a spark there and we both move in, but then we don't.

He gets back into the car and they pull away. I stand there and watch from the sidewalk. I watch for what seems like a very long time, then all of a sudden realize that I am still standing there and turn to rush into my building. Despite my fatigue I take the stairs two at a time, noticing how thirsty I am. In only seconds I am at my own door, unlocking it and walking in. I remove my shoes and set my purse on the coffee table, but before I make it to the refrigerator I notice the message indicator light blinking on my home phone. Immediately I know what the message will be and I cannot believe that I have forgotten.

"Hi honey," says my dad's voice at about eight the night before, long after I should have been home from the parade. "I just want to let you know we're going to leave a little later tomorrow. About nine-thirty instead. I wanna go out to Grandma's for a while before we go."

"Oh shit," I say out loud to myself. "Oh shit, shit, shit."

My dad's message continues. "All right. See you tomorrow. I'm really lookin' forward to it, kiddo. Can't wait to spend some time with you. Bye babe. I love you."

For two weeks I've planned to meet my dad at my parents' house this morning, forty minutes from my own, and ride with him to Pennsylvania where my youngest sister has just started graduate school. She needs a dresser and a table and I've offered to make the trip with him, to help transport these things in his truck. I have to be there in an hour and a half, which means I have to leave in fewer than sixty minutes, and I cannot imagine that. I cannot imagine doing anything other than chugging this soda and crawling into bed to sleep and sleep and sleep.

I pick up the phone to call and tell him I can't go and he answers on the first ring. "Hey babe," he says brightly. "Did you get my message last night?"

Shit, shit, shit.

"Yeah," I reply. "Well, I got the message *from* last night, but I got it just now."

My father laughs deeply and I am instantly filled with the sound of him, a sound I love so much. I know that from my few words and the tone of my weak voice, he knows why I only just now got his message from twelve hours ago. He knows, but then again he doesn't know at all.

"I take it the St. Patrick's Day parade was a blast," he says, that pure and loving timbre in his voice.

"It was," I tell him.

"I'm so glad," he replies. "Where'd you go?"

I pause for a moment, consider pajamas and my bed, a heavy blanket pulled all the way to my chin. And I consider the table legs he took off for me too, the subs we ate with tear-filled eyes.

"I'll tell you when I see you," I say. "I have to get ready now. I'm just waking up."

CHAPTER TEN
Good Morning Beautiful

It's another Monday morning, but this a good morning, beautiful. The sun is shining again and it's still warmer than it should be for March. The snow has melted along with a lot of the pain I've been feeling since October when my heart was freshly broken. The blood seems to have stopped dripping and the wound isn't as sore and stinging to touch. There seems to be more of a dull ache now.

I am aware that it might be because someone else is filling the void though, filling it up with joy and anticipation so that there is less room for sorrow and fear. It's coming from the outside I think, but then I don't. I don't think.

Just as I'm pushing away this worry about fleeting and risky joy, my blond friend suddenly walks in through my open classroom doorway and fills the space with the scent of cherries and almonds. She gently closes the door behind her, and when we hear it click she says, "What the fuck!" I set down the books I am carrying and turn to her. I'm already laughing.

"Pennsylvania?" she questions. "You went to Pennsylvania yesterday?" She begins to laugh wildly and it catches me too, right in the belly. My laugh becomes louder.

"I told you, I forgot," I say, still laughing.

Through her high-pitched giggles she says that she thinks I probably forgot a lot of things over this weekend and I tell her that I remember everything, just with a few fuzzy parts. She laughs and laughs. "I cannot believe this. I really can't," she says.

"Which part can't you believe?"

"Tell me about it," she says. "All of it. I can't believe any of it." Her laughter rolls then, tumbles around me, and I can't help being so very full.

"So?" I ask her. "Have you talked to The Kisser?" She laughs again, puts her hand to her mouth as we sit down at a table.

"He called yesterday. We're going to dinner tonight," she says with surprise.

"Oh my God!" I say, leaning toward her. "That's awesome."

A huge smile mixes with giggles that slip out every couple of words and she says, "Yeah, except we'll probably have to go somewhere with booster chairs and those place mats they let you color on." The end of this statement is almost swallowed by a chortle.

"Stop. He's not that much younger."

Composing herself she says with horror, "He's twenty-six. He's five years younger!"

"Ten. Remember we agreed to take five years off, to account for male dumbness."

Her head falls backward and her face turns toward the ceiling. Her upper body arches dramatically over the back of the small chair and she lets her arms fall in mock exasperation. Looking at me again she says, "Thanks a lot!"

We laugh and laugh and I love her so much right now. She is my medicine.

"Seriously though, just go with it," I tell her, and I mean it. "We wouldn't search out a guy this age for you, but since you stumbled upon him . . ."

"Speaking of stumbled upon," she interrupts. "Did you call him last night?"

"No," I say.

"So, when are you gonna?"

"I don't know. Maybe I'm not," I say, but don't know if I mean it. "Can we get back to you please?"

"What? Don't be ridiculous."

I reach for a small stack of books, pull them onto the table we're sitting at and shuffle through them as if searching. I think about getting up to put them away when she reaches over and grabs one.

"Hello," she says, waving a book at me and laughing.

"Come on," I start. "If I hadn't called it off, I'd be a newlywed right now. This is too soon."

"I get that," she says, placing the book back into the pile. "I really do. Nobody says this has to be serious though." I stop rifling and look up at her. She shifts, straightens her body, pulls her shoulders back and looks at me in earnest. "Listen," she tells me. "Obviously you two are very attracted to each other. Your PDA in the bar and the blanket wedged into my couch cushions are proof of that." She laughs and I do too, then look down, my elbow on the table and my hand at my forehead as if the sun is too bright in my eyes.

"So you have that," she continues, "and just, I don't know, you really hit it off. I think you could use this, just a little fun for a while. That's all."

I pick up my head, put my hands in my lap. "I wonder if maybe I'm not ready for that either. Just a little fun."

She looks at me with a slightly titled head. "You deserve to have some fun and you're good at it, you know?" When I don't respond she says, "Can you just have fun, not worry about anything else?"

"I guess so," I tell her, but I don't know if I can anymore, if I ever could.

I look out the window and suddenly I remember looking out another window and I remember so much pain and I remember thinking I knew what was causing it, but now I'm not so sure. Now I think maybe it was there long before I noticed.

Four Years Earlier

It was after six o'clock in the morning and I'd been up waiting since close to five, staring out the window and repeatedly pushing the blinds apart with my thumb and forefinger to find that it still wasn't there. His truck. It still was not in its new parking spot next door, where he'd moved to from our apartment less than a week before so that he could have room to think, to think about getting married. Right next door.

I couldn't fucking stand it anymore and I got up from the seat beside the window and walked into the bedroom. I moved toward the double bed he'd brought up from the basement because he'd taken the king-sized one next door to his new place, and I crawled back in. As soon as I had the blankets pulled up though, I felt trapped and I threw them off, walked back out to the kitchen again. I sat down and pulled my legs up into the chair. My chin rested on my knees, and once more I pushed the blinds apart, much like I did that day all those years ago when he was in the driveway with his ex-girlfriend and she was screaming and asking and hurting. I was like that. I was screaming and asking and hurting as I looked across to his driveway that was separated from mine by only a thin row of grass and shrubs.

But really it was separated by so much more.

I let go of the blinds and stared across the kitchen, watched the water dripping in the sink. Drip. Drip. Drip. I turned my head back to the window, pried open the blinds again. I looked at the driveway, looked away, let the water drip three more times before I turned my head back to the window and lifted the blinds. I looked at the driveway, looked away again. I let the water drip. I looked back. I lifted the blinds. I looked away. I did it again. I did it again and again and again.

It became six-thirty in the morning then and still he was not home. He had said that he didn't want to lose me and that his moving out wasn't the end, just different. It was not the end. It was just different. But he had been out all night.

Drip.

Drip.

Drip.

I opened the blinds again, looked out again, turned my attention back to the sink again.

Drip.

Drip.

Drip.

Finally, my thoughts became overwhelming and I started to cry and didn't look back out the window. Instead I put my brow on my knees and wrapped my arms tightly around my legs as the tears fell hard.

What seemed like hours passed before my crying subsided and I heard the drip in the sink again and looked up suddenly, wondered how many drips that had been. How many drips had that been and when had I last looked out? I turned my attention quickly back to the window and pried the two plastic pieces apart, then drew in a shallow breath, stunned.

His truck. It was there.

I stood. I opened the blinds wider. His truck was in the driveway where I had spent the last two hours looking for it, but he was not in it and the door to his apartment was closed. He must have pulled in, gotten out and entered his apartment all as I cried and drifted off on my sadness. So many things happened when I wasn't looking. Too many.

I went to the door and hurriedly slipped on my clogs. I walked out onto the small porch in my pajamas with my hair falling out of a ponytail and my face tight with dried tears. I closed the door behind me and quickly crossed my driveway, walked over the grassy median between our two parking spaces, then hurried to his door. I turned the knob. It circled only a fraction before stopping abruptly. Locked.

But this wasn't the end, right? This was just different, right?

I knew it wasn't. It wasn't right.

I knocked and it hurt my heart. It sounded so loud, just like the drip, drip, drip. Knock, knock, knock. I thought I'd have to knock again, but he answered the door in only a moment, so quickly that I wondered if he'd been standing right behind it breathing deep breaths and expecting this. He did not look surprised to see me. He looked alert and even a bit annoyed, and suddenly I felt totally exposed, naked.

"What's up?" he asked.

Those two words. Those two small dismissive words rang out like gunshots, sent me deeper into a haze of fear and rejection. They sent me deeper into rage.

"What's up?" I said evenly. "Are you seriously going to be that big of a fucking asshole?"

I didn't wait for him to respond. I had waited all fucking night and I wasn't going to wait a second more.

"What's up," I said, "is that it is almost seven in the morning and you're just getting home and I know nothing about that. Nothing."

He took in a deep breath, let it out quickly.

"I told you I needed a little space," he said, as if that would explain it. But the words hit me like a ton of bricks, hard and solid and painful. I tried to mask my grief, but the mask was flawed.

"You need a little space to stay out all night?" I asked.

He took just an instant too long to form his reply, and like a twig suddenly underfoot, I snapped. I preferred the snapping though. The sound of it covered the sound of so much hurt.

"I'm sorry," I said scornfully. "I guess I thought by a little space you meant the taking all your shit and moving across the driveway kind of space. I didn't know you meant the staying out all night space too!"

I took in a breath but didn't miss a beat. "I thought you meant the not seeing each other every morning or the not splitting bills anymore kind of space. You know, not sleeping in the same bed every night, but not sleeping in someone else's bed," I said.

I paused, but he offered nothing, so I replied, "As stupid as I am though, I draw the line at the staying out all fucking night kind of stupid."

Through an exasperated sigh he said my name then, and I knew it was serious. It is so serious when they say your name, and then he said, "Jesus fuckin' Christ."

"You know what?" I bellowed. "Fuck you!"

I started slowly to turn away after that, so slowly that he could have stopped me. He could have stopped me, but he didn't, and so I turned back. As always, I turned back.

"You are such a motherfucker," I said flatly, but full of longing too.

I spun then and rushed toward my own apartment, placed absurdly on the other side of our two driveways, and I listened for him to call after me. I listened, but I didn't hear a thing, until finally I did. Finally, stepping onto the first porch step, a sound rang out.

I heard the sound of his door closing. I heard that little latch on the knob falling into place in the door's frame, and I turned to look back. I turned to look back and it hurt like hell. It always did. It hurt so much to look back.

Later, more than four hours later, I had cleaned my already clean apartment. I'd done laundry and cooked things and rearranged drawers and had to stop several times to catch my breath and hold my heart. Then, mercifully, I'd fallen on top of the comforter of my freshly made bed, the one he'd brought up from the basement when he left the week before.

About an hour after that, as I slept, he let himself in with the key he'd not given back. He took his shoes off at the door and walked the several steps to the bedroom we used to share and crawled onto the bed next to me. I woke up as he was wrapping himself around me and I turned into him. Just as if nothing had happened. As if he had not moved out last week. As if he had not stayed out all night. As if he had not just closed the door behind me.

I turned into him and he folded me into his arms and said he was sorry, kissed my face and said it again. I looked up at him with eyes barely open and I started to ask. I started to, but then I didn't. I didn't ask what he was sorry for.

"I love you," he said. "I love you so much."

I gathered my breath then, my courage too.

I whispered, "I don't know if you do. Not in the way I need."

He pulled me into him and held me tightly then, so tightly I felt almost restrained, but it felt good, so much better than being let go. I was drifting back to sleep when I heard him say, "I do."

It is now the fourth time I have flipped open my phone to stare at the number Big Mistake dialed into it on the morning before, and I'm thinking about this other morning, the one on top of the comforter, before the girl and the gifts and the kitchen counter biting into my back. It was before all of that, but surely I had known that it was coming.

It's Monday night, close to eight o'clock, and if I don't push the green button soon then it's going to be too late. That's what I always think, that it's going to be too late, and so I don't let anything unfold naturally. I fear that I have to take it all apart myself before it takes me apart, sends me into so many little pieces.

Then finally I do it. I push the green button and my heart begins to race and only a second later I hear the ring in my ear.

"Please, please go to voicemail," I say out loud.

"Hello," says Big Mistake. Oh fuck, I think. Fuck, fuck, fuck.

"Hi there," I say with a voice I don't recognize.

He pauses a moment then asks knowingly, "Is this the little leprechaun from two very long nights ago?"

I stop pacing and sit on the bed, savoring the quick bud of self-assurance that starts on my lips and blossoms into a smile. I say, "Top o' the evening to ya."

He laughs that low deep laugh and I'm transported to the warm dim corner of a bar on Saturday night. We are sitting in chairs opposite each other. One of my legs is between his two as he tries to pull me into his chair and laughs when I say that I don't lap dance in public.

"What's up gorgeous?"

My budding smile is now in full bloom as I ask how he is and he takes in a deep breath, lets it out with the words, "I'd be better if I weren't filling boxes with shit from my kitchen cupboards."

"Why are you doing that?" I ask, confused.

"I'm moving, remember? I'll be out there by April first so I need to get packing."

"Right. I remember," I say, and it is only in that very moment that I do remember.

"Well then, aren't you counting the days until I'm just around the corner?"

"Not quite," I say firmly, trying on this false bravado, wanting to be healthier than I am.

"Well that's not nice," he says, and seems to mean it.

"I mean, I just haven't known you long enough or sober enough to be counting days until you move here," I explain, and it feels like a lie.

I hear the noises in the background settle down then, a quieting of pans and utensils. I remember packing and unpacking my own things just a few months ago. I remember when My Ex packed his to move next door because he needed some space, a year before we were engaged, two years before it was all over. I've seen too many boxes filled with things. I hate them.

"So, the tough-girl routine of Saturday night wasn't an act, huh? You really are this tough?"

I choose my words gingerly, careful not to tell him too much. "I'm not very tough, really. That's the problem."

I'm cautious. I say little. I don't want him to know anything, and then again, I do. He doesn't respond right away and it is quiet between us and I feel him searching for words. I'm searching too. Finally he tells me, "You're tough about what you will and won't allow."

That is a strange thing to say, I think. It is also true and real and I feel totally drawn in. We aren't small-talking. We are getting right to it.

"I think that's reasonable," I say, then lie back on the bed, becoming comfortable, more in control.

"So how long will that go on?" he asks intently, surprising me.

"What do you mean?" I ask.

"How long will you have these rules or something?"

"Rules? I'm not sure I have rules. I have boundaries and I will have them for as long as it takes."

Suddenly I realize that this is too much too soon and it feels confrontational and I think I should back down a bit, but he is quick.

"As long as what takes?" he challenges.

I pause, unsure, but then I say, "As long as it takes to figure out what I've learned and make sure I don't do the same things again," and surprise myself once more. I'm telling this guy more than I want to, saying things I didn't even know I wanted to say. How can I be talking to a stranger like this? I was supposed to be married for two and half months now. I was supposed to be a lot of things.

I think of our green desk, of the drawer that falls out and the journal I tore apart.

"I get that, but you could probably let your guard down just a little, don't you think?"

I bristle. "Why do you feel the need to worry about my guard?"

"Ouch," he says, and seems to force that low deep laugh he has.

"Oh, did I hurt you?" I tease.

"You didn't yet, but I have no doubt you could."

I think about this, wonder what kind of hurt he might be talking about, feel the power in the possibility of hurting him. Maybe that would help. Maybe it would lessen my own pain if I could dish some out.

"Are you still there?"

"Yes," I say.

"Thinking up ways to keep me away from you I bet."

"Now why would I have called if I wanted to keep you away from me?" I ask reasonably.

"Good question. Actually," he says, and the kitchen noises start again, "I didn't think you *would* call."

"Why not?"

"Why? Because of everything we just said, about you being so guarded. That's why."

"Hmm," I mumble, thinking about that. "I'm maybe not as guarded as you think. I mean, I did spend the night with you only hours after we met."

"Ah, this is true and I am so grateful for that. But of course, I couldn't even get my hand up your shirt."

I laugh uncomfortably, a little startled by this intimacy. My face gets warm. He continues.

"I gave you my number so I'd know you wanted to talk to me," he says. "I figured if I called you, you might just answer to be nice."

"Oh, and I'm the guarded one?"

He laughs again and it sounds so real.

"I can't believe all the shit she left here," he then says all of a sudden.

"What?" I ask, surprised.

"My ex-wife. You wouldn't believe the shit she just left that I'm stuck sorting through."

Immediately I bristle. I don't want to talk about this.

"No, I probably wouldn't," I say with irritation that he doesn't seem to notice.

"Yeah," he says. "Bullshit."

I listen to him rummage through things I can't see and I imagine dinnerware he doesn't know what to do with, too many spatulas and knives and serving spoons. As if hearing my thoughts he says, "Oh, and don't get me started about the cookie sheets. Why did we ever have so many cookie sheets?"

I imagine his ex-wife then, wonder if she is at all like the girl I met at a jewelry party last month, the one who admitted she had walked down the aisle just hours after a huge fight with her fiancé and how every step of the way, passing friends and family in her long white gown, she imagined not doing it. She imagined turning around and running out. Then she looked at me with something like envy when she told me that I was brave to call off my wedding. I said that really I was scared to death and she reminded me that being brave doesn't mean you aren't scared.

He is going on about the things she left in his kitchen, but I'm not answering. Instead, I'm imagining all the couples who saunter the aisles of Target and Pottery Barn choosing the vases and towels and plates they want purchased for them, even though they know they'll be splitting it all up in the not-so-distant future. And they allow it. They allow it because they're afraid.

Maybe I didn't do that, but I did other things instead, because I have always been scared too. I am starting to see that I have always been so scared and that maybe it makes me cling and cling, white knuckles on life and love. Maybe I thought I could hold him that way, but maybe that's not how it works.

"I should let you go," I suddenly say to him, because I need to go. I need to think about this.

But abruptly the sounds cease and he says, "Shit. I'm really sorry."

"It's fine," I say. "It's just a bad time for you. Give me a call back when you're not so busy."

"I am no longer busy," he says. "I may be an idiot, but I'm not busy."

"Why are you an idiot?" I ask. "I mean, besides the obvious reasons." He starts to laugh.

"I can't believe I waited all day for this abuse," he says, his laugh getting heartier.

There is a short silence and then he tells me that he has been waiting all day for me to call and that he did not mean to spend this time bitching about his ex-wife and throwing shit around the kitchen. I think about fear and white knuckles, kicking and struggling, always kicking and struggling, and I know I should hang up, but knowing doesn't make it so.

"You waited all day for me to call, huh?" I ask.

"I did," he confesses, and then something hits me.

"Wait a minute. You gave me your number by calling your cell with mine. That means you have my number in your caller ID."

"That's true," he banters.

"So you could have called me," I realize.

"Right, but I wanted you to call first."

"What if I hadn't?"

"I had insurance I guess."

"So you would have called?"

"Of course. Maybe not today, but eventually I would have."

"Oh. Is today too early? Did I break a rule?" I ask, joking mostly, but unsure. I haven't done this in a really long time. I was supposed to be married less than three months ago.

"No, I don't care about that shit. I wish you'd called yesterday," he says and I smile, once more savoring a bud of self-assurance.

Once more from the outside in.

"I have some pressing questions for you that can't wait three days," he continues.

"Pressing questions, huh?"

"Yeah. We're gonna try to get to know each other, right?"

I pause, surprised by this. "I guess," I say.

"Don't be so excited," he tells me.

"Yes, we can get to know each other," I say with more energy.

"That's better," says Big Mistake.

"So, what's one of your questions?" I'm intrigued by the idea that he wants to get to know me, that he has questions.

"Well, seriously, I do have a lot of important questions, but first, can I ask you one that's not as important, but that I really want to know?"

"Sure," I say, delighted.

"Do you have some secret workout for getting that hot little ass of yours?"

I draw in a deep breath. I am surprised, excited, so unsure, and trying to hold onto what Cherry Almond said this morning. "Can you just have fun," she asked me, "not worry about anything else?"

"I guess so," I told her.

But I don't know if I can anymore.

If ever I could.

The next morning I am so tired. I hold frozen spoons over my closed eyes trying to make them less puffy, but feel grateful that the tired and puffy come not from insomnia and crying, but from staying up way beyond my bedtime acting like I'm less broken than I usually am.

I place the spoons in the sink now and make my way toward the front door, take a loving look at the couch and feel the odd energy that comes from anticipating an afternoon nap, from a kind of tired that makes you feel alive and alert, that soaks right into your skin and feels like healing. When I reach the door I gather my knee-high black boots and put them on, then stand up straight and drop the hem of my skirt so that it falls just above my calves. I take one last peek in the mirror by the door and I feel good.

But then I remember.

I slip off my boots, unable to make even the short trip to the bathroom wearing shoes. Shoes can never touch my carpeting because everything will be ruined then, and I think about that and I know it isn't right, but knowing doesn't make it so.

In the bathroom I open the medicine cabinet. I pull out the bottle. I push down on the cap and turn it, gently shake out one small pill, then wonder if maybe I can stop now. I wonder for just the shortest moment, not even measurable, then quickly realize that one night of feeling full cannot undo months and months and years and maybe even forever.

I set the pill on my tongue.

I replace the cap and the bottle, slide the mirrored cabinet door back in place and look into it as I swallow the pill and as I swallow more. I swallow fear and shame and self-doubt and think how unlikely it is that anyone would ever know just by looking at me. They would never know that I am so full of these things that it empties me out. They would never know that I am often sad, riddled with a sorrow I'm realizing does not come from just this loss. I've been reading about life with My Ex and seeing the constant pulse of worry that has been with me always. A constant pulse that maybe helped pushed us apart. And this pill, it helps. For now, it helps soothe me, calm it all down to just a gentle rain rather than a roaring storm, though I know I must find a better way. I just haven't yet.

My gazing into the mirror, lingering too long, is interrupted when my text message signal goes off, and I think it can't be him. It can't be. It is only seven-twenty in the morning and we were on the phone until after two. It can't be him already.

I run to my purse that is hanging on the doorknob. I reach in for my phone. When I flip it open I see the familiar envelope icon and I see his name above it. A smile is already forming as I press the button that will open the message from Big Mistake, and a moment later I read his words and they fill me up. From the outside in I am filled up and I know that this is a dangerous way to live. I know I have to find a better way. I just haven't yet.

He writes, "Good morning beautiful."

CHAPTER ELEVEN

A Country Song

"You know that's a country song right?"

"Of course I know that," I say lightly.

"So it was a perfect message to start your day."

"It was," I tell him.

"I mean, you're a country music fan and it was morning and you're so beautiful."

I wait a moment, a little anxious, mild fear setting in again, fear that he is trying too hard. I am starting to know what that looks like. I ask, "Are you always this sweet or is this just what you do when you're still trying?"

"Aw, man. Here we go," he says, sounding frustrated.

"I know. I'm sorry. I should keep things like that to myself, figure it out on my own," I repeat, using words he said last night.

"Right, because you'll see that this is me. It's not an act."

"Yes, and it's not like you would tell me if it was an act anyway," I say.

There is a pause then.

"I think you're going have to tell me more about this guy you didn't marry," he says finally.

"What? Why?" I ask, stunned.

"Because then maybe I can understand what you are so scared of."

I don't know what to say. His words take me by such surprise that I can't speak, but I take in a deep breath. "Are you there?" he asks.

I let it out. "Yes." I say.

"You can let me in you know?"

"I am," I tell him.

"*This* is letting me in?" he asks.

"Yes," I say irritably. "I mean, what exactly do you want? I've known you for two days."

I feel his silence then. It is coming through the phone heavy and thick. I think I should hang up, but then he speaks.

"I'm sorry," he tells me. "I'm being an ass. I just really like you."

Again I don't speak. I breathe deeply. I know this is too much too soon, but I need it.

"I'll stop talking about it," he continues. "I'll just show you and stop pushing. Okay?"

"I think that would be great," I tell him, but I don't say that I really like him too and that I'm putting more of myself into this than is reasonable, more than he can see, trying to fill my holes from the outside in with someone I hardly know.

"Oh wow," he says all of a sudden. "I love this song. Can you hear this?" He turns it up and puts the phone closer to the speaker. The music fills the space between us and I hear a song I love, a song that breaks my heart and makes me smile at the same time. It tells a beautiful story and stories are always good, even the ones with unhappy endings, even the ones that require little white pills for a while.

Five Months Earlier

Aimlessly turning the pages of a Redbook magazine, I sat next to a fireplace in the large early-eighteenth-century converted home, when the oversized wooden door finally opened and a nurse said my name. It's always serious when they say your name, I thought, pushing back tears and an upset stomach.

Quickly I replaced my magazine on the battered coffee table and gathered my coat and purse. I followed her through the big oak door and down the creaky hallway to the scale. I removed my shoes, though she didn't ask me to, and stepped on top of the black box. It wobbled beneath my low weight, which wasn't as low as it had been the last time I'd been there for the same thing.

"This way," the nurse said hastily, as I slipped my shoes back on and followed her around the corner where she pushed open another large wooden door and stepped across the small room to the counter. I sat down in the chair closest to the door and looked away as she flipped the pages of the clipboard she'd been carrying, then asked coolly, "You're here this morning for anxiety?"

"Yes."

"I see you were prescribed Paxil before. Three years ago?"

"Yes," I said again.

"You're not taking it anymore though?"

"No."

She opened the papers on the clipboard again and I tried to figure out what she might have been thinking of this and if they would give it to me again.

"So you stopped on your own?" she asked, dropping the papers back into place.

Well, if on my own means waking up naked in a hotel room and then, because it was easier than any alternative, letting my boyfriend, who later became my fiancé, convince me that the Paxil had fucked up my head, yes. I'd stopped on my own.

"I did," I replied, but then didn't mention how forty-eight hours later my anxiety was so severe I threw up and didn't eat again for three days and slept hardly at all. I didn't mention the fourth day, how my hands had stopped shaking enough that I finally wanted to eat, so we drove all over trying to find a place that didn't make me queasy when we pulled in. Eventually we found one and ordered a bowl of fat-noodled soup that I said was the most delicious I'd ever had, and we pretended everything was normal, even as my spoon shook when I brought it to my mouth.

I did not want to explain any of that and I didn't want to explain how, as I sat there three years later, I needed a prescription again because again I could not manage. Ten days after I'd called off my wedding, I simply could not manage.

From the outside in. Always from the outside in.

"The doctor will be with you in just a minute," the nurse said abruptly, and then she was gone and I was alone with my worry and with my legs, which I crossed then uncrossed, crossed then uncrossed, then crossed. I wiggled my foot and read and reread the information on the wall about the flu, the circulatory system and breast cancer detection. Then I traced the edges of each poster with my eyes. I traced them just like I did when I was a kid and didn't have control of situations, didn't think anyone else did either. I tried to gain control, stay in the lines, and my mom thought I had trouble seeing when I tried to explain to her why I wasn't following closely in the grocery store. She thought I had trouble seeing when I told her that I had to go back an aisle because I wasn't done tracing the shelves and the boxes and the tiles on the floor. So she'd taken me to the eye doctor, but he didn't understand either. My eyesight was fine. It was my thoughts that were blinding me.

Just then the door swung open and a doctor entered. She stared down at her stack of papers and absently pushed the door closed with the sole of one foot as she offered a muffled greeting and I wondered where my own doctor was.

Her entire presence filled the room as she moved herself to a low spinning stool and continued going over what was presumably my chart, while I wondered what she was reading and thinking and planning to do with me. A moment later she looked up over the top of the glasses perched on the end of her nose and smiled. Abruptly then, she dropped the pages so that they fell back into a neat pile and she pushed the glasses off her nose, let them hang by a beaded string. She folded her hands in her lap and wheeled herself a little closer to me. Then she asked me what was going on.

I stumbled over my words a bit and looked away. When I looked back she was still staring, and I blinked at tears as she picked up her glasses and poked at the corner of her mouth with one of the ends. I finally found words and numbly replied.

"I was here a while ago. My anxiety had gotten out of control. I was given Paxil and it really helped. Then I stopped taking it because things got better. But they're not better anymore."

The "because things got better" part wasn't really true and guilty tears stole the rest of my words.

"It's okay," she said.

"I'm having a hard time managing," I mumbled.

"Uh huh," she said, still looking at me with her head tilted slightly down and her eyes cast up, hands folded and glasses dangling. "I saw some notes there about your anxiety," she said, and tipped her head toward the clipboard as she set it on the counter. "It's been going on for a long time, ever since you were a kid, just gets worse during times of stress."

I swallowed and agreed with her.

"Tell me about the stress that brought you in here three years ago and the stress that's brought you here today."

Torn between wishing she'd just write the prescription and appreciating that she wanted my story, I took a deep breath and wondered what to say. It all seemed too big to explain in the few minutes she probably had before her next patient.

"Three years ago my boyfriend cheated on me. I found out after it had been going on for over two months and I couldn't handle that."

"I don't know if I could handle that either," she replied. I swallowed and found a soft smile, grateful and sad.

"His lying was the worst part. That was the part I mostly couldn't handle."

She nodded.

"There was that, but there was not knowing too. There was not knowing how to leave him and not knowing how to stay and it made life unbearable." I licked my lips, swallowed hard, continued. "Now we've been engaged for a year and nine months and our wedding was set for two months from today, December thirty-first, and I called it off ten days ago." I started to cry even more then, and she took a tissue from the nearby box and handed it to me across the small space between us.

"So this anxiety, like three years ago, is situational, and we need to get you some relief during this time. We can do that," she said, pulling a pad of prescription slips and a pen out of her breast pocket. She began writing as she said, "You have general anxiety too though. You're anxious daily, weekly, what?"

"I guess normally it's on about a weekly basis. Sometimes daily."

"Uh hmm."

"I don't know for sure. I know that I almost always feel worried and I feel it in my head and in my stomach and in places

I don't know. Sometimes there seems to be a good reason, but sometimes there doesn't."

"Right. Do you eat when you feel like this? Do you go to work? Do you sleep?"

"Right now I don't eat much, but normally, when it's just my usual anxiety, I eat. I go to work. I don't always sleep well though. That's hard."

"That part's hard even with just your normal anxiety?" she asked, then looked up from writing and tore the top sheet from the pad, put the pen back into her pocket.

"Yes," I said. She handed me the prescription and I scanned it quickly to see that she had given me the same medication that had worked so well last time. A small flow of relief began.

"So we need to get you working on how to cope with this anxiety and maybe even reduce it. The Paxil is fine right now and I think you need it, but that's not what I want to see you using for the long term. Okay?"

"Yes," I responded carefully.

"What you need to do is see someone, a therapist, counselor, whatever title as long as you talk to a professional. Someone should help you toward some, you know, new ways of thinking, ways to work through your worries."

I couldn't speak.

"Do you know how to find someone like that?"

"Yes."

"How?"

"I used to see someone through a program at work."

"Okay," she said, with a question at the end of her voice.

"I'll contact them again," I promised.

Yes, I thought. I need to talk to someone. I need help.

"That's good. That's for now though, temporary. You need something long term too. You can start with that and they can get you in touch with someone more permanent."

"All right," I said uncertainly.

"You understand what I'm saying to you, right?" she asked.

"Yes," I said. But I didn't really.

"This is important," she said then. "You don't have to feel so unsure all the time. There doesn't need to be all the not knowing. Or if there is not knowing, it can be okay."

I didn't speak. I just nodded, tried to let that idea soak in, become true. There didn't have to be all the not knowing. Or at least it could be okay.

"Very good," she said with finality as she grabbed my chart once more and began to write on the first page. "Get that counseling started right away or call our office if you need help finding someone. Then I'll see you back here in three months. Sound good?"

"Yes," I replied slowly.

"Great," she said, and pulled the top page from my chart. She handed it to me and said she'd see me at the end of January. I couldn't help but think I should be married for a month by then. But not anymore.

I thanked her and stood. I gathered my purse and jacket and held tight to the paperwork in my hands as I turned toward the heavy door. She stepped in front of me, pulled it open. I walked past her and she told me to take care as I headed back down the creaky hallway alone. I returned to the big oak door from which the nurse had called me less than twenty minutes before, then walked through it and made my way to the window where a receptionist sat waiting. I folded the prescription and tucked it into my purse, then handed over the page the doctor had given me.

The receptionist asked if I had my insurance card and I wanted to ask if there was insurance for heartbreak and doubt and fear and shame, for the kind of worry that rushes at you as surely as the sun comes up in the morning. I wanted to ask if that kind of stuff was covered.

Instead, I just said, "I do."

A song is playing on the radio. It sings about when I get where I'm going, and I think it's fitting as I talk to Big Mistake while he drives on Thursday evening, just five nights since I met him.

"So where are you now?" I say, at least an hour into our third phone conversation of the day. Three too many, I think.

"I just passed exit forty-five."

"You should have taken that one," I tease.

"No, forty-six is more direct, no cutting through the city."

I'm nervous to say what I'm thinking and I'm nervous to even be thinking it, but I say it. "If you'd gotten off at forty-five you could have come for a visit."

Admittedly though, I'm also relieved that he has already passed my apartment. It's almost nine at night and I'm planning to get up at five-thirty in the morning, already dressed in My Ex's oversized sweats, his T-shirt and a pair of his thick winter socks. My face is washed of all makeup. My hair is in a ponytail.

"I'll turn around," he says suddenly.

"You can't turn around on the thruway," I say, sure he is not serious.

"Wanna make a bet? I would have come to see you in a heartbeat if you'd asked. I just thought it was too late." I don't know what to say and he's quiet for a moment too, then suddenly says, "Shit, hold on."

I wait, and after a few seconds his deep voice fills the phone again. He tells me that he has turned around in one of those spots you are not supposed to turn around in and that he can be to my house in about fifteen minutes. He asks for the exact address.

What the fuck, I think. What the fuck am I doing? I shouldn't be doing this. The song is still singing about shedding struggles and getting where you're going and I feel panic rushing in as I tell him that maybe it's not a good idea.

"I'm already headed your way," says Big Mistake simply. "I wanna see you and I know you wanna see me too. Come on, gorgeous."

I know better. I really do know better, but knowing doesn't make it so, and a moment later I'm running to the bedroom already half out of My Ex's clothes and pulling my hair from the ponytail. I catch a glimpse of myself in the mirror of my new armoire and my face is flushed, eyes wide. When I get where I'm going, I think. Will I be okay?

Four And A Half Months Earlier

Abruptly I reversed my direction on the one-way street, making an awkward K-turn because the lane was not wide enough and I'd made my decision to turn around at the last minute. Just like so many other places in life, too narrow and too late.

I'd been on my way home when My Big's name appeared on my cell, My Big who had called repeatedly since she'd heard the news close to two weeks ago, news I didn't know how to make anyone understand, or to hear myself not understanding either. By her third call, I knew I had to talk to her, and I pulled into a parking lot down the street from our apartment where I could see the kitchen light on. I flipped open the phone and said hello to my friend, eleven days after calling off my wedding.

"Sweetie, I'm so sorry," her voice soothed over the phone.

"Hey," I pretended. "How are you?"

"Oh Little," she said, her term of endearment from over ten years ago, since we met in college and became Big and Little. "What are you going to do now?"

I hesitated, but then I told her.

"Well," I said. "We went to Pre-Cana over the weekend. Even though the wedding is called off. He said he wanted to try."

In her silence I heard my words.

I hated them.

"Pre-Cana? Why would you go to Pre-Cana if you are not getting married?" she asked.

"He wanted to," I replied slowly. "I did too, but it was his idea."

"Hmm," she said tentatively. She did not understand. I didn't either.

"He said he doesn't know what he's doing, that he doesn't want to lose me, but he's scared."

"Scared to get married you mean?"

"Yes," I said. "I know it sounds crazy and probably is. I can't explain it. It doesn't make sense really, but it makes more sense when you hear it from him. He loves me. He's just not ready. Well, he wasn't last week anyway." I could feel the slow start of flutters in my stomach, the indecision and fear, the horror of my own words, the excuses.

"He wasn't ready last week?" she asked.

Oh fuck. She could hear it too.

"Yes. Before I called off the wedding he wasn't."

"And now?" said My Big.

"Now he might be. Now it's different," I told her, even as the words made me feel sick.

"Okay," she said slowly, and then there was silence. Neither of us knew what to say to the other until finally she found a way to fill the space.

"So how was Pre-Cana?" she asked, and I was thankful.

"It was great," I replied, with too much enthusiasm for a girl who had just called off her wedding then received premarital counseling with the man she was not marrying.

"We discussed this compatibility test that Mother sent a while ago," I continued. "He finally filled it out after I called off the wedding. I mean seriously, the next day he was at the kitchen table filling it out."

"I don't understand that," she said to me.

"I know," I replied. I didn't understand it either and saying it out loud made it land heavy on my heart and all around me. The absurdity of it seemed to fill up the car so that there was almost no room for me.

"So," she said. "He changed his mind? He wants to get married after all?"

I heard the question and it was deafening, so I pushed the button for the radio, turned the dial so that the volume was low and I could just barely hear the song, but still it helped to break up her words, words that didn't make any sense. My pause was long enough that she added, "Has he given you back the ring?"

I tried for a deep breath, but the weight of her question made it too hard to breathe deeply. "No," I admitted.

It was so loud in that car, just so fucking loud.

"Right," she said simply. Then she was quiet and her silence was worse than words.

"We spent almost four hours with her, with Mother, and she thinks we're very compatible," I continued. "She said a lot of things that are hard to explain, but we have so much to hold onto." My friend didn't speak and I added, "I just don't know how at this point, to hold on."

"I know," said My Big. "I don't know how you can either."

Oh please quiet down. Please. This is just too loud.

Then I said, "She told us one thing that I just can't get out of my head."

"Oh. What's that?" she asked.

"She said that maybe we only called off the wedding, not the marriage, and that she'd still marry us on New Year's Eve if we want, as long as she can see us at least once more before then. It's just the party that isn't happening anymore. That's not the same as the marriage."

My friend listened, then responded gently, so gently.

"That's true, but why would you have to call off the wedding, the party part," she corrected, "if it was still going to be right to get married?"

No, no, no. Stop being so loud.

"I know," I told her. "I don't know."

That's when I started to cry, soft and silent tears that dropped in slow thin lines down my cheeks. There was no sound for too long after that and I couldn't believe she wasn't talking, worried that I had finally stunned her into silence. I said her name, but she didn't respond, and I said her name again before I took the phone away from my ear and looked at it. The connection was lost, the lights and words on the screen gone.

All at once then, the silence from the phone made me aware of the sounds that filled the front seat where I was sitting, the words of a song I loved to sing along with, that I knew every word to but was hearing now for the very first time.

There were words about promises and a better life, and I gasped. I heard her singing about dreams that don't exist and lies that fill canyons, and my tears that had been falling slowly and quietly suddenly poured out loud and fast, and I knew. I knew.

The girl in the song wondered why she was waiting and waiting, and my tears became faster and louder as I dropped my head to my hands and choked on my sobs. I had called off our wedding and was looking for a new apartment and getting movers and didn't know where my engagement ring was, but I was still waiting. Still kicking. Still struggling. Still trying to keep a shattered windshield from falling into my lap.

And then she sang about questions, all the questions her friends kept asking, and the phone rang again and I saw My Big's name, but I couldn't answer. I could only listen to the lyrics about how everything was a lie. Every single thing.

"Don't you know?" the song asked.

Yes, I thought. I do.

It is nine twenty-eight on the clock in my bathroom and that same song is playing now, the one I heard in the car when my friend's words were deafening. Then, suddenly, my apartment buzzer sounds and startles me even though I was expecting it, and I remember four months ago when that buzzer sounded and My Ex came in to look around my new apartment, trace his fingers over our green desk. I never would have thought then that someone else would ever ring that buzzer and that it would be this late at night or happen so soon.

I take one last look at my light eye shadow, the few strokes of bronzer, a trace of lip gloss and that one swipe of mascara on each lash. I look down quickly at the white sweats I've changed into and the pink toe polish that peeks out to match the T-shirt I put on. Underneath all of this are my best underwear and bra, but not because I expect them to be seen. It's because I need them so I can feel good, confident. The wine is helping with that too, and I grab the almost empty glass from the bathroom counter as I head to the front door thinking that I should not be doing this.

I get to the door and pull the lever that unlocks the main entrance downstairs. I open the door just a pinch so he will know for sure which one is mine, then hurry into the kitchen to pour a dash more wine and open his beer. I'm closing the refrigerator when I hear a gentle tap and a soft hello. My stomach lurches and I step out of the kitchen with the wine in one hand and beer in the other. I try to take a deep breath as I move forward. That breath gets stuck when I see him.

"Hey beautiful," he says, and takes me in with one subtle drop of his eyes. He looks back up with a pleased smile that fills me with enough confidence to let out some of the breath I'm holding. He tries then not to turn around while he reaches to close the door behind him, and I spot the red rose he's holding at his back and feel the rest of the air finally leave my chest. We step toward each other, and as soon as I'm in reach he leans down to kiss me as he brings the rose between us and his other arm goes around my lower back. With his lips on mine, he pulls me closer as I naturally bend away just a little, like my body is trying to send my heart a message. The kiss lands softly, but memories come hard. My Ex. Just four months ago he was here like this. He was here.

"Where did you get a rose at this time of the night?" I ask, using the flower as a convenient distraction. Another deep breath comes in now and I let it out with less effort. It's getting easier, but I have to be careful.

"Your favorite place," he says.

"Wegmans. They have roses all night."

He takes the rose and sets it on the coffee table next to our drinks, then pulls me into his arms as he says, "And I'm going to have you all night."

"Oh really?" I say teasingly, marveling at how easy this is, and how it shouldn't be. I have a guy in my apartment at nine-thirty at night, a guy who is not the one I was supposed to marry three months ago. He's calling me beautiful and holding me against him like he's done this all his life, and I have to remind myself that I met him only five days ago. I have to remind myself.

He holds onto me as I think that I can't trust this. I can't trust that I'm seeing it all clearly after so little time to put myself back together, after maybe having never even felt whole to begin with. A quiet voice says I need to be alone, even if I think I can't bear it, and I remember what the doctor said. She said I don't have to feel so unsure all the time. There doesn't need to be all the not knowing. Or if there is not knowing, it can be okay.

But it's not yet.

I'm still me. Just me, which seems harder tonight without the thick shield of alcohol or long-distance phone lines. There is nothing except me and more than eight years of working on a puzzle that never ended up fitting together, full of too many missing pieces, pieces with broken edges, loose-fitting pieces. Then there's the picture that came on the front of the box, the picture I'm still holding. I have not yet let it go, thinking there might still be time. Maybe I will find a piece under the couch, make an edge bend back into shape, finally fit a corner tightly into its spot. I know it is just too soon for a new puzzle. It is just too soon when I am still holding the cover of that other box, wanting that other picture.

"Hey," he says gently, trying to bring me back, but I pull away from him, hoping to stop this freight train that wants to run through my heart when I haven't even unloaded its last shipment yet. He holds onto me though, kisses me gently. I try not to kiss him back, but his lips are melting into mine and one hand is on this spot at the small of my back that makes me feel weak, that I remember only now he found the other night too. He knows it. He knows he's found something, and I sink into him and kiss back even though I hear the sound of the train with all of its boxes of broken promises, its crates stacked with disappointment.

He pulls back and looks into my eyes, then all around my face. It feels as though he is drinking me in, and if I don't think about anything else, about regret and worry and doubt, then it feels good. If I don't think about rejection and fear and hurt then I start to find some contentment in this moment, in just this moment, and suddenly it is not that hard. I find it, a piece of it anyway, a little bit of letting go, and he sees this on my face, feels it as I soften.

"Ah, finally. I must be doing something right," he sings, as I close my eyes and lean into his warmth.

"I know those words," I tell him.

"For you," he whispers, "a country song."

CHAPTER TWELVE
Pieces

Two nights later it is Friday, the real St. Patrick's Day, and I am with Cherry Almond and some others I don't know as well, drinking rum and Cokes and thinking I cannot let this happen. I cannot, I think. I cannot be shattered this soon, going to pieces.

"What the fuck," says Cherry Almond, opening a text.

"What's it say?" I ask, feigning disinterest. I know I can't care this much this soon. I cannot be waiting like this for a guy I have known for just six days.

I push around the appetizers again, pretending.

"It says they just got to Salinger's, but doesn't ask us to meet them, even though it's like two doors down. It doesn't explain why he said they'd be here two fucking hours ago either!"

I laugh a hollow laugh because the wounds are too open tonight and I can't make any of my joy stick. I'm fixated on this guy and where he is and what he's doing and who he's with and what he's thinking and why he hasn't called me. Doubt has taken hold, the need to be important and the fear that I'm not, and I wonder why my comfort with myself seems to depend on a guy I met less than a week ago. It seems to depend on a lot of things that aren't me.

"It's no big deal," I tell her.

"It's no big deal?" she replies. "Oh my God. Come on! I've spent almost every day with him. You've spent a good share of time on this too. Now suddenly they are out with their fucking friends and we can just sit here and wait?"

Our friends begin to chime in, but I can't hear them over the banging in my own head telling me that I'm a fool. I am such a fool to have allowed things to get this far and a fool if I don't let go right now, get up and walk out and not wait for him. I was never good at that though, at not waiting and not waiting and not waiting, and this feels like so many things. Mostly though, it just feels familiar, like a bunch of lessons I still haven't learned.

"I'm calling him," Cherry Almond says, but I hardly hear her as I think about that pretty girl in the coffee shop and wonder again if I've never really been that happy because I've never thought I was pretty enough, as pretty as I think everyone else is, as we are supposed to be. I wonder again about her house and if it was like mine, one that made her feel sad and ashamed and angry, even though she was loved. Can houses really make you feel that way or are you already sad and ashamed and angry and just blame it on the house, and on not being pretty enough? I feel ashamed and angry again. For not being happier.

Cherry Almond is talking on the phone now and she's motioning to me, but I'm gathering my things, readying myself to go. These thoughts are too big for me to sit here being this small.

A short time later, he is sitting beside me and I listen as he tells me that he was just trying to fit back in with his friends, that after he left them to get married it was not the same anymore and now that the marriage has ended he is trying to make up for lost time. He couldn't call because he was trying to show them that he won't let a girl take him away from his friendships again, and I don't know why I'm even listening to this. It is the same things all over again with a new person, and I just want to be more than this.

I need to leave, to just get up and walk out. I can smell the smoke and hear the alarms, see the flames that will consume me if I don't go. It is all right here, so obvious, and so I edge a little closer to the end of the bench when he says, "I don't fit in with these guys anymore though. That's what I realized as I was with them tonight, wanting to be with you."

No, no, no. Edge closer to the end of the bench. Go. This is too familiar. This is a big mistake, just like his T-shirt said a week ago. I should have read it more carefully.

"Well, you probably just have to give it time," I say, trying to sound supportive, strong, like I don't need this. I reach for my purse.

"I don't think so," he replies. "Too much time has passed."

I slip my hand through the strap and edge closer to the end of the bench, slide the purse further up my arm and fumble for my jacket. That's when he reaches for me.

"What are you doing?" he asks.

"You'll fit in with them again," I say, swinging my purse strap over my shoulder and wiggling a little, trying to gather everything, my courage mostly.

"I don't even want to," he says slowly, staring right into my eyes and attempting to drag me into him with a firm and steady gaze. But I look away, and when he realizes that it is not working he reaches out with one arm and wraps it around my waist. He pulls me to him and says, "I want to fit in with you."

Our faces are inches away now and I'm pressed right up against him. I want to stay and I want to run away screaming, and I know better. I've done this before, been in this same spot. I know that I will let him consume me if I don't go, so I start to slip a leg out and stand up just as he leans in and places a slow kiss to my lips. He lingers and lingers, then pulls back only a little and looks me right in the eyes, and his own are full of tears, and I need to leave. I need to fucking leave, but he presses his cheek against mine and whispers into my ear.

"Please don't go," he asks.

And if you do, I think, take me with you.

The purse strap slides off my shoulder.

Suddenly then, a waitress comes to the table and sets down several plates. They are all filled to overflowing with different foods. Another waitress is behind her and sets down more plates and the table becomes full and his friends gather and I am disoriented. I look around as if just waking up and I am not sure what to do or what I was just thinking and I blink my eyes, look at him. Cherry Almond suddenly appears next to me in the oversized booth and tells us to move over, and Big Mistake laughs as he moves, pulling me with him. I tell him that I have to go, but his grip tightens and he tells me to stay and I say that I can't.

"Come on. Look at all this food," he says.

"I don't want anything," I tell him.

"Well, I want something," he tells me. "I want you."

Today would be nine years. If I hadn't left in November, we would be celebrating nine years together, April twenty-fifth. We would have been married four months ago, maybe already divorced by now.

"I can imagine this for the rest of my life," Big Mistake tells me, and I am startled.

"What?" I ask.

"This," he says. "Can't you?"

We are at his house and have just finished a dinner he made. It included a beautifully set table and candles and wine, and I have been completely overwhelmed since the moment I walked in the door, because it is just a Tuesday night, and I know that this is not how Tuesdays should go.

He notices the look in my eyes, but he goes on. He says this is how our entire lives can be. Our entire lives, he says again, and I tell him not to say things like that and he wraps his arms around me as I stand at the kitchen sink rinsing dishes. He places his lips on the back of my neck, takes a deep breath.

"Come on. Can't you see us someday down the road?" He doesn't wait for me to answer. "I can. I see us inside some awesome house, washing dishes while a couple of kids who look just like you run around outside. I can see it," says Big Mistake.

I am stunned and don't speak, but I think no, no I can't. I turn off the water. I reach for a towel to dry my hands and turn to face him. He hasn't really let go of me though, hasn't stepped back at all, and so we are pressed tightly to each other.

"You can't say things like that," I tell him.

"Why can't I?"

"Because it's too soon. I've told you before. I have this bad habit of listening to words and not actions and I can't listen if you're always talking." I wiggle, but he tightens his grip.

"I mean what I say," he says, followed by my name, which rolls gently from his mouth and into an ear that he kisses.

He kisses my cheek too, and then his lips trace a line down the side of my neck and I cannot break away from him.

"Let's go upstairs," he says slowly, as slowly as he has said it so many times over this last month. I break away from him and tell him that I should go home.

"I don't understand," he says. "Why?"

I'm not ready and he knows it and I am not going to say it again.

He reaches for me, pulls me back to him as I look over his shoulder at the television. Taylor Hicks is announced on *American Idol* and he begins to sing. I free myself and walk toward the television saying that I really want to see this. Truly though, I just want to get away. I can't do this today, the day that would have been nine years.

I feel him holding back, still standing by the sink, waiting and watching as Taylor sings about giving it one more try, and I start to come undone. I haven't cried since March tenth, more than a month ago, and I wonder how I know that it was March tenth, but I know how. It's because I count days, the same way I used to count how many times my foot brushed over the vent on the bathroom floor when I was a kid. I count everything, keep track of things. And I make it all mean what maybe it doesn't really mean. But I don't know how not to.

Now I am here with another guy who is telling me he sees a future for us, but all I see is that day in our apartment with all the boxes piled around, when My Ex was sobbing with his head in his hands, when he looked up and asked how he was supposed to live without me. How?

He must have figured it out. He must have, and it hurts so much still, hurts so much to be let go, to be not good enough.

I take a deep breath, try not to sound like my throat is full of tears. "I think I'm gonna go," I say, turning to face him where he watches me, still leaning against the sink.

"Why?" he asks, and takes a step in, then another, a quicker one after that.

"I just need a minute I guess."

"You need a minute?"

"I'm sorry. I know I'm being weird right now."

"I scared you, didn't I?"

"Everything scares me."

"Don't go," he says coming closer, and I think about how many times I have heard that.

"I'll call you before I go to bed all right?"

I'm at the door now, my purse and jacket already on.

"Are you ever gonna let me in?" he asks, then takes my hands in his.

"I have let you in. It just needs to be slower than this."

Gently I pull my hands back, wrap my arms around his neck and go up on my tiptoes just the way I always did with My Ex. They feel so much the same, too much, and when I close my eyes I can hardly tell which one is holding me, which one I am kissing goodbye.

Tears begin streaming down my face before I am even out of his driveway, and before I pull to the intersection at the edge of his complex I am sobbing. Almost as soon as I move onto the highway I have to pull over into a hotel parking lot that reminds me of the time I stayed in a hotel twenty minutes away from our apartment because I had given my ring back to him and he didn't speak of it and I was going crazy.

I am trying to catch my breath when I hear a text message and look down at my phone. Through a blur of tears, I see that little envelope next to Big Mistake's name, and find that it reminds me of the email from My Ex, the one that came only days after I'd called him when the sixty day rule had ended and he'd been out of town, when I'd been on my living room floor sorting candles.

Two Months Earlier

Numb from pain and regret, I walked into the office of my new apartment and sat down at the green desk. Mindlessly I opened my laptop and typed my email address into the search window, waited.

A few moments later I typed in my password as a deep and tired breath escaped. It was Thursday and I had been out of school all week on February break, but it was really no break. Instead, it was just more time to mourn what I had lost, ache to get it back. It was the week after the sixty days, the phone call and the last goodbye.

A list of email messages appeared and I began highlighting them, pressing the down arrow and preparing more and more messages to be deleted, thinking how much I wished I could delete more than just emails. I wanted to delete mistakes too, turn them into a long gray line like this and erase them all with the touch of a button.

Down, down, down, the list got longer and darker and I almost looked away, but then I didn't. I looked at the messages. I looked at the highlighted names and addresses and then I saw another one. I saw one right below the highlighter, a name and address still unshaded by the down arrow.

It was his.

I gasped, and my heart beat wildly and my hands shook and everything inside me became frantic as the world around me went quiet and still. I clicked on the message. It opened.

Hi there. I'm sorry I couldn't talk the other day. I've been thinking about you all week though. I thought maybe I shouldn't write to you but then I decided I really wanted to. I hope it's okay.

I want you to know that I miss you. I really do. It's not that I didn't want to talk to you during these last two months that we agreed not to talk. It just seemed better for us both if we didn't. I miss talking to you though. I miss you in so many ways. Our song is playing right now and you know the song. This fucking song gets me every single time. I guess that is why I am writing. I am so sorry for all of the bullshit that occurred between us and I realize right now that I am still very wounded by a lot of it. I don't mean to say that you aren't too. I know you are. I just want you to know that so am I.

You are such an amazing person and the life I lived with you was incredible. One thing I know for sure is that if I had a choice to give it all back and not experience that life with you, I would still choose you, regardless of knowing how it turned out. You made me a great person in so many ways and we had incredible experiences together and I would not change that for the world. I love you very much and I always will no matter how much time passes.

Please don't think that this is a farewell letter. I know you will read into it. You are so good at that. Don't forget, I know you very well. Things happen for a reason and I have no idea what will become of us, but right now I know that for some reason we need time. This letter just sort of surfaced. I didn't plan it and I hope it does not upset you. Even after everything, you are still the only one I can open up to.

PS: I was watching the winter games and Vonetta Flowers was on. I got the biggest smile and even laughed out loud. I remember how you thought her name was Banana and then you loved that name and wanted me and everyone else to call YOU Banana. It lasted for months. You never cease to amaze me with that mind of yours. I miss it. I miss you. Love, Me.

I didn't even realize when the crying started, when the slow and steady tears began their descent down my face. Suddenly they were just there, dripping off my chin and landing in my lap. And then I cried harder, so hard, as hard as I had ever cried. I cried as hard as I did when he told me for the first time that he didn't want to talk about getting married. I cried as hard as I did when he moved out and then took another girl to dinner, and when I gave my ring back and when I packed my things and when I first slept alone in my new apartment. I cried as hard as I did when I called him just days before, after the sixty day rule, and he didn't want me back.

I cried and cried and read the letter and read the letter and let another goodbye seep into my flesh and bones and tear everything apart, and I thought I would die from the pain of it. I thought that literally I might not be able to find another breath, and then suddenly I was out of the chair and moving to the rug beside the green desk. That green, rough, wonderful fucking desk we bought at the Salvation Army so many years ago.

I leaned heavily against it and the metal drawer handle dug into my back and I let it. I let it dig in as his words seemed to fill my head and the room and the whole building, and then so did everything else, everything he didn't say. It was so loud, the sound of his unwritten goodbye, his letting me go. His letting me go again.

But he loved me too. He loved me and he let me go and that felt like something too hard to ever understand.

I covered my ears then, tried to keep out the roar of his voice on the page. I bent my legs, brought them close to my chest, wrapped my arms tightly around my shins. I rested my forehead on my knees and tried again to let go. I tried to let go for the first time and the last time and every time. This had to be a real goodbye and so I said it out loud. "Goodbye," I said, choking on deep sorrow. "I loved you. I really did. So much."

My pain filled the room and pressed me into the green desk, and then I curled up beside it and tried to drift away. I imagined rolling out to sea on a wave of sheer loss, devastation.

Within moments though, the phone rang, and despite the haze of despair I felt compelled to look at it. I saw my sister's name on the screen then, like a life vest thrown into the current. I reached for her and tried to answer, but my sobs choked me, crushed the words in my throat.

"Oh my God," she said. "I'm here. Just tell me when you're ready."

I tried again to speak, but the words were garbled, like a mouth full of water, like drowning.

"Do you want me to talk for a minute?" my sister asked, knowing. "Want me to just talk?"

Humbly I managed to reply.

"I do."

We are laying on his bed now, ten days after I left because it was absurd to talk about having a couple of kids while My Ex's goodbye email still filled me with fresh pain. Streetlights and a cool breeze stream in through the windows and our bellies are full from another dinner, Mexican to celebrate Cinco de Mayo. I'm flush from the thrill of a warm Friday night, two glasses of wine and him on his side, his body tucked up tightly against mine. One hand holds his head and the other is stroking my face. I can feel my heart beating.

Slowly I look away and gently he reaches for my chin and turns me back to him, meets my gaze. "Why do you always do that?" he asks softly.

"Why do you always look so serious?" I retort, trying to hide.

"I *am* serious. About you."

His words put yet another chip in my armor and I feel myself soften and he feels it too. "Wow," he teases. "You're actually looking at me and not running away or making a joke."

I continue to hold his gaze and he seems poised with unspoken words, and as I look at him I recognize myself. I see the fear and rejection. I see the self-doubt.

Lightly he kisses my lips and instantly I'm warm all over but scared too. I should have been married less than five months ago and healing is supposed to take a lot longer than this and I need more time.

I pull away a little.

"Your distance hurts, you know? It's actually hurting me."

His words stun me and I can't form a reply.

"Not just right now," he continues, "but over these two months. You keep putting so much space between us."

All at once I am irritated and I find my voice.

“Space? Oh, you mean because I won’t sleep with you?” I attempt to sit up. Lightly he presses me back.

“No. Of course it’s not just that.”

“But you admit it is that too,” I say.

His gaze becomes intense, like he would swallow me with it if he could, and I can only think that I want him to. I want to be consumed by someone so that I will know I’m something worth having. But I don’t want him to know either. I don’t want him to know how desperate I am.

“I just care so much about you that this distance hurts,” he tells me then, and I think that it’s time to go, that this is too much too soon and I have too much left to learn.

I try to be light, not heavy and wounded. With a small smirk I say, “I bet I know where it hurts.”

He doesn’t laugh.

He doesn’t even smile.

He reaches for my hand.

My own smile fades and our eyes lock and I try to look away, but he holds me. He brings my hand toward him, rests it at his heart, presses it so firmly that I feel it beating.

“It hurts here,” he claims.

I’m shocked and terrified and exhilarated too. It has not yet been five months since I should have been married, even less time since the last words My Ex ever spoke to me, and yet already I am in a bed next to a person who is holding my hand on his heart. Healing takes longer than this. I know it does. I know. But I don’t.

I swallow hard as I look into these eyes that are holding so tightly to my own. I think about the last two months. I think about eight and a half years. I think about how I’m supposed to be newly married, but I’m newly broken, or maybe not so newly. I think about how I feel like nothing. And I want to be something.

That was five days ago. Five days since he didn't laugh, didn't even smile, when he reached for my hand in his bed and rested it at his chest. "It hurts," he'd said, pressing my palm firmly to his heart.

I pick up the phone again, and again there is nothing. For almost two whole months he has texted before eight o'clock in the morning with passionate pleas to be with me and ardent descriptions about all that I am, but now, five days later, there is nothing. There is just nothing, and I want to be something.

Suddenly I have to read words, find evidence, look for answers. Kick. Struggle. I locate his text from yesterday. I read it again and again I notice. I notice that it says quite simply, "Have a good day."

It just says to have a good day and I realized it then, but I understand it now, now that the thoughts that have been bouncing around in my head start to settle into a certain spot, a knowing spot. My stomach lurches and I get warm, warm in the way that you get when you have a fever, are fighting a hurt that's gotten inside of you.

It's been a subtle shift, barely anything, hardly noticeable. That's why I didn't understand until now, because these things that are barely noticeable are the ones that feel the strongest once you do notice. They feel like bricks coming down on your heart, shattering that already broken windshield of your life.

Doubt has me in its grip again, the need to be important and the fear that I'm not because he is letting me go. I can feel it. He is letting go of me and I hate myself for that and I wonder and wonder why I let my worth depend so much on the attention of this guy. Why do I let it depend on so much that isn't me?

Two days later he opens his front door and tentatively says, “Hey.” I step back inside and slowly pass him. He closes the door behind me and I stand facing away, terrified, angry, broken. He walks around me and turns. He looks confused, surely because I just walked out the door a few minutes before, got into my car and pulled out of the lot. What he doesn’t know is that I couldn’t stop thinking about that farewell email, the one I got after more than eight and a half years, after a wedding that didn’t take place, and I want this goodbye to come sooner. It’s clear that I haven’t learned much, but I’ve learned at least that. Goodbye shouldn’t take too long.

“What’s up?” he asks, choosing words far too causal for this, the same ones My Ex used that day outside his door when he hadn’t come home all night. I want to punch his face in.

“What’s up,” I say, mocking and contemptuous, “is that this is bullshit and I came back to tell you that.” He straightens and I try to steady my voice, lower it. I need to be brave. All of this anger isn’t brave. It’s something, but it’s not brave.

“I know things have been weird lately. I tried to explain,” says Big Mistake, such a big mistake.

“Just stop,” I demand. “Stop with your bullshit. I came back because I can’t go home and continue pretending I’m not waiting for you to call, waiting for you to start acting like the person you pretended to be in the beginning.”

“I was never pretending,” he tells me.

“Oh, please shut up. I’ve heard enough. I came back to officially end it instead of dragging it out any longer. You know it’s what you want, but you’re too afraid to say it.”

“It’s not what I want,” he says.

I should turn around and leave. I know I should, but I don’t. I say, “You wanna know why this is so hard for me? You wanna know?”

No, I think to myself. Don’t tell him that. Do not.

"It doesn't have to be hard. We can work this out," he says flatly, because he doesn't believe it. He just wants to ease his own guilt by telling me things that aren't true but don't hurt. I've been here before. I know what it looks like, what it feels like. Still, I don't leave when I should. I don't leave because I want to be consumed by someone so that I will know I'm worth having.

"It's so hard because somewhere along the course of this game you've been playing, that I've been trying to learn the rules for . . ." I gulp. I won't say it.

"It hasn't been a game," he interrupts.

I find my voice again. "Yes it has," I say. "It's been a game. I didn't know it though, until tonight, when it became so clear that I was losing because we don't play by the same rules." He doesn't speak and I think I shouldn't say the rest. I should not. But I do.

"This is so hard because somewhere along the course of this game something happened." Don't tell him what happened. Do not tell him. It might not even be true.

"I'm telling you, it's not a game," he says. "I care so much about you. I'm just sort of confused."

"Yes, suddenly you're confused. Just when I think I'm maybe falling in love with you, you're confused."

I said it. I can't believe I said it and right away I want to take it back. Take it back, I think. Oh God, take it back.

He says my name and then I know this is serious. It's always serious when they say your name and I hate the sound of it and I hate when he reaches for my hand, so I don't let him have it. I step away and wish that I had not said those words and wish that I could save myself, so I try.

"Maybe I'm not. Maybe I just want to fill this hole in my heart so badly and you knew that and you took advantage of it." He starts to respond, but I don't let him. "It's probably that. It's probably not love, but it sure has a sting like that."

I take a deep breath and try not to sob as he again reaches for me and I again step back. Reaching for me is an easy fix and he's going to have to do more than that, but he won't. I know he won't. I've learned that much.

"Can you come and sit down, please?" he asks.

"You know, don't you? You know it's done and you want it to be. You just want me to say it because you are a fucking coward. I've done this before so I know what it looks like. You know that though, that I've done this before!"

I take a deep breath and look at him and I recognize the look on his face. He is looking at me with regret, with so much regret that he is overflowing with it. I am too.

"I told you," I say. "I told you so many times, but you made promises and plans and now, almost out of the blue, everything has changed. Just like that."

I take another breath and it gets quiet, too quiet, so I continue. "We've been going on in this shit for a week now because you're a coward and so am I. We're just two fucking cowards."

"We're not cowards," he says, then starts to say more, but I interrupt.

"We are," I tell him. "We're just cowards about different things."

Suddenly I feel weak and foolish and not worth a damn and mad too, so fucking mad. I'm mad at him for making promises he cannot keep and being a selfish asshole, and I'm mad at myself too because this feels just like before. It is like before, only without all the years and a ring to give back and a wedding to call off, an apartment to pack up. This time there is none of that, but it is the same.

"Oh my God," I say out loud, because suddenly I know that standing here is doing so much more damage than if I had just gone home and let myself quietly grieve, let him slowly slip away and wonder. Instead, I am standing here broken, frantically trying to put myself back together and constantly dropping shards that cut me again and again, and letting him see, letting him see too much.

"I should never have come back here," I say angrily.

"Yes, you should have," he says. "We need to talk."

"No. We don't," I reply, then feel how much more devastated I'm about to become and know that I have to save myself. I have to, but I don't.

"You made me believe things and I wasn't ready for those things not to be true and I told you that. I fucking told you so many times."

I begin to cry now, and before I know it I am crying hard and I don't know how to make it stop and it's too late. It's just too late. The sorrow is all pouring out and he's going to see, but fuck it. Let him see.

He does not speak. He looks down.

I yell, "I should never have let you in and you should never have come in because I told you. I told you how scared I was, but you said you weren't and that I shouldn't be."

I pull all the air into my lungs and then it spills out of me in profanities mumbled under my breath as I run my hands through my bangs and down my neck, pausing to grip the hair that hangs around my shoulders. I'm starting to lose it, and I try like hell to rein myself in as he stands there staring at me. He stands there staring and doesn't look away. That's maybe the only true thing he's ever done. He doesn't look away.

"You should not have allowed this, you fucking asshole," I say, and he winces, but I go on, wanting to hurt him, knowing I'm not. I'm not hurting him. He's just wincing because he wants this to be over and so do I, but I'm crying much harder now and I can't make it stop.

"I knew this was all wrong, but you were relentless. You talked me into you, into us. You talked me into all of this after I told you I wasn't ready. I wasn't ready for it not to be real."

He reaches for me and again I jerk away.

"Don't touch me," I yell at him, and I hear my voice and it sounds so damaged, but still I haven't totally lost it yet. A part of me that's buried but still beating is reaching up to hold me together, not letting me shatter completely. I put my face in my hands and try to find my breath, so I don't see when he reaches for me again. I just suddenly feel his hands wrap around my back and I tense, but I don't pull away because pulling away when I'm in his arms seems somehow crazier than what I'm already doing. I don't want to be crazier.

He steps into me, but the hug is so mild I'm not sure he can even feel me, like the way you'd scarcely feel a butterfly in the palm of your hand as you gently preserved the broken wing. I almost can't feel him either, his bones or flesh or embrace, but I know he's there because what I can feel is his warmth. I can feel it slipping away. It's escaping through the cracks that have formed, leaving a draft where the heat of us used to be.

After too long my crying subsides and I pull back and look up and I am alarmed. I see a sadness in his eyes that reminds me of my own and I think suddenly that it is one thing to have changed his mind, to have moved too quickly, to have misjudged. It is another to have never even meant any of it in the first place. I have to be worth meaning it in the first place.

Please make me worth it.

"Just tell me if this was all a game to you," I say. "Was it like your selfish need to be fulfilled by someone else and I got to play the part until you felt better?"

He looks right at me for a moment and his gaze is intense. It is as if he is seeing me for the first time and I wait for him to respond, but instead he looks down. He puts his hand to his mouth and shakes his head back and forth and I cannot take all of this not knowing. I cannot fucking take it!

"Stop being such a coward," I say heatedly. "My God, I am so sick of shit cowards," I say. Then I think, shit cowards? Where the fuck did that come from? I have no idea what that even means. Does that mean you are afraid of shit or that you are shitty at being a coward? Oh fuck. I'm not even making sense anymore and I think that I am going to start to laugh and go insane, but then suddenly I don't. I don't laugh.

"I don't know what to say," he says.

"Oh, but you knew what to say when you were trying to talk me into your heart, your life, your bed. You knew exactly what to say then. Remember how you saw us in a house with kids? Remember how your heart hurt when I wouldn't sleep with you?"

He opens his mouth, but still he doesn't speak, and after a quiet moment he softly says my name. There it is again. So serious.

He looks up at me. I wait. A moment later he closes his eyes and looks down again.

"Jesus Christ," I say. "Everything was a lie."

Abruptly he looks up and meets my gaze once more and this time his eyes are as sad as I've ever seen and he drops his right hand from his mouth. Falling down his chest, it seems to rest by chance at his heart, and I wonder if this is killing him and I hope that it is. I hope he drops dead right here in front of me. Just over a week ago he brought my hand to his heart and told me that he cared so much for me that not sleeping with me was actually hurting, hurting his fucking heart. How could I have ever believed that?

He reaches up and runs his hands over his head, drops his chin toward his chest, and now I see him. I see the man I was supposed to marry, My Ex. I see him sitting in our living room, head in his hands, boxes all around. I see his shoulders shaking with his sobs and hear him ask how he is supposed to live without me and I remember that I didn't think he'd be able to. I didn't think so, but in the end he must have figured it out because not too long ago I sat at our green desk and read his email and he didn't ask for me to come back.

I want to wind up and just punch Big Mistake right in his face, but instead I simply whisper that I absolutely hate his fucking guts and I turn and grab the handle of the door. As I do, he reaches out and takes a hold of the back of my shirt. With some force, he pulls me to him and turns me around. He looks right into my eyes, right down deep into a place that hurts so badly I absolutely cannot stand the pain of it. It is killing me and I make a tentative plan to drive off a cliff on my way home, just drive right off of it.

He moves his hands to my wrists and holds tightly as he says, "I swear. I never lied to you."

I look at him and realize what is happening. I realize that just like another time, this one too is letting me go. So easily he is letting me go and it hurts so badly. It hurts and hurts and hurts, the truth of it burning into me as I pull my arms away and reach back for the doorknob.

My hands are shaking. My heart is too.

We are still looking right at each other when he confirms his goodbye, when he admits that it is over, that he is letting me go. We are still looking right at each other when he pleads, "Don't hate me. Please don't."

I hope you don't leave, I remember. And if you do, please, take me with you.

I don't look at him a moment longer. I turn away. I open the door. I walk out. I do not look back. For once, I do not look back.

I hurry toward my car, swallowing hard and trying to breathe, and when I get there I slide in quickly and fumble through my tears to get the key into the ignition. The radio comes on and I hear words, but I don't hear them because I am trying so hard to get out of the parking spot. I am trying so hard to get away without looking up. I don't want to know if he is standing at his door or not because I can't take the pain of it either way. Just like that day outside My Ex's new apartment. Just like that.

Hurriedly, I put the car in drive and pull out of the lot and I can't see through my tears, but suddenly I can hear. I can hear something other than the throbbing of my broken heart and the pain pouring down my face and dripping onto my lap. I can hear the song on the radio. It is about leaving the pieces when you go.

CHAPTER THIRTEEN
Not Okay

I wake up several times but don't get out of bed. Instead, I turn over and pull the blankets in closer and hurt. It's like the flu, a broken heart is. A broken heart that's been broken again before it was even healed. I'll have to rest and get plenty of fluids, not do too much for a while, not do too much ever again maybe, because I'm not okay. I am just not okay.

The next time I wake up it has gotten worse. I can't think or see or breathe or feel anything besides intense pain, a devastation I know I've mostly inflicted upon myself. I know that I am to blame, but I don't know what I've done wrong. It's like realizing you took the poison, but having no idea which bottle it was in.

I get up slowly, so slowly. I walk the few steps to my bedroom door, the same one My Ex stood in not too long ago, looking around and telling me how beautiful I make things. I must not make things quite beautiful enough though, or he wouldn't have written that goodbye. Big Mistake wouldn't have said, "Don't hate me. Please don't."

Walking out into my hallway I am dizzy, and it gets worse with each step. Finally I have to put my hand up and steady myself with the wall as I turn toward the green desk and see the clock that says it is one in the afternoon. I think I should eat, but the thought makes me sick, and I think instead that I will go back to bed, but I have slept too long and not long enough, and at once I am overwhelmed, completely incapable of anything. It's like the ceiling is getting lower and the walls are caving in on my heart. I sit down at the green desk and put my head in my hands. I don't know what to do or how to take care of myself, and suddenly and profoundly I don't think I can be alone.

Carefully I stand and head back to my bedroom. The phone sits on the nightstand, the one I had to buy when I moved here only seven months ago, and I know that it was too soon. It was too soon, and so I pick up the phone and dial my parents' home and my mom picks up on the second ring. She says hello and uses my nickname and I can't speak.

"I will be there in less than an hour," she says. "I'll be right there."

"Okay," I choke.

She hangs up without asking anything. She asks nothing. She doesn't need to. She knows. She knows what pain sounds like. She's heard it before and I fear that she carries around much of the same and she's my mother and words are not always necessary and it's a relief.

I set the phone down and open the closet. I reach in for a bag. I start to pack it with things. I don't even know what I am packing or why and I don't know where I am going or for how long, but still I fill the bag and it feels like something. It feels like I am doing something to help myself.

Fifty minutes later the buzzer goes off and I jump. That fucking buzzer again. It is my mother this time and I push the button that will let her in the front entrance and then I wait. I have changed into clean underclothes, jeans and a T-shirt. The bag sits beside me. I pick it up. It feels heavy, too heavy. I look inside because I'm not sure what I packed, and I see mismatched pajamas and changes of clothes and more underclothes and one pair of socks and I don't know if it's enough and I don't know if I packed my toothbrush. I really don't know anything at all.

I put my hand on the door just as my mom knocks, and when I open it she simply steps toward me, takes me into her arms. She doesn't ask what happened or why I am so upset or what I want to do. She just hugs me and then pulls back, takes the bag and turns to walk out again, and it reminds me of when she had to stay with me during those days when I couldn't eat my oatmeal or go to work, when she had to sleep next to me in my bed because he had been with someone else.

She doesn't really know what happened this time, but she does know that it is too soon, that it has been only months since I didn't get married. Maybe she knows how for much longer than that I have been unsure and scared and ashamed. Maybe she has been too. And maybe she too wonders about pretty girls and nice houses.

I step out behind her, close and lock my apartment door, then follow her down the steps and out the front entrance to her car. She opens the back door and puts my bag in while I open the front door and slip into the passenger's seat. I recline it a little and slouch down and close my eyes, which burn with fatigue and heartache. A moment later she is behind the wheel starting the car, and as she looks over her right shoulder to back out of the spot, she takes me in and says softly, "I'm sorry, honey. I'm so sorry."

"Thanks Mom," I say, holding back tears, suffocating on them. "Thanks for coming to get me."

"You know if I could take this pain away from you and have it for myself I would. You know that."

"Yes Mom. I know."

She is quiet for a moment as she gets the car in drive and steps gently on the gas to move through the parking lot, and as we pull away she says, "Everything will be okay. I made sauce."

It's been a month and three weeks since that day my mom came to get me and I stayed on my parents' couch for more than forty-eight hours, eating nothing, sleeping a lot and taking small sips from the things they set beside me. I knew it would be easier if I just did that. If I just drank a little bit, it would be easier for all of us.

Then, on the third morning, I got off the couch close to noon and went to my bag of mismatched clothes and found nothing left to wear. There was nothing left and I just stood there, head bent, arms hanging, staring into the bag before numbly walking out of the bathroom and asking my mom to take me home. Just like that, I asked if she would take me home, and she asked if I was sure and I wasn't, but it just seemed too absurd to stay without having another change of clothes. Crying and sleeping and not eating for days was bad, but when you can't even change your clothes anymore, something has to give. And so I went home.

For almost two months now I have continued to grieve, to ache for things I can hardly even name. It all seems to take up so much of my energy that I barely have the strength to eat, and that worries me at times, but mostly it has offered an odd bit of relief, a pleasure that I know isn't quite right, this getting smaller. There is something about that, about getting smaller. It feels somehow like a win, like I'm adding value by taking away my body. Not for the first time, I stop to think about this, to wonder at what it means and if it's true. I don't think it's true, but I think we are meant to believe it anyway.

I think we are meant to believe in pretty girls. And nice houses.

Cherry Almond and Paddy and Guinness and My Big and my sister and more and more friends have been part of this grief, part of the joyful times that interrupt it too, and I am really grateful for these women who are helping me get over this man, these men. Maybe they are helping me get over more than that too. Maybe they are helping me get over myself. Because maybe, if despite all my self-absorbed grief, they still want to be with me and I can still hear and see and love them, then maybe I'm more than I think I am. Even as I revel in becoming less, smaller, maybe I am more.

And so we go out a lot. We order layers of French toast for breakfast and drink too many margaritas in someone's backyard. We wrap our hands around warm coffee mugs, wrap our hearts around each other. They sit on my couch and I sit on theirs, and when I run out of things to organize in my apartment I go to their homes and help redo their kitchens and their closets as we laugh and cry and heal and break, and I see that it is not just me. They hurt too. They too feel small and broken and they too are trying to move on. And so we do it together.

Something more is also happening, something I never expected, that I didn't even know existed. I have found a healer. She was recommended by the doctor who gave me the medicine all those months ago, the one who thought maybe I needed more than that because so much sadness and holding on and fighting back does not make you well. Rather, it requires a kind of help I never knew to ask for until I found myself with a mixed bag of things, sleeping on my parents' couch.

This healer uses a thing called Reiki, an energy therapy I don't fully understand yet, but that I know is something. It is taking hold of bits and pieces of the self-doubt and fear, the worry and sadness, burdens that seem to drive me, and it is moving them over to make room for other things. I don't know exactly what it is making room for. It's too soon to know anything other than that I can't go on this way, and the way I'm going on seems to be about a whole lot more than lost love and a cancelled wedding. It seems to be about something much deeper and scarier and harder to get over.

It seems to be about me.

So on the same day my mom brought me back to my apartment, having not showered for days, with a randomly packed bag of clothes and giving barely a fuck, I got out the number and picked up the phone. I picked up the phone because maybe I did give a fuck somewhere. Somewhere deep down I was interested in finding something that would really heal this pain, a pain that maybe did not need to be this bad.

I called her on a Wednesday, and later that day I walked into her office. I had only mildly showered since Friday and was in some hybrid of pajamas and gym clothes, with unbrushed hair and no breakfast, getting smaller and smaller, but it was too late to care about any of that when I sat down across from her and she spoke.

"Would you like to tell me your story?" she asked gently, and I answered right away. But not with my voice. Instead, my reply came out in tears, storytelling in salty water instead of heartfelt words, and as I cried she picked up the tissue box and slowly handed it across the low table between us. I took it. Like a drowning girl takes a raft I took it, and as I put a tissue to my nose she started talking to me about pain and fear and grief and how these things can live in your body and in your mind. They can live there, she said. And I didn't know any of that.

But I did.

Yes, I told her. They are living in me, always have been, and I'm ashamed of that because nothing really that bad has ever happened. I should be better than this, I said, and she told me that it was not for me to judge and that if my pain was real then that was all that mattered.

"But it is also part of your journey to heal it," she said. "You can heal."

I wiped at my nose and eyes and she continued to talk about my power and my choices and her voice was soothing and genuine and something else too. It was knowing. She knew.

I remember how I looked up at her then and I noticed. I noticed the gentlest smile and eyes that seemed to hold me in such care. I noticed her open palms and her heart facing directly at me and both of her feet anchored firmly to the floor. I noticed the cool air of the room and the dim lights, soft music and glowing candles. I noticed the scent of fresh laundry.

All of it wrapped me in a warmth that suddenly felt like so much peace and hope, and although slivers of glass from that broken windshield of my life were still cutting, I could feel a promise of something else. I could feel a promise.

Once my tears had subsided, she had me lie on my back on a tall massage-like table and she put a heavy blanket over me so that I became suddenly aware of my whole body, but not the way you do when you stand in the mirror wanting to be smaller. It was an awareness that felt like power, like here I am taking up this space and counting for something. I closed my eyes and she placed a small pillow over them. It seemed filled with little bits of oatmeal so that it took the shape of my eyes and my nose, my forehead. It smelled like lavender and something else too. Maybe ease.

She began moving around me, but I couldn't hear her or feel her touch. I could just sense her. I could sense her presence around my entire body and I started to tingle, to come completely alive as slow tears dripped out from under the pillow filled with oatmeal, lavender and ease. A moment later I felt her near my head and then, as slowly as anything has ever happened, so slowly, something was placed on me, something that seemed to wrap around my entire skull like a soft warm helmet. Then, within moments, it felt like a gentle magic was pulling out every fear I had as my head and face buzzed with an energy I'd never felt, and I wondered what she had done to create such calm.

After some time, the intensity of the sensation started to settle and all at once I realized what it was, what was on my head. Her hands. Her hands were on my head. That was all. And that was everything.

I've been going back every few days since then and feeling a little less sorrowful and fragile, a little less like I'm not enough and like I'm too much at the same time. Things are shifting in my body and my heart and my head, not profoundly at all, but just enough to notice, and with the constant suggestion that if I am patient there will be more. I'm still not totally sure what this shift is getting rid of or what it is making room for, but I'm trying not to push and pull and struggle. I'm trying to simply let it happen because it seems like maybe it's just me. Maybe what it is getting rid of and making room for at the same time is just me.

So now, almost two months later, with the beginnings of something that feels like confidence, I am trying to figure out how to work the friggin' latch on the chain I've chosen to wear on a date.

Yes, a date.

I probably shouldn't be doing this. I probably shouldn't. But among all the things I am learning, one is that right now I am not made to be alone. Whether or not I like it, that is who I am for the time being, so I'm going on a date because I am also learning that maybe losing this love isn't what has made me so sad and fearful all the time. Maybe I already was. It may be that I have never felt like enough and that I hold too tightly because I think that something else will fill in what I am lacking, but it never does because maybe only I can do that.

Maybe.

So I'm going to test it out, this learning to like myself thing, this budding confidence. I want to wear it like a new dress that you really love on the rack but aren't as sure about when you put it on. It's pretty, but it feels a little tight, uncomfortable. I need to move around, stretch it out some, and practice not looking back so much or waiting either, waiting for what I think should be next. I want to figure out how to get close to someone just for the experience of it instead of because I think they can make me into something I'm not, because perhaps there is nothing I'm not. And if there is, if there's something I'm not, maybe only I can make me into that. This is the kind of date where there is a lot to learn. I have to figure out which bottle that poison is in after all.

And I don't know if I believe any of this. It could all be utter bullshit. But I do like the way it sounds. And I do need some new noises in my head.

So he's a blond accountant I met online, a place I've been having a lot of fun in the last two weeks, bantering behind the shield of the laptop that sits on my green desk. I've been testing my wit and charm, discovering a little more about what I'm made of.

I tell them a lot, but I don't tell them that I'm looking for self-worth that isn't wrapped up in what they think about me, and I don't tell them that I'm worried all the time and I'd like to stop feeling so broken and sad. I don't tell them how I'm fully aware that if these are the things I want then maybe I shouldn't be dating, that I should spend a lot more time alone because the person I really need to be comfortable with is me, but I'm not yet comfortable enough for that.

In all of this guy's pictures he is really handsome, with blue eyes and a soft smile, wholesome. He says he's five feet nine inches tall and that seems a little short, but I'm doing things differently and I might as well start with height. When we exchange emails, his words are careful, not like Big Mistake, with all of his grand gestures and convincing monologues. All of his lies.

He's safe, this accountant. I don't think he can hurt me and that's what I need right now, to not be hurt.

Ready to go, I realize I haven't tried too hard. I'm not wearing much makeup and my hair is straight, but not pin straight. I'm wearing a simple pair of jeans and a fancy tank top. I smell of shampoo and cocoa butter, a hint of lemon. I'm not wearing jewelry since I can't get the clasp to work and it's better that way, simpler. I slip my feet into a comfy pair of flip-flops that show my pink toes and I grab my purse and keys.

I walk out the door of my apartment, but not like that day close to two months ago when I was following my mom with a mismatched bag of clothes. This time I feel more like myself, whoever that is.

Arriving at the bar just moments before our eight o'clock meeting time, I pull easily into a front-row spot, then reach for the visor, flip open the mirror and linger. I need one more thing, I think, and so I open the inside pocket of my purse and remove a slender tube. I slide out the wand and apply a coat of clear gloss to my lips. Immediately I feel even better. I also immediately know that it is dangerous to let these things outside of myself bring so much of my confidence and joy, but that's where I'm at. I can only make one step at a time. Just one.

Getting out of the car, I note how crowded the place is and I'm glad. We won't stick out, me and this blond accountant who is only five feet nine but very wholesome and safe. I follow behind a small group as they enter, and when we get inside I look toward the bar. He said he would wear a pink polo shirt and I see him right away. He takes what looks like a final swig of his beer, sets the bottle on the bar, then turns as if he knows I have just walked in. He sees me and prepares to stand up. His smile is wide and welcoming, the same one I liked in his photos, and immediately I feel the wholesomeness and the safety that I've felt in all of our emails. This could be just what I need, no expectations, simply a handsome distraction as I try to heal this brokenness.

As I get closer to him though, almost close enough to touch, he comes off the stool. He stands just feet from me and immediately I see. I see that there is no way. There is just no way in hell he is five feet nine inches tall. Maybe standing on a stack of bullshit that's true, but here, standing in front of me in my flat flip-flops and all of my five feet seven inches, there is no way. He is not even my height. Our eyes are not even level. I can see the top of his head!

As he reaches out to hug me, I come back to the moment and hope that my face has not betrayed my thoughts. He is so handsome and so wholesome and so safe, but he is so fucking short. And he lied about it too.

This isn't going to work. I've had enough men coming up short in my life and this is not going to work. He is saying something and I am listening, but also I am suddenly trying to not laugh. I am trying hard to not absolutely die laughing, and eagerly I attempt to hide my silliness with a huge smile and pretend excitement. I don't want to hurt him. I really don't, but I simply cannot believe that I am on a date where I can see the top of this guy's head, the spot where all of his blond hair meets at a little circle. And it is becoming hilarious, absolutely fucking hilarious.

As he puts his arms around me, I realize that I could rest my chin on his head, and I am about to lose myself in unbridled laughter as I think that maybe the universe is talking to me. Maybe the universe is letting me know that things are not always as big as I have let them be.

Maybe I am bigger.

Awaking a little before eight in the morning, the sun is already streaming brightly through my blinds when I reach for the phone, wanting to silence it. Why is someone calling so early?

I look at the display screen and see with surprise and delight that it is Cherry Almond. Today, the twenty-second of July, is the wedding of a mutual friend. It is just six months and three weeks after what would have been my own wedding and that is why I am invited to hers. My broken heart made a lot of room for those who were just on the verge of being my friends and who, once tragedy hit, were drawn deeply into my life.

I fumble with the phone and finally answer.

"Happy wedding day, briiiide's maid," I sing, dragging out the long vowel sound.

"Oh my God, tell us about last night," says Cherry Almond.

"Are you kidding?" I say. "How can you care about this right now? Aren't you getting ready for the wedding?"

"We're just getting our nails done so we have time. Our Bride is here too. Now tell us what happened!"

I marvel at how these friends of mine can be so interested in my life even on days that are so important in their own. I marvel at how I have found them, how I have found beautiful friends like this and how they have found me too. They've found me.

"Well," I begin, "let's just say that I will not need that plus-one option."

"Shit, really?" Cherry Almond asks with genuine disappointment.

"Um, yes, really, but I still had a great night. He was a good guy. It's just not a match."

"Are you sure?"

I begin laughing and tell her that I am very sure, then pause, trying to figure out a dramatic way to tell the rest.

"Let's just say that if I brought him to Our Bride's wedding today, we'd need a booster seat for dinner."

She bursts out laughing and my own laughter starts to rise and immediately gets hearty, completely infected by hers. She tries to speak, but it comes out through all kinds of giggling.

"Wait, so he was short?" she asks, then almost snorts with laughter.

"Oh my Christ," I say. "I felt like an absolute giant!"

Her laugh becomes even more pronounced, and through her fits of hysteria she asks why his profile didn't give his height. I tell her that it did and that he must have lied and she asks if I called him out on it.

"No," I say, laughing again. "I decided this is one lie I can let go."

Cherry Almond laughs, then relays the details to Our Bride, as I sit grateful that on this wedding day, gathered among champagne and painted nails, they care about me.

"So, listen," I tell her, "It's not like you have anything that important to do today. I mean, you should have plenty of opportunity to play matchmaker. Our Bride too."

Laughing, she says, "We've got your back, and let me guess, you want a tall guy, right?"

"Even fucking medium height!" I yell, and she laughs and laughs and I think that these girls are everything. They are every single thing.

A phone is ringing again. It is a soft ring, like wind chimes gently rousing me out of my sleep on this morning after the wedding. I am groggy and not well rested. My head is heavier than it should be.

Another morning after a wedding.

Slowly I open my eyes and turn onto my back, a deep breath coming in and out as I look up at the ceiling remembering last night's dance with the tall gorgeous guy who bent forward and talked with warm breath in my ear. He said I was amazing. He said he'd never met anyone more beautiful. I flush now at how tempted I was to turn into him as his hand pressed against my back and pulled me closer. But I remember how he also reminded me of that Fourth of July wedding, the one in the yellow dress, and how he reminded me of Big Mistake too.

So I didn't. I did not turn in.

Still facing the ceiling, the phone continues ringing as I think about how just an hour after the warm breath and a hand at my back, I found myself with another good-looking smooth talker. My smile widens as I remember how at the same moment I started to turn away, he reached for me, and how that fumble caused my entire glass of Captain and Diet to fall to the floor, hitting his left foot and filling his loafer with the light brown liquid. But that's not all. It was followed by several pieces of ice and that skinny red stir stick, and I thought I might come wildly undone. There it was, just sticking straight up out of the space between his foot and the edge of his glossy black loafer, like a beacon.

"Oh my God," I'd said to him, covering my mouth to hide the brewing fit of laughter. "I am so sorry."

Really, I wasn't though. Really, I thought it was a delicious experience made even more satisfying when I turned toward my table of friends and found them all in varying stages of laughter, and that's when I lost it too, almost had to double over with the pure joy of it. We all watched then as the smooth talker sloshed off with a shoe full of booze, and I knew it wasn't right, but it didn't feel so wrong either.

I am remembering all of this now as I hear the phone on its sixth ring, but still I don't answer. I don't answer because it is not my phone, and I move onto my side and see him fumbling with it, bringing it to his ear as he turns to smile at me.

"Hey Mom," he says, and I am mortified.

"Sure. Let me ask her." He turns to me and presses the phone against his bare chest. "My parents want to know if we can meet them for breakfast."

My eyes grow wide. I look at him. I try not to die. We?

I met Young Blood last night at the wedding, along with his mother who is on the phone now, and his dad and sister too. I met him only minutes after dropping that tumbler on the other guy's foot, back in line at the bar with Cherry Almond and Our Bride. He'd come up behind us at just the moment I'd staggered back, my heels not sure of the uneven outdoors or five glasses of Captain Morgan. He'd reached out and steadied me and then let go, no warm breath in my ear or hands on my back, just a hearty laugh when I said I'd stumbled on purpose, that it was part of my charm. After that we didn't stop laughing. Not until just a few hours ago.

He is talking to me now as I think that this is familiar. It is not completely unlike my conduct at the Fourth of July wedding, but different too, very different. I am in my own bed. I am not naked and I know exactly who I am with. I remember everything, and while I wouldn't be here like this without too many Captains, I don't regret what I've done and I can't get this smile off my face.

"Oh my God, you are kidding!" I whisper loudly to him.

"No, I'm not. You know my mom thinks you're great. Everyone does."

Everyone?

I pull the covers over my head in not-so-mock horror and tell him no. I say that I absolutely cannot go to breakfast with his family this morning. The whole time they will be thinking that I just had sex with their son who is eight years my junior. They'll have no idea that we didn't, and it's not exactly something you announce, but I'll want to.

"They won't be thinking that," he tells me. "Don't worry."

It's not just that though. It's something else too. It's that going to breakfast is too intimate. It is saying too much, things I don't want to say. This was just supposed to be fun because fun is healing and I need to get well. I don't need anything else. I don't need my comfort with myself to depend on a guy I just met or anything outside of myself really.

"Come on," he urges from his position beside the covers I am hiding under, before suddenly his head appears inside the sheet with me and he is holding the phone outside, his arm extended. He kisses my forehead, and when he pulls away and looks back at me I realize that even though I have only known him for twelve hours, and I don't really know him at all, I do. I know him very well, not like the guy in the black and purple tie at the Fourth of July wedding. It's not like that. I didn't know him. I know this.

He pulls me back with the clear blueness of his eyes and a grin that begins and ends in just one corner of his mouth, and I want to thank him for reminding me how much I am able to be put together, despite all of my coming undone. I want to thank him and tell him that I need more of this, this waking up and looking around and letting go and feeling and trusting and breathing and being.

Our eyes lock then and his seem to beseech me because I think he suddenly knows what I know. He knows that this is all there is for us. There is just this one night, and it makes sense, but it is sort of sad at the same time, and as I look at him it seems incredible, the capacity for connection even if it can't last. This won't last. Many things don't. It's the ability to connect that matters, even if briefly. I forgot about that. I'll have to remember the next time I forget.

As if he is reading my mind, his bright eyes flicker, and with no more prompting he simply tells his mom that he will call her back, then pulls the covers off our heads and pulls me into him so that my cheek rests on his chest and his arm comes around me, and I think how lucky I am. I look at this guy I just met who is huddled in my bed with me and I am so glad this has happened, really powerfully grateful. But I am sorry too. I am so sorry that it won't last beyond this day, because while they are rather easily drawn in, they do not easily stay, and I can't bear that again so soon. I simply cannot bear it. So I have to let him go, and then I have to figure out a few more things. And by a few I mean a lot.

I whisper that I cannot go to breakfast and ask him to understand, to thank his parents and just tell them that I have another commitment. He tells me he understands, but his eyes betray him. I see his disappointment. I recognize it there on his face, what I have felt so many times.

"You're not going to give me a chance, are you?" he asks suddenly, and I wish I could tell him that when you can't love yourself you become desperate for someone else to do it, and I don't want to be desperate. I need time to learn how to stop all of this kicking and struggling, I want to tell him, but I think somehow he knows. I think he knows because he pulls me closer. He pulls me closer and we fall asleep. We just fall asleep, me and this guy I hardly know, but then again I do, and I have such gratitude for it.

So that night when he calls, it breaks my heart a little that I don't answer.

Later I am dressed for bed and lounging on the couch in front of the television when one earring suddenly falls out of my ear. I jerk to catch it, but instead I have to dig for it in the oversized Superman T-shirt I'm wearing, the one that hangs over the waist of the baggy Syracuse sweatpants that are so long they wrap around my ankles, and I notice.

I notice that I am dressed in them. I'm dressed in Big Mistake's shirt and My Ex's sweats, and the weight of it becomes painful and I don't want it to mean this much. I don't want to be so damaged by the shirt that falls over these pants, blends right in so that I cannot even see my own shape, can only see theirs, and I wonder if everyone feels everything this deeply for this long, like a cold hand constantly on the heart, squeezing and twisting and breaking.

Why can't I just wear an oversized Superman shirt that a guy gave me a couple of months ago and not think about how he probably lied to me and I never really meant anything at all? Why can't I just wear baggy sweatpants that I first slipped into nine years before and not think about how he never called after sixty days and how our wedding date was seven months ago?

I get up from the couch now and walk toward my bedroom, dressed in clothes that hide the shape of my legs, my hips, my stomach. They hide me, until I pull the too-big shirt over my head and toss it angrily at the floor. I turn toward my armoire and shimmy out of the extra-large men's sweatpants I've been wearing for years and years. I let them fall.

Then, in only my underwear, I look in my new mirror that is in my new bedroom in my new apartment in my new life, and see that I look the same and completely changed too. I look like someone I know and also like a total stranger. I'm not sure about anything anymore, when before I was so certain. I was so certain and maybe that was a lot of the problem. Maybe there is no certain.

The next weekend I am on the phone with my sister. "I'm gonna let you go," I say to her. "I'm just pulling into the parking lot."

"Call me as soon as you leave," she tells me.

"What if I don't leave alone?" I say back.

"You'd better leave alone!" she demands, a hint of jesting in her voice.

I laugh and tell her I'll call her later and we hang up as I pull into a parking spot and take a deep breath full of excitement and maybe more, maybe enchantment. I'm a little enchanted, but I know better, so as I reach for the car door I focus on just enjoying this experience and not making it anything it isn't. I remember my Reiki master's two feet anchored to the floor, and when I take my first steps on the pavement leading to the bar, I plant my own more firmly.

He's a lean blond thirty-two-year-old with the bluest eyes and a birthday just one month before mine. He's been calling me, texting me, emailing me multiple times a day for the last week. Every day, at all hours, completely sweeping me off my feet, and I have known since the very first message that he could be dangerous for me, that it's too soon. The ease with which we have teased and flirted, the chemistry without ever having met, is very familiar. I've recognized it for the risk that it is. I can totally see it, a beginning with a fiery end. Still, I am here.

At first, I told him that I would not meet him. I said I had too many other dates set up, which hadn't been a lie. I was enjoying as many experiences as I could, trying to find my footing and trust myself, even though I know it is maybe not so wise to try to mend a fragile self-esteem and broken heart with dinner dates and good night kisses. Still, knowing something does not make it so, and until him it had seemed safe. Until him there had been nobody to keep me on the phone until three in the morning or make me rush to my email and sit at the green desk without crying.

So I'm walking into the same bar where I met the too-short guy less than a month ago, and before I have even let go of the door behind me I see him. I see him and am completely stunned by his presence. Sitting on a barstool at the smaller and more secluded bar a few paces beyond the main one, he is swigging his beer with his back to me, but I know it is him. I know his blond hair, his wide shoulders, even his right hand. I've studied his photos and I've studied him and I even know his right hand, the wide palm and the rope bracelet he wears around his wrist.

I don't need this, I think. I really do not. It is too soon, and I know it even more now that I am here. I should turn and leave, but it is too late. It is already happening and I am reasoning with myself, saying that the cracked windshield of my life might not shatter again if I just drive slowly, look more carefully around the little lines of splintered glass in front of me.

Then suddenly I am totally propelled, pushed forward as if not by my own choosing, my feet less planted than they were just moments ago. I am moving toward the bar where he is setting down his beer bottle and turning in the direction of the bartender, politely raising his hand. I reach the stool where he is sitting and without missing a beat, with all the confidence in the world, I slide casually into the one on his right. I simply sit down, not like I have just arrived and we are meeting for the first time, but like we have been here for a while and I am just returning to my spot beside him. Then, in the split seconds before he turns to me, I notice something I could not have known from calls and texts, pictures and emails. I notice what I could not know until I am right next to him, right where I should not be.

He smells so good. He smells like cologne, but not just cologne. It is something else too. Maybe it is his soap or shampoo, maybe the laundry detergent he uses. It could be the scent of a candle from his house. I don't know exactly, but it is so good, and I sit there and take it in. I take in his blond hair again too, the wideness of his shoulders and hands, the bracelet at his wrist. It all hits me with a force I had not expected, and I try to be careful as I sit for what seems like a very long time. Really though, it is only a second or two before he gets a hint of me and turns slowly in my direction, lighting me up with his eyes.

Blue.

His eyes are so blue as I smile and raise my brows, say, "Hey there," like I have always known him, like I have known him my whole life.

It is so easy, too easy, and now his gorgeous face fills with a breathtaking smile, the same smile from his pictures. His eyes dance with it, those brilliant blues, and I get warm again, only this time even warmer, much closer to the fire. He turns more toward me and I notice immediately when his right knee grazes my left and I am reminded of that day in the car after the St. Patrick's Day parade. Big Mistake. I admonish myself for giving so much meaning to something so simple and wonder again if everyone feels everything as deeply as I seem to, a cold hand constantly on the heart. I don't want it to matter that his knee touches mine. I want it to just be one knee touching another, nothing more, and so I push the feeling away as his eyes pierce me with their baby blueness and he sets down his beer and stands.

"Come here," he says, and without hesitating, as if it is the most natural thing on Earth, I move into him. My arms slip between his arms and his body, and my palms reach up to press against his back. His own hands press into the base of my spine and I touch my chin to his collarbone as his head tilts down and his cheek presses against my hair. I breathe him in and he smells so good, even better this close. It is all happening so fast, too fast.

I am already in his arms and I'm not sure where my feet are, but they are not planted.

He pulls back then and looks down at me, says so slowly, "You. Are really. Fucking gorgeous."

This is surprising and amazing and filling and dangerous because I don't believe it myself, but I like to be with people who do. I like to hear it and to think that it might be true, and I notice that I am once again looking outside of myself for what I need and I know that this is not safe. I know that I am not paying careful enough attention and that unlike the connection with Young Blood, I might not be willing to let this one go.

"Well, it's not like you're seeing me for the first time," I reply, trying to handle the warmth, being this close to fire.

"No, but we both know people can look fantastic in photos and then in person it's not the same. Remember your guy? Cousin It?"

I laugh and remember telling him about that and think how it's like we already have a history when really, we are meeting for the first time. I need to be so careful. Some connections just aren't meant to last.

"Tell me about it," I tease, raising my eyebrows and tilting my head in his direction to suggest that he is not the same in person as he is in his photos. I make a fake attempt to turn away from him then and he catches me by the waist, such a simple grasp that I notice too much. It seems packed with intimacy, and when he pulls me back to him I feel weightless, consumed.

From the outside in. Always from the outside in.

"I see you are as much of a brat in person as you are on the phone," he says.

I love that. I love it. I love that he knows me and gets me and likes me, but I also know that this is just too fast. I know this and yet I don't because I won't stay long enough with any knowing other than how gorgeous he is and how gorgeous he makes me feel and how it is like I have known him my entire life, even though I know better.

He seems to sense my hesitation, quickly takes my hand. He pulls me back up to the bar, then motions kindly to the bartender, just as he did earlier when he didn't know I was watching. He turns back to me then and his smell continues to fill my senses as he asks what I want, and his gestures seem easy and self-assured, yet still humble somehow. His eyes seem to drink me in as a soft new smile forms on his lips and it all catches me by surprise. I want to stay next to him, get even nearer than I am now, but I know I'm already too warm. If I get any closer I will burn.

As the bartender approaches, it is like we are both coming out of a spell. We turn to him so slowly as he asks us what we'd like to drink.

"What are you having?" I ask Blue, this guy who is too warm and dangerous for me.

"You," he replies. "I'm having you."

Ten Months Earlier

"You did the right thing calling it off," my sister said to me.

"It doesn't feel right," I stammered between hard tears. "It feels like everything is over, like my life is."

There was a long pause then and I cried and she breathed and we just held onto our opposite ends of the phone line. She'd been gathering courage maybe, courage she knew I needed.

"Why do you even love him so much?" my sister asked slowly.

"What?" I asked through my tears.

I asked her what, but I knew.

"I mean, I know he has tons of great qualities. Don't get me wrong. We all love him too, and you guys have had a very good life together in many ways, but in a lot of ways you haven't. I'm sorry," she told me. "I just feel like I have to say that."

I started to cry harder then, but she continued. "I don't understand why you can't let go when you are so hurt and sad all the time."

I don't understand either, I thought, and I wanted to tell her that it was because I loved him, but I knew that wasn't enough and I knew she knew it too. "I know," I said through my tears. "I know."

I did. I knew she was right. She was right and it broke my heart and pissed me off and embarrassed me that she knew this, that we both did.

"Maybe it's just that it's been so long." I paused, gathered my breath, not even sure the words were true, but feeling them, feeling maybe they were. "There's just so much history now and it seems like such a waste. I didn't want to let go in case we could get it back, what we had at first, before we didn't."

"I know," she said simply.

Suddenly more words came and it was like I didn't even know them until they were out of my mouth, out of a buried spot in my head and heart.

"I think it's like I decided that I love him and once I made that decision, I couldn't undo it." I paused again, gathered more breath. "I think I decided that I didn't want to undo that decision."

"I understand," she said simply, and she did. She understood because she had her own story, one she told to me almost as often as I told her mine. "I understand hanging on, not wanting to risk the undoing."

"Yes," I said through slowing tears. "It's a risk. It seems like an even bigger risk than hanging onto what isn't working, the undoing does."

"I know," said my sister.

"There's more though," I told her. Then I thought. What is it? I know there's more, but what is it?

"What?" she asked, echoing my thoughts as I breathed in and out.

"I've never danced with anyone else," I told her suddenly, then started to cry soft tears that dripped slowly. "I mean really danced, in that way that isn't even dancing, but being held, being really held onto." I was crying harder by then, crying and crying. "I've never woken up and had someone watching me, just watching me sleep like I was everything, like I was every single thing."

Gently my sister said my name. She tried to wrap it around me.

"Nobody will ever love me like that again," I sobbed. "Nobody will ever love me like he has loved me, like I'm everything. And since I can't love myself like that, I needed him to."

Except for the sound of my sniffling and swallowing, it was quiet until she said simply, "I don't know what to say."

"You don't have to say anything," I said. "We both know that he doesn't either. He doesn't love me like that either. Not anymore."

She didn't pretend. She was just quiet.

"And maybe, when you can't love yourself that way, you become desperate for someone else to do it and you think if you just hold on long enough, they will. If you kick and struggle they will finally get it and love you enough and then you'll know you are worth it."

I was explaining this to my sister, but really, I was explaining to myself.

"I know," she said, and she did. "Do you think you can get through it, just wait it out this time?"

I didn't answer. I didn't know.

"I think you can," she told me.

"It just hurts so bad," I said finally. "That's why we keep going back, because it hurts so much to be apart and we forget. We forget that maybe it hurts even more to be together."

She wasn't deterred. "I think you have the courage," she repeated.

I knew she was right, that if I could just wait it out, one day it would stop hurting. If I could just wait.

"I think you do," my sister repeated.

I didn't want to commit.

"I don't know," I said. "I don't know if I do."

My building buzzer sounds. It rouses me from this memory with my sister, our words from the day after I called off my wedding only ten months ago, not nearly long enough.

I get up and walk toward the button on the wall that will unlock the main entrance and then I open the door to my apartment, leave it slightly ajar. I sit down on the couch again and pick up my glass, my courage serum.

I don't even know why I'm doing this, why I've agreed to have him here. It's over. It should never even have started and I've already grieved, grieved deeply another loss, a third in so short a time.

Because when you can't love yourself, you become desperate for someone else to do it, and you think that if you just hold on, they will. If you kick and struggle, they will love you and then you'll know you are worth it.

I hear his footsteps on the stairs and I remember what my sister told me later, what her own counselor had said, how sometimes we think we have to linger in our mistakes just because it took so long to make them, and I remember how I was shocked by that, still am. I am shocked by how long I can linger, for days and months and years even, for all my years. I can't this time though. I cannot linger.

I hear his footsteps in my hallway now and I think about Big Mistake and My Ex and then suddenly he is tapping lightly on my door. He is at my door tapping lightly, just over a month since I walked into that bar and found him sitting on a stool with a beer in his wide right hand, a rope bracelet on his wrist. It is only about a month later and already pain is at my door again and I shouldn't let him in, but I will. I will let him in so that I can linger in grief for a guy I met only thirty-eight days ago. Thirty-eight days. Who cares about thirty-eight fucking days? I spent over three thousand days with someone and came within seventy days of our wedding and that ended and I survived and now I am crying over this? What the fuck. I have lost far more than Blue and his thirty-eight fucking days.

Slowly I feel the door open, but a split second before that I smell him. I smell the freshest laundry and shampoo and cologne and something else we could never decide on. It wraps itself around me now the way it has for the last thirty-eight days, only this time it is cloaked in a profound sadness, devastation that so much can happen in so little time and so much can end too. In so little time so much can end because some things are just not meant to last and I cannot linger.

His smell tries to consume me now, tries to change my mind as it fills me with that same powerful awareness of him that has been present all the times we've been together, since the day we met in that bar and I sat down without saying a word. His scent has lingered on my clothes and my hair and my car and my couch and my sheets, lingered like a mistake, a mistake you can't stay in just because it took so long to make it. I take a bigger sip of wine, just trying to survive. From the outside in.

"Hey," he says softly.

I turn to look at him then and maybe I shouldn't have because even now, even through such clouds of anger and hurt, I can still see how handsome he is. I can feel it actually. I can feel how handsome he is and I am shocked by it. It is as if I am seeing him for the first time, and I fear that I will come undone as his bright blue eyes plead with mine, his red lips slightly parted, ready to speak, but unsure. He takes my breath away and I don't know if I am ever going to get over this or anything else.

Gently he closes the door behind him, but not in his usual whirlwind, not in the quick and grand way he's done most things. Instead it is softly, as though it will break, as though I will. It is not like the time only two weeks ago when he told me to be dressed by six o'clock, then swept through the door with fancy cheese and crackers, a huge bouquet of flowers that I didn't even have a vase big enough for. It's not like that time at all, when he set the cheese and crackers on my coffee table beside a bottle of champagne and fat purple grapes, then laid a blanket out on my living room floor where we sat for two hours eating and drinking and talking until we got hungry again and he drove us to a restaurant he had already chosen. There we sat side by side on a cushioned bench for hours more as we ate and laughed and made plans.

It is not like that now.

"Hey," he says again.

I stand up and feel weak, try to be stronger.

"I'm thinking it wasn't a good idea for you to come here," I say, partly because it wasn't, but mostly to shock him into saying something to counter that, to convince me. I have used this tactic many times, trying to get them to convince me that I am wrong in letting go, that I am worth more. Sometimes it works, but really it never works at all.

"I know. It probably wasn't, but I don't want to end things on the phone," he says.

Again, there it is. The end. Being let go. I want to throw up and cry and burrow into my blankets, but instead I snap.

"Well, don't do me any favors," I say.

This is one reason it's ending. My tough-guy-fuck-you routine. Nobody ever knows it's not real, and before he can reply I continue, even though I just want to be quiet, curl up on the floor with my hands over my mouth, over my heart too.

"I guess you just dropping off the face of the earth for like four days should have been my first clue, right? I probably don't need you to confirm it by coming here," I say.

He says my name then and I wince. Not that again. Not my name.

"I did not drop off the face of the earth," he says. "I had a competition and I was out of town. You know that."

"Yes, you've had competitions and been out of town almost every weekend since I met you, and yet you've always found time to call or text or both, many times a day. Many!" My voice is rising and I try to regain control, but it's hard to regain something you never really had.

"This time was different. I tried to explain that," he tells me.

"This time was so different that you could not call or text for two entire days?" He does not reply, so I carry on. "No. This time wasn't different. *You* were," I spit out.

"I just don't want to do this. We've been doing this since Saturday."

"Yes, Saturday. The day you finally decided to throw me a bone."

I have to stop. I cannot linger.

"It was not like that." His voice is starting to rise and I want to end this. I know that I am not doing it right. I know that I should let go. I know that I am wounded and weak and not equipped for this, that just like with Big Mistake I should grieve quietly on my own and let him simply slip away. But I can't. Or I won't.

"Please don't bother telling me all of your bullshit excuses again. I can hardly stand it. Poor cell phone reception. Leaving your phone in your room. Being so tired. Not wanting to wake me up. Oh my God, it's like you could not decide which one you liked best so you used them all," I say.

That's when he snaps. He just snaps and I don't expect it.

"Oh, and let's not forget that my fucking aunt died on Saturday while I was competing," he yells. "So I rushed home to be with my family yesterday and not you and you couldn't fucking stand that!"

I am completely stunned, silenced by his raised voice and angry tone, his sharp words and the wild look in his blue eyes. I start to shrink. I don't know who I am. Who am I, arguing with this guy I didn't even know thirty-eight days ago? I should have been married to someone else for close to a year by now. For close to a fucking year I should have been married, but instead I am standing here fighting a fight that has already been fought and lost too. It's been lost. Who am I?

I struggle to hold back tears now. What he's saying is not true, but surely that's how it appears to him. I don't know how to reply because I don't really even know what is true or why this hurts so much and why I feel so unsafe, with him and with myself and with everything. I don't know what's happening and I don't know when that started, the not knowing and the fear and the doubt, but I know it did not start this past weekend when he didn't call and I felt he was slipping away. It started so much longer ago than that, with a little girl who never thought she was pretty enough, whose house wasn't a nice one.

And maybe it started with even more than that.

I am so confused and hurt that I can't think. He is saying something more, calming down now, but I can't hear him because my heart is pounding so loudly and with so much uncertainty, with a fear that has settled securely into my bones and my blood. I am not afraid of losing him anymore. I know I have already done that. The fear instead is of being this person forever, this girl who just can't make it work, can't stand firmly on her own two feet. I'm afraid of being this girl who will just never get it right.

Suddenly other thoughts start to get loud too, so loud. They rush into my head and try to save me by filling all of the space where fear and doubt reside, moving them over to make room for anger. Anger seems safer. It seems like I will be safe if I'm mad and I've learned that this is not true, but once again knowing doesn't make it so. I know now that the only thing to save me is letting go, but I simply cannot do it. I simply cannot let go because my holding on is so strong. It is so practiced.

"Look," he says more calmly now. "I'm sorry. Can we just try to start over?"

Start over? Now he wants to start over? So where will we start? Will we start back at thirty-eight days ago when he would excuse himself from a business meeting just to answer a meaningless text from me and call me every two hours to confirm dinner plans, when we spent every night together in my bed or his? Or will we start back at Friday, when he didn't return a text or a call for two days and I sat like a fool on my floor and cried, cried alone beside the green desk?

Again.

After all of his promises, ones completely broken now, ones about caring so much he couldn't stand it, we will never start over. I hear his words so clearly and they all sound like nothing but bullshit, another Big Mistake. He's just like him and he's just like My Ex, who took back my ring and never told me where it was and let me put a wedding dress in a hope chest and place the veil on top. He is just like both of them and I am just like me. I am just like the me I have always been, that I don't want to be anymore.

Suddenly I find myself thinking of that receipt in my back pocket, the one showing two rooms in Buffalo, two rooms even though he had continued to insist that he'd only gotten one. I'm thinking of the girl he dated before we were engaged, the one he bought birthday presents for and took out to dinner and fucked in the apartment I set up for him. I'm thinking of how he swore he needed to take a job in another town to get his career more stable so he could be ready for our life together. I'm thinking of him, always thinking of him with that same lump in my gut and tightness in my heart. It's the same, only it's not the same, and I can't even tell the difference between this and that. The pain seems all to be coming from one place, but I don't know where and I wonder again what this pain is all about and if it is like this for everyone. I wonder if everyone feels everything as deeply as I seem to, that constant squeezing and twisting and breaking of the heart.

Blue is saying something more now, but I don't hear him because I am thinking about what I will say, how I am going to say everything that needs to be said, spell it all out for him. I am going to tell him what a motherfucker he is and how he had no right, how I had no right either. I had no right to trust him.

"You know what?" I say.

Softly he asks what as he steps toward me, and his eyes are pleading and edgy when he touches me, and all of a sudden the entire room seems to shift and soften. Just like that. Suddenly everything is just not so awful and I am shocked, stunned by how quickly I can let someone soften me because I am not strong enough. I can't seem to stand in my own space alone and certain. I am so desperate that I'm ready to go to him, step into the arms he has opened up, because the fear of myself is greater even than my fear of him.

Then, all at once, my throat seems to close and it's as if wings are trapped inside of it, flapping wings. I begin to cough and I try to stop and I do stop, but when I go to speak again suddenly the coughing starts anew and then I can't stop. I cannot stop coughing.

"What happened?" he asks quickly, and as he reaches out for me there is that scent again. The scent of him. It is all around me, the freshest laundry and shampoo and cologne and something else I could never quite put my finger on.

My words. They seem to have gotten caught in my throat. I cough more and more and he goes into the kitchen and I hear him open the cabinet with the glasses, hear the faucet turn on. He holds a glass under it and fills it with water, turns off the faucet and returns to the living room where I am now sitting on the couch. The coughing is under some control, coming in shorter and less dramatic spurts, but still coming so that I can't talk. I can only think about how he knows where my glasses are, that they are in the cabinet to the right of the sink.

"Drink some water," he says simply, holding the full glass out to me. I take it and drink from it, and as it pours down my throat, so do all of the words I had planned to say, the angry ones and the soft ones, all of them. I realize that I am not going to say any of them because they are gone. Like the water from the glass, the words are gone so that I cannot use them to prove my point or plead my case or be right or start over. I cannot use them to demand answers or apologies or forgiveness because they are gone and none of it matters anyway. Nothing matters but letting go, and I know that my holding on is practiced and strong, but it is also what makes me so weak. Maybe my body knew that. Maybe my body knew and created that cough.

Then all at once, he surprises me. He lifts my chin toward him and he says, "I'm so sorry I hurt you this weekend. I really didn't mean to. I didn't mean for it to get this far."

He didn't mean for what to get this far?

I don't understand and I want answers and apologies. I want so many words. I want to say them and I want to hear them, but that's just because I'm used to them. I'm used to these conversations that are like glue, like hinges, like rope that allows me to hold on when what I need is to let go. So I'm not going to ask or demand or speak one sentence. I'm going to just keep my words locked up, even if they feel like pieces of glass cutting into my cheeks, my tongue, my gums. I am going to seal them tightly behind my lips no matter how they cut my mouth so that it bleeds right down my chin, drips onto my heart.

I cough again.

He continues.

"I was just trying to give you a taste of your own medicine," he says. " It backfired."

I look at him and I don't understand. I do not understand what he has just said, have no idea what he is talking about. I have no idea.

Softly, through another cough, I ask him what that means, and my voice is strained and shaky. Holding onto these jagged pieces of words is hard. It hurts.

He looks down when he replies.

"I mean," he says, "I've asked you to commit to me and you won't. I know you say you are committed, but you're not really." He looks back up then, holds my uncertain gaze as he continues. "You play it safe, keep me at a distance. It hurts. I wanted you to know how it feels."

At first, I don't even know what he means. I have to think, to replay these words he has just said, replay them over again in my mind more slowly so that they make sense.

And then they do. And then I am shocked.

All weekend he was not answering my texts and calls, not communicating with me in any way because he was playing a game, one he had planned to win. The prize would be me. He'd win me by playing me, but he had no idea how badly I would lose. He still doesn't. He has no idea.

He says my name then. He says my name because I start to cry and shake my head and he knows this is serious. It is so serious.

"I'm sorry. I'm really sorry. I fucked up. I didn't think you would react so strongly."

I know what he is saying to me and then again I don't, and while I know it doesn't matter and that no amount of words can change that, a few seep out anyway, just a few. "A taste of my own medicine?" I ask breathlessly.

He looks down, closes his eyes. “Yes. I know you aren’t seeing anyone else anymore and you say we are together, and we are, but it’s with restrictions. You keep me at a distance. You won’t even sleep with me. I just wanted to wake you up, I guess.”

I am stunned and I don’t speak and the silence between us becomes deafening and so he fills it while I just hold my words like pieces of glass in my mouth that hurt so badly and trickle out of my eyes in salty tears.

“I’m sorry,” he tells me again. “I know you said you needed time. You were protecting yourself. I didn’t believe it. I thought it was me, that you didn’t care that much about me. I see now that you do. I’m sorry.”

I start to cry harder now and he reaches for me and I smell him. I smell that something else we could never quite decide on, and I think that maybe I know what it is.

Maybe it is fear.

Maybe he too is full of fear. Maybe he is a lot like me and I should go to him, tell him how much I understand. Instead though, I pull away. I cannot make sense of him when I have my own questions and doubts and hurts to figure out. And I have to. I have to figure it out.

So I stand up. I plant my feet firmly to the ground. I make room, create the space to let him go because I cannot linger. My comfort with myself cannot depend on a guy I’ve known for thirty-eight days. It cannot depend on anything that isn't me.

I have to let go.

And I have to be okay.

CHAPTER FOURTEEN

Here We Go Again

"Here we go again," I tell my sister.

"Oh just call him," she pleads with me.

"Seriously, will you give it a rest? I am not calling."

"You said yourself he was a great guy and you hated having to choose between them."

"But I did choose. I chose the fucker who told me to choose, then gave me a taste of my own medicine."

"Yes," my sister says casually. "I know. Did he call again today?"

"Yes," I tell her. "Twice."

"Do you think you should give him another chance?" she asks tentatively. "I'm not saying you should. I'm just saying I think he's maybe less of a dick than he seemed during that bad weekend. Maybe he's more of what you had during that first great month."

I soften a little, imagining his scent and blue eyes, the wide hands and shoulders. I imagine flowers and a blanket and the restaurant where we both sat on the same side of the table, a part of him touching me the entire time we ate.

"I pick dicks," I tell her. "That's what I do. I pick dicks."

My sister ignores this and says, "I think it's possible this new guy is not a dick though."

"Well, did you think the first two were?" I ask, referring to Big Mistake and Blue, but before she can respond I remind her that she didn't, that she didn't think they were dicks, and then I say what she is thinking. I say that I know everything went way too fast with those two and that I got in too deep. I admit that I let them sweep me off my feet with well-placed words, fancy dinners, beautiful flowers. I admit that I was trying to fill in my gaps, light up my dark spots. I admit that I've been desperate and unsure and broken, just like in the life I had with My Ex. More and more I see it there. I see how he loved me, but how he had to let me go.

Then I repeat that I cannot call him. I cannot call this other guy I met online two months ago, around the same time I met Blue.

"You can," she says, "but you don't have to."

"Do you know what he said when I told him that someone else, Blue, was asking me to be exclusive, that I was going to give it a try?"

"No. What?"

"He just said that was one really lucky guy."

There is silence for a moment before she asks, "What's wrong with that?"

"What's wrong with that?" I say agitatedly. "He didn't even try to fight it. I don't think he really cared."

There is silence again and I sense that my sister wants to say something, the same thing maybe that I am suddenly thinking. She wants to say it, so she does.

"Don't you think that might be a good thing?" she asks cautiously, like she's tapping her toe in a pool of water before jumping in. When I don't stir, she continues. "I mean, you haven't had much luck with the ones who fight it."

I'm quiet. I don't really understand this and I want to deny it, but somehow it seems right.

I don't want to call this guy who posted pictures of his trip to Iceland, the one with a deep smile, perfect white teeth. I don't want to call this guy I met for the first time at a coffee shop, where it was so easy to talk to him and he looked me in the eyes the whole time and he had something about him, something not like anything. I don't want to call this guy who didn't fight, didn't find well-placed words or make promises, whether he could keep them or not. I don't want to call this guy because he's different and I don't understand that, and I want things to change, but I only know how to make them stay the same.

"Don't you agree?" my sister asks more confidently now.

I wait and I remember what my Reiki master tells me, the woman I met when a broken heart made it so that I could not take care of myself and had to call my parents, sleep on their couch and barely change my clothes. She tells me that there are other ways of thinking. There are other ways, she says. I don't have to choose from fear and self-doubt, from the feeling that I am lacking. I can think differently.

Then again, maybe I shouldn't be doing this at all for a while. Maybe that is part of the problem too, that I find it so hard to be alone. I find it just so hard.

My sister says my name then, puts a question mark on the end of it. And it is always so serious when they say your name.

Two days later I am sitting at the green desk. I am writing and deleting and rewriting and deleting again, and then finally I text Iceland. "Hey there," I say. That is all I could come up with, all that seems to make sense, and already I am sick of the familiar anxiety that comes from always trying to get it right, to be enough but not too much.

Several minutes pass and I am impatient the whole time. I am looking at my phone every few seconds even though I know there would be an audible indication if he'd written back. I don't need to look, but I can't help myself, worry creating obsessions I can't seem to let go.

More minutes go by and I think that he is not going to text back. Why would he? Three weeks ago I told him that I was not able to see him anymore, that someone I met first was asking me to make a choice and I wanted to give it a try. It was Blue, who smelled the way he smelled and asked me to pick him and so I had, and Iceland, the guy I'm texting now, thought that Blue was a lucky guy. I fucking hate that. I hate it, but my Reiki master tells me that I can think differently. She says I can.

I leave my phone on the green desk and go into my bedroom to distract myself with putting laundry away. I turn on the radio, make the volume loud enough that I can't hear my text message indicator because I cannot allow so much of my happiness to hinge on the attention of these men. I should not even be contacting him to begin with, but my sister thinks I am not meant to be alone and that there is no shame in that as long as I don't settle, and clearly I am not settling. I'm giving rings back and calling off weddings and breaking up with people every chance I get. That's definitely not settling, right?

Five minutes later I have put all of my socks and underwear away and placed all of the sheets and towels in the linen closet. I go back to the desk to check for his message on my phone, but there is nothing, and I am angry and I am sad and I don't care. I start to return to the laundry and right then I hear the ping. I stop. I walk toward the desk.

Then I think maybe I won't look at it now. I'll wait and not be so eager and spend some more time on my own. Of course I don't though. I pick up the phone.

"Hey there?" his text reads. He puts a question mark at the end. It's been twenty-eight minutes. I wonder why there is a question mark and I wonder what took him so long and I wonder if I will always need answers that I just don't need. I wonder if I will always try to remember too much and predict too much, to live in the past or the future even though there is really no room for me in those places. There seems to be no room for me right here either though, right where I am.

Now I'm the one to be silent because I simply don't know what to say. I wonder why I contacted him in the first place. I wonder why I can't just be alone. But I know.

Finally, after at least ten minutes of waiting and wondering and worrying, I text back because I have to say something, even though I don't know what to say, and so I write, "Whatcha been up to?"

His next text comes quickly, within a minute. "Aren't you supposed to be dating someone?" writes Iceland.

Oh shit, I think, and don't know what to say. Yes, I am supposed to be dating someone, but he said that he was tired of me being aloof and holding back and thinking he was like the others and not giving him enough of a chance, even though I had given him a lot of a chance that he just couldn't see. He couldn't see it because he expected it to look like something else, so he decided to let me feel what it was like to be the one trying to get the attention. He wanted me to want him because despite his blond hair and blue eyes, his wide build and good smell and all of his talents, he was unsure and needed me to show him his worth. He was just like me.

I don't tell Iceland that though. I just write, "Well, that didn't work out so well." But I don't send it yet.

I stare at the phone and think about how I'd coughed so hard that night and how Blue had gotten me a glass of water, how he knew where my glasses were, but he didn't know so many other things. He didn't know that giving me a taste of my own medicine would be opening a bottle of poison. He didn't know I'd react so fiercely, jump to all sorts of conclusions and come totally undone. He didn't know about the receipt in my back pocket or the girl and her birthday presents, and he didn't know that I was broken and unsure and afraid.

I should have known though. I should have known.

I'm still looking at my text. "Well, that didn't work out so well."

I'm still not sending it.

Iceland wasn't really my second choice, someone I'm just contacting because the other guy didn't work out. He is a totally different kind of choice, not even in the same category. I picked Blue because he challenged me. He fought for me. He was relentless. That's why I picked Big Mistake too, and My Ex. All those years ago, My Ex. He fought for me. They all did. But not really. Not in the end.

There is nothing I can say to convince him that he isn't my second choice, but rather a different first one. I cannot try to explain that and so I just keep the words I've already written. I hit send.

I hit send, and exactly at that moment a text comes in. We must have been writing at the same time, I think, but then realize that the text coming in does not show Iceland's name, only a number I don't recognize. I open the text and read it. I still don't understand. It reads, "Hey there. How ya doin'?"

For another moment I don't get it, until suddenly I do. I notice the area code and then I notice the whole number and then

I realize that it is him. I deleted his contact information from my phone the night I left, but still I have not forgotten it. I have not forgotten Big Mistake.

I read it again and cannot stop reading it. "Hey there. How ya doin'?" I cannot stop reading it and I cannot believe what I am seeing, cannot believe he is sending me this casual text now, three months after I stood in his kitchen crying and he told me that he'd never lied to me and not to hate him.

I absolutely cannot believe it as I try to form words to Iceland, this guy who might be a better choice for me, even if I shouldn't be choosing at all. But I cannot form words and my heart races as I close the text window and do not reply. I do not reply to either of them. Instead, I turn and leave the phone behind. I just leave it there on the green desk.

Waking up the next morning I'm struck quickly with pangs of guilt and anxiety. I didn't text Iceland back last night and I didn't care, but in the light of day I do. I think how full of shit I must seem to him. We didn't speak for more than a month and then suddenly, on a random Wednesday night, I text a couple of words to get his attention, and when he gives it I don't reply. I wonder what he thinks of me and I want him to think that I'm more than I am.

I spring quickly out of bed. Moving always brings at least some relief to the streams of worry that plague me, and I make my way hurriedly from the bedroom to my phone on the green desk. My feet are bare as I step across the threshold and imagine the relationships I've had like debris spread all around me. I have to walk softly, careful not to step on something sharp, a jagged memory that hurts still. It seems like I can't step anywhere without landing on loss. To think about any of them is to think about all of them and they feel like fishhooks in a bowl, tangled and twisted, each jabbing at me as I try to pull out only one at a time.

I grab the phone. I turn it on and head toward the bathroom thinking that I don't want to add this new guy to the bowl of mixed-up pointy fishhooks. I am a bad picker, so I fear he's going to become another sharp place, more debris. My phone is in my hand and I turn it on. Within a few seconds I see a message. It is from Iceland, this guy I don't want to pick.

It reads, "Hey, you still there?"

It was sent last night, about fifteen minutes after I'd gone to bed because it seemed impossible to explain Blue to Iceland and because Big Mistake wanted to know how I was doing, but My Ex does not.

Fishhooks!

I go into the bathroom and turn on the water. I get my cleanser and squeeze a dime-sized amount into my hand. I create a warm and gritty lather that might scrub away some worry and doubt and this need I have to not be alone.

Reaching for the towel that is always hanging so neatly on the bar, I bring it to my wet face. I begin dabbing and patting and trying not to be so scared, and when my face is dry I refold the towel and hang it perfectly back on its bar. The little white daisy is facing out, exactly in the center of the towel, and I wish that I could fold my life as perfectly as I fold linens. If only I could get it to face in just the right direction, be centered.

I find his message again. I hit reply. I type.

"Good morning. Sorry for last night. I was wondering if you want to come over tonight for football?" I hit send. Just like that, without even thinking. I just do it and then wonder what the fuck I'm doing.

What *am* I doing? I know he loves college football and that there are games on Thursday nights, but other than that I have no idea why I am doing this. Last week I was still crying my heart out over the second guy since I called off my wedding only ten months ago. Only ten fucking months. I don't know if I want to do this and it seems like I'm doing it without thinking, without choosing. Of course that's not true though. We always choose. Even when we don't, we do.

Before I can set the phone down to turn on the shower water, the text message indicator goes off and I am surprised he is responding so quickly. I look at the phone, but his name does not appear. Instead, it is that same number from last night, the number I know is Big Mistake.

He writes, "I really miss you."

I cannot believe it and I feel like I have to move so I walk to the living room and sit down on the couch, stare at this message. I just stare.

He let me stand in his apartment close to four months ago crying and shaking because he had changed his mind, and then he let me walk away. He let me walk away, but now he misses me. So does Blue. After he gave me a taste of my own medicine and I stood up and asked him to leave, he started calling and texting and wanting to start over. They have both changed their minds, much like My Ex did so many times. Until the last time.

The last time he didn't.

That night my apartment buzzer sounds at almost nine o'clock. That fucking buzzer, I think. It seems to bring so much pain to my door.

I take a little too long thinking and fretting and wondering and so it sounds for a second time, but this one is different. It is softer, without so much urgency, like he didn't push it all the way, was just trying to alert me. It never reaches that piercing pitch that makes me jump and rush and cringe, so immediately I settle down, some worry and pain retreating for a moment.

Maybe he really is different.

The thing is, I don't know if I am.

So I don't go to the door. I stand beside the coffee table, the one with the candles inside that I rearranged that day on the phone after sixty days had passed, and I think about ignoring the buzzer, ignoring Iceland. I think I don't need this and I'm bad at it anyway. I think I should not let him into my apartment or my head or my heart, that I should spend time alone with the person I am most afraid of.

Me.

I should spend time alone with me and so I wait and it seems like a lot of time goes by, too long maybe. He might be gone because the buzzer doesn't sound a third time, and then I get nervous and think I'm doing the wrong thing and don't know what the right thing is and wonder if there is really such a thing as letting things unfold on their own, not having to tear them open.

I don't think there is.

The next morning my alarm goes off so early, the same time as always, but so early. Exhausted, I roll onto my left shoulder and reach for it with my right arm, but I miss it, and so I reach again, but still I cannot get that tiny fucking button. Finally I have to sit up, grab hold of the entire clock. I bring it into the bed and find the too-small switch and silence the radio. Then, the device still in my arms, I fall back onto the pillows, angry with myself for staying up too late, and angry maybe for more.

Finally, last night, I'd unlocked the main door. From the couch I had listened as he'd taken the stairs slowly and then, with almost no sound, tapped softly on my slightly opened door. He'd peered in with a small smile on his face, but wide enough that I could see his teeth, the same bright teeth I'd seen in that first online picture he'd posted from Iceland.

After short and awkward greetings, we'd sat side by side on the couch and we were tentative. We were slow and quiet and unsure, watching college football for over two hours, and talking and drinking beer and not being like what I am used to, nothing like it.

It was obvious that very first time I met him a month and half ago in the balcony of a city coffee shop and it was more obvious last night, increasingly clear as the evening progressed into the earliest hour of the morning. Something seemed to be missing, yet at the same time everything felt very much there.

Slowly I slide from bed now and close my window because this September morning is cooler than mornings have been lately. Rubbing my eyes, I head for the kitchen where I will start my morning coffee, but first I see our beer bottles sitting in a tidy row of six along the edge of the sink. He'd gotten up each time last night and rinsed each pair, placed them neatly in this spot. He'd then retrieved us each another, and every time he was gone I'd stared at the wall that separated us and wondered what was happening.

He smelled good too, I think now, reaching for the coffee bin. He smelled good, but in a different way than Blue did. His smell was more real, like maybe just a hint of the simplest soap and then something like oatmeal. Oatmeal and soap. Oatmeal and soap never hurt anybody, and he wasn't wearing any glaring T-shirt either, nothing about a big mistake. I think about this as my coffee makes its brewing sounds and I walk the few steps from the kitchen across my narrow hallway into the bathroom.

I turn on the water in the shower and look in the mirror. I don't look so bad after sleeping only four hours, and I thank God it's Friday. That's why, when football ended last night, we found reruns of *Saturday Night Live* and laughed and laughed, because I knew today would be Friday and somehow it's easier to be exhausted when the week is almost done. I also let him stay until two in the morning because I was drawn to him, drawn to that real and unfamiliar scent and to the way he was so reserved and careful, like there was a sleeping baby next to us and he didn't want to wake it. I was drawn to him even though he seems nothing at all like what I am drawn to. Nothing.

The hot water starts to fog up the mirror and I leave my wandering thoughts and strip down, fold my pajamas to neatly place on the counter. I turn on the radio and turn up the volume so I can hear it over the drum of the shower, then step in. A new song begins, and I try to listen as water runs over my head and I grab my hair and pull it all behind me to get wet. The announcer says the name of the song then, and I cringe a little.

I keep wetting my hair. I try not to listen anymore, but I hear. I hear them sing about moments and days and roads and where they lead.

And then they sing about choices. They sing about my choices and his choices, and my hands drop to my face and my head falls forward, and before I even know it is going to happen I am crying. Slow and gentle tears bubble right to the surface like a backed-up drain, all at once and without warning. I am totally overcome by the words and then they continue, the lyrics and the tears, and I'm afraid I will always be like this.

There are words about not looking back and not forgetting, about forgiveness and regret. There are just so many words and so many tears, but I keep going. I have to. I get the shampoo bottle and squeeze some into my palm, rub it into my hair, make little circles with my fingers like it is the most natural thing in the world to wash my hair as tears roll down my face and small sounds of pain come from my throat, my heart really.

I hope you know that you are loved, they say next.

I hope you know that you are loved.

These words hit me hard, harder than the others, and I think that I do not. I do not know that I am loved as I bring my soapy hair into a fat pile on top of my head and turn my face upward so that the water can hit all of it. It can hit the soap and the tears and the heartache too, wash everything down, all the way to my feet, where it lands and swirls away from me and I imagine it is all of my pain and broken pieces, all of it going down the drain. It is making room for something else. I don't know what it is, but it has to be something else.

"So I'll give ya a call or text after the movie," Iceland says, "let you know."

"Sure, sounds good," I say, though secretly I wish he'd just decide now if he's going out with his friends after the movie or coming here instead, to watch more Saturday Night Live as we sit on the couch and drink from beer bottles that he later rinses and lines up on my counter. I don't like not knowing and I don't like that he isn't willing to give me all of his time, get wrapped up in a fiery mess with me like everyone else, and I don't like that I'm thinking like this because I know it doesn't work. Knowing, however, doesn't make it so.

We say goodbye and hang up and I set the phone on the coffee table, the same one with the drawer full of sorted candles. I get up and walk into the kitchen, pour iced tea into a tall glass and gather up a place mat and the container of Chinese takeout I came home with just a few minutes ago. It's from the restaurant Big Mistake introduced me to. But I don't think about that.

I walk back to the living room and put my food and drink down, then slide onto the floor in that spacc between the coffee table and the couch, that same space where I sat with Blue only a month ago, eating cheese and fancy crackers. I don't think about that either.

I eat my brown rice and broccoli and watch a home design show and look around my small apartment and think I will paint the walls, add a large area rug. I get an idea for my closet too, imagine bins in all the same sizes, shapes and colors lined neatly on that top shelf. I see them full of purses and scarves and I start to feel better. I start to think that maybe being alone isn't so scary. It's just something I've never done before and I know there is a difference between scary and something you've just never done before. I know. But I don't.

When my meal is finished, I walk down the short hallway into my office and step up to the desk. That green, rough, wonderful desk. I pull out the wooden chair that's tucked into it and I sit down, touch my laptop keys so that the screen comes back. I log into my email and immediately a message appears from instant messenger and I can't believe it. Twenty-two minutes ago Big Mistake wrote, "Hey beautiful."

I stare at it, just stare. More than three months before, and with what seemed like ease, he let me stand in his kitchen with my back against the door crying and swearing, then turn around and walk out, my shattered heart falling behind me. I should not say one word to him, not one word more than the no words I've been saying to him every time he has tried to contact me in these last two days. Before I can decide not to reply though, he writes again. He asks, "Are you there?"

Without fully thinking, I have typed yes and hit enter. I don't know why I've done this and then again I do, but I don't have time to think about that because immediately he replies. He asks how I've been and I say that I've been fine, even though I know it makes no fucking sense at all to talk to him.

Big Mistake: Did you get my texts the other day?

Me: Yes.

Big Mistake: I thought I would hear from you.

Me: I'm sure you did.

Big Mistake: What do you mean?

Me: I'm sure you thought you would hear from me, but I had nothing to say.

There is a long pause after this.

More than a minute goes by.

Big Mistake: I'm sorry.

Me: For which part exactly?

There is another long pause and then he replies.

Big Mistake: For everything, I guess. I was confused and scared. I didn't mean to hurt you. I fucked up.

Me: I'm over it.

Big Mistake: I just didn't want to get hurt again.

Me: So you just suddenly thought of that? Because the whole time we were together you never mentioned any possibility of getting hurt. I did, but you didn't.

Big Mistake: I know. I'm sorry. You didn't deserve the way I was at the end.

I don't reply.

Big Mistake: I think about you and I see what we had. I can't help but wonder if there is still more.

There is another long pause now and I am stunned. I lean back, away from the computer keys. I bring my hands to my mouth. I breathe in.

Big Mistake: Are you there?

I breathe out.

Me: Yes.

Big Mistake: I'm sorry. It's just that I'm thinking about you all the time now. I fucked up. I know I probably have no right to tell you any of this, but I've been talking to friends and we thought maybe I should just reach out.

Me: You've been talking to friends about me, the same friends that are my friends too?

Big Mistake: Yes. I've been telling them how much I miss you and that I never should have let you go.

I pause again, sit back once more. This is everything I thought I would want to hear, everything, but it does not bring the comfort I imagined. Instead, it brings more pain. It brings a hurt that comes with knowing that I want these words from someone else, from the one I spent so many years with, who put a ring on my finger and then put it somewhere else and never told me where it was and I'm not ever going to know either. I'm not ever going to know what happened and I'm not ever going to hear from him again, and at this point I don't even know why I want to. Maybe it's just to know that I'm not so bad. I want to know that I'm not so bad, because I don't know. I simply do not know.

He doesn't wait any longer, and as I sit staring blankly at the screen, another message comes. He tells me that he started dating a girl a month ago and that he broke up with her last week because he realized she didn't make him nearly as happy as I did and I cannot fucking believe it.

I don't wait to reply this time. All at once I know precisely what to say.

Me: Are you fucking kidding me?

Big Mistake: I don't understand.

Me: No, you definitely don't.

Big Mistake: You hate me.

Me: Yes, pretty much.

Me: You have no idea what you did, do you?

Me: It's not all your fault though. I'm at least as much to blame for falling for it.

Me: I want you to leave me alone.

Big Mistake: You didn't fall for anything. I never lied to you. I told you that. I cared so deeply for you. I still do.

Me: You didn't seem to care so deeply for me when you weren't returning phone calls for days and when you let me stand heartbroken in your kitchen. I didn't notice any deep caring then.

Big Mistake: I know. I was scared. I'm sorry.

Then, just like that, I log off. It just happens. I didn't even know it was coming. I just shut down the entire conversation and close the laptop. I stand up and push in the chair, tuck it neatly into its space under the green desk we bought at the Salvation Army so many years ago, then move to the floor beside it. I sit down in front of it, a drawer handle touching my back just as it did almost a year ago when I moved in here and was all alone, and I think that I will not do this. I will not repeat this pattern, all of this hanging on and hanging on.

I take a deep breath in and the handle of the drawer pushes into my back and acts like a trigger so that I stand up and walk out to the couch. I lie down and close my eyes and I am not sure how much time passes when I wake up and see that it is ten minutes after ten o'clock. It is close to forty minutes since Iceland's movie would have ended and I reach for my phone on the coffee table and look for a message from him.

There isn't one.

Iceland, the one I think is so different, was supposed to let me know what he was doing after the movie and it should have ended forty minutes ago and he hasn't called and I decide immediately that he is worthless and that I am sick of waiting. I am sick of days and months and years of waiting and waiting and waiting.

I text him. I ask if he knows his plan yet, if he thinks he is coming over or not. But thirty minutes later, after checking my phone a dozen times, he has not responded. I am in pajamas with my face washed and moisturizer applied and I am pulling back my bedding, climbing in. My phone is on the nightstand and I reach to check it once more, but there is no message from him and I am crushed. I really thought he was different, but it seems he's not and apparently I'm not either.

Very soon I fall asleep, and only an hour later I wake up suddenly. Was there a sound? I turn and realize that my phone is lit up, so I reach for it and find a text message, but not from Iceland. It is from Big Mistake, and my heart races as I read again that he is sorry and that he knows he fucked up. He asks if he can see me, if I will give him just a few minutes. He's free for coffee tomorrow, he says. Will I meet him? For a moment I wonder. I wonder why Iceland has not called me and I wonder if I should hear what Big Mistake has to say.

I start typing then. But not to him. I write to Iceland, "Are you alive? Since you are not responding I can only assume you're dead. It was nice knowing you." I think of adding a quick fuck you, but then I don't. I'm trying to be something else. I'm not, but I'm trying.

I turn off the phone. It's easier to stop waiting for it when the power is off, even easier if you throw it across the room. So I do. I throw it through my open doorway, where it loudly hits the wall before landing in the hallway with a thud. I turn over in bed then and cry myself to sleep.

Here we go. Here we fucking go again.

CHAPTER FIFTEEN
Different

I've been awake for two hours and have retrieved my phone from the hallway, from the spot on the floor where it landed last night after hitting the wall and leaving a ghastly mark. I've been turning it over and over in my hands, then putting it down and picking it up and putting it down and picking it up, and wondering if it's too early to type a nasty message to Iceland because I haven't heard from him all night, and because I remember another time when I waited all night. I remember watching water drip in the sink and opening the window blinds over and over until finally his truck pulled into the driveway. I won't do that again. This time will be different.

Three hours go by and there is still nothing. It is ten o'clock. I am showered and getting dressed for the gym, even though I'm not likely to go, and that's when my phone rings. It just suddenly rings, and too quickly I pull it from the side pocket of my gym bag. I look at the screen and it's him. Iceland. He should have called or texted at least twelve hours ago, and I hate myself for waiting all that time, so I silence the phone and tuck it back in my bag.

I go to the door and slip on my flip-flops. I force myself to walk out, and as I turn to lock the door my voicemail indicator sounds and I cannot help myself. I have to listen. I unlock the door and go back inside. I set down my bag and take out my phone.

His voice.

It is deep and gravelly, and I like the sound now as much as I did the very first time I heard it, as much as I have every time since. There seems to be texture, not all smooth or all rough either, just solid, something you can feel. There is a sense that his voice is a living thing, wrapping itself gently around my face as he speaks, softening my features. I take all of this in as he says that he is sorry about last night, that his phone died during the movie and he did in fact end up going out for a beer after, a couple acutally, he teases. He says he got home near one o'clock in the morning and plugged in his phone, but by the time it got enough power to come on it seemed too late to call. He wonders then if I am free for lunch and says he is going to jump in the shower, but that he hopes to talk to me soon.

Then there is silence. The deepness and the gravel just end, and I stand there holding the phone and looking out the window and thinking of his voice. It is so steady and clear, so certain and matter-of-fact. It is not like anything else I know.

He doesn't mention that I texted three times and that the last two were sarcastic and cross. He seems to not notice this, or maybe not consider it worthy of discussion. What's more, even though he says that he is sorry, he isn't really apologizing, not in the way people usually apologize, a way that suggests a need for forgiveness, a wish to release guilt. Instead, his apology is just an acknowledgment, recognition of an undesirable situation. He offers facts as he sees them and doesn't suggest there is anything more to it than that. It is all completely unlike anything I am used to, not tragic or pleading or false or self-absorbed. In fact, there is hardly any emotion at all in his tenor or his words. There is just ease. There is a statement of his position as if it is to be accepted, not questioned, and I am stunned.

I continue to stand in the silence that follows his message, holding the phone and looking out the window, disoriented, but knowing that somewhere deep down, in a place I don't fully recognize, I appreciate this. I appreciate this steady hand, this certainty. I want to feel more of it, to be matter-of-fact, unquestionable. Another part though, a part I am more familiar with, wants to argue, wants him to prove that this is not all bullshit.

He didn't have to let his phone die. He could have texted at one o'clock in the morning. He could have called much earlier than ten o'clock the next fucking day too, and everything he said could be all lies and I can't take the chance that it is. On the heels of everything else, after putting my ring on the bathroom counter less than one year ago, I can't take chances.

So I dial his number and it rings several times before his voicemail picks up and I am glad. It gives me courage. "Hey," I start. "I got your message. A dead phone, huh? That's not very original, you know? I take it you're a late sleeper too, since your message is coming pretty late in the morning." I take a breath. I want to stop, but I don't. I haven't learned enough yet.

"Anyway, you don't have to feel obligated to call back. I'll see ya." I push end on my phone and then immediately wish I could take it all back. Immediately I wish I was not so much like myself.

I move from the window to sit on the couch, put my face in my hands and think that maybe he really is different. Maybe he is, but I'm not. Then the phone rings. The phone suddenly rings and my heart beats and I stare at the phone, but Iceland's name and number do not appear. Instead, it is Big Mistake, and I don't answer and finally it stops ringing. I put it back in my bag and head for the door again, and as I am locking it I hear the signal, the one that indicates a message. It took a while to come so it must be long and I don't want to hear it. Still, I sit on the steps outside my apartment and pull the phone from my bag.

"Hey," he says, then pauses. "I know I upset you by contacting you last night. Well, I mean, not just that." He pauses again. "I know you're still hurt by everything that happened and I'm sorry. I'm so sorry. I just really want to see you." There is a shorter pause. "I miss you so much. I totally fucked up. I know."

There is a long pause then and he takes in a deep breath. He lets it out. I wonder if he is pacing back and forth from his living room to his kitchen, past the dining room table where he lit two tall tapers and served me food he cooked himself. I wonder if he stops in front of the window over the sink, the one I was looking out of when he asked if I could picture us with children running around outside after dinner. I want to throw up. I want to scream. I want to cry tears that come from way down deep, from years before this, and so I start heading back to my apartment as the rest of his message plays.

"I would love to go back and start over," he continues. "I would really love that. Can you call me? I just want to talk to you. Call me. Bye babe."

Tears then, from way down deep, from years before this, from the pit of my heart.

Back inside I place the phone on the coffee table and stare at it, then lean back on the couch and close my eyes, try to keep the tears locked way. Just then, the phone rings again. Startled, I open my eyes and hinge forward to see that the screen displays Iceland's name, this guy who now more than ever seems exactly the same as everyone else because he didn't call. I can't untangle them, like a bunch of fishhooks in a bowl. They all come out at the same time, though I try only to tug on one. Fear comes out too. Self-doubt. Shame.

Pretty girls. Nice houses. Not me.

"Hey," he says in his voicemail. "I got your message. Can you call me back? Thanks."

I push replay and there it is again, that deep gravelly voice, that steady hand. He is not tragic or pleading. He is nearly devoid of emotion. I'm not though. I feel everything deeply, a cold hand squeezing and twisting and breaking the heart.

So I don't call back.

The next morning, another Monday fucking morning, I pull into my parking spot at school and I'm tired. I rest the back of my head against the seat, close my eyes.

That's when suddenly my text message indicator alerts me and I see his name across my screen. Iceland. I have not heard from him since early yesterday, when he asked me to call back because he didn't understand my edgy message about his dead phone and being a late sleeper. I didn't call him back though, because I didn't understand it either, and because I didn't understand him not defending himself or apologizing. I didn't understand him being so much of something else.

I look at his text and it is very simple. "Are you okay?" he writes. That is all.

I just sit then. I sit paralyzed by the simplicity of his words as a sort of calmness wraps suddenly around me, softens my features. I sit and think how only moments ago I was cursing him for not calling back again yesterday, not apologizing more, not trying to rouse me from my pain. But suddenly, like there is no other answer, I think that he was telling the truth about the other night. With little sentiment and no dramatic displays, he was simply telling the truth and I just didn't believe it because I can't stop feeling that receipt in my back pocket. I can't stop feeling like there's always more to the story and like maybe I'm not enough. Not pretty enough. Not a nice enough house.

His phone died during the movie and he went out for a beer after so he'd gotten home too late to call and that's all there is to it. Suddenly I know. I don't know many things, but I know this.

I pick up the phone and tap my finger in the message reply box. I start typing, and as I do I wonder if it's possible not to feel so lost and broken. I wonder if I can just trust someone. I wonder if I can trust myself.

I hit the keys, telling him that yes I am okay and thanks for asking. I tell him I was just confused about not hearing from him Saturday night and that I made assumptions. I apologize. I hit send. I try not to be the same as I've always been.

Fifteen minutes later I've already wondered half a dozen times why he has not yet replied and then a text comes in. I pick up the phone, read his words. He writes that he didn't mean to upset me and that nothing he said was bullshit. He asks if he can give me a call tonight. I tell him that he can and he tells me to have a great day and then I don't hear from him again. I check my phone a few times each hour, but there is nothing, and it is so unfamiliar that I can hardly think straight until that night when finally he calls.

We don't talk long. We make plans for an early dinner the following evening, and when the call ends after only about ten minutes, I sit on the side of my bed bewildered.

This isn't like anything I know. There is no urgency. There is no fire that seems to consume me as I sit with my feet dangling, staring into the open closet where there are now neatly lined bins on the top shelf, all in the same size, shape and color, and feeling flustered. I'm flustered by the ease. It doesn't make sense. It should be harder than this. Shouldn't it be harder?

I see a scarf hanging out of one of the bins, and as I rise to go and tuck it in I think of the last year and how I have been running into burning houses, attracted by the flames and heat, the rush to make it out before we both turn to ashes. It was like that for the eight and a half years before too, with My Ex, whom I met in a little bar in my hometown after a softball game and went home with that very night. We were supposed to end in marriage and start a new life from there, but we never started. We just ended.

This isn't like that. It isn't like anything.

There doesn't seem to be any smoke now, no flame-filled heat, and I feel it. I feel it missing, but not exactly the kind of missing that feels like lack. It just feels different, like instead of a raging fire that you have no choice but to put out when it gets too hot, this is soft embers glowing in a hearth. You are still drawn in, but by warmth and light, not a hot and fiery mass that you can't even see through. This is contained, safe, exactly what I haven't had and maybe haven't even wanted. Until now. Until I just can't take any more heartache and loss.

I can't take burning again.

At six-twenty the next night I am waiting for him to pick me up for our casual early dinner at six. At six. But it's six-twenty now, so I am frustrated and anxious, wondering what could make him so late and without even a text, though this is our fifth time seeing each other and he's been late every time, once by more than a half hour. That time, while I waited for him in the same coffee shop where we first met, a younger guy who had been watching me since I'd walked in, finally snuck over and asked who was keeping me waiting so long. He said whoever it was should be worried that someone else would steal me away. He sat down next to me after that and was still with me when Iceland finally arrived, running late, he'd said. Just running thirty minutes late. I think about that now and wonder if he even cares if someone else steals me away.

Then I get a text. It is six-twenty-two. I read it and see that he has just pulled into my complex and wants to know if I'm going to come down or if he should come up. I want to write that I just worked all day long and then rushed at the bank and the grocery store and my workout so that I could be ready for this date, and he is twenty-two minutes late and doesn't seem to care.

Instead, I just write that I guess I'll come down. I use the word "guess" on purpose, like I had to think about it and finally decided to see him after all. I put a period at the end to show I'm pissed. I wish I wasn't.

I gather my things, and as I walk out my door I realize how accustomed I have come to waiting even though I fucking hate it. I hate it, but I'm used to it, used to waiting for people to show up and keep promises and tell the truth and hold on and let go. I'm used to not knowing too. I'm used to not knowing and being forgotten, and I'm sick of it. I'm worth more than that, or at least I want to be, and I'd like to stop being reminded that maybe I'm not. I'd also like to stop being so fucking angry about it.

When I get downstairs, he is parked outside the main entrance, and as I approach the vehicle he reaches across and opens the passenger door. I hear music and it reminds me of something and suddenly I know that it is my twenty-fourth birthday it reminds me of. It sounds like a song that was playing as I danced on the hope chest and My Ex reached for me with a sly smile on his face. It reminds me of when my knees buckled and I fell into him.

"Why do you even love him so much?" my sister had asked close to a year ago. "I mean why?"

Because I could dance on a hope chest with him and he could make my knees buckle and because I always fell into him. I always fell into him. Until one day I didn't. One day he just wasn't there anymore and that hope chest now holds my wedding gown. The veil sits on top.

"Sorry I'm late," Iceland says with an uncertain smile, and I snap out of my fear and doubt, my anger. He's been late every time and I've been less than thrilled every time. I think he knows this and I don't want him to know, but then again I do. I don't want to care about it either, but then again I do. There are worse things than being late. Cheating and lying and broken-down hearts are worse than being late and I know I need to let it go, but knowing doesn't make it so.

"Oh, you're late?" I say mockingly. "I hadn't noticed."

"Sorry." He is clearly uncomfortable and suddenly so am I, and I don't want to be.

"Where are we going for dinner?" I ask, trying to let go and let go and let go.

He tells me the name of a place I love and asks if I like it there, and I tell him that this place is perfect as he puts the car in drive, pulls onto the lane that winds through my complex, just like my mom did all those months ago when I packed that bag of mismatched things and couldn't be alone. He asks how my day was, and before I can answer I feel his voice again, the way it is so gravelly as it softly wraps itself around me. I tell him that it was good, and as we talk I am struck with how just last month I told this guy that I could not see him again because Blue had said he cared so much about me that he could not continue to be with me if I was seeing someone else too. So I'd chosen Blue over this guy who is not the same as anything and always late and doesn't really act like he is even all that interested in me.

"Hey," I say as we wait at the stoplight. "What was the name of that little dive of a place we went to for fries and beer over the summer?"

There is a pause and then, "Before you dumped me?" he jabs.

I am surprised. We have never spoken of this and now suddenly here it is. "I did not dump you," I throw back, a wide smile on my face. I'm a little uncomfortable, but also I like this. This feels like something I know.

He reminds me of the name of the fries and beer place and I say, "Ah, right. I can't believe I am saying this, but I've been wanting to go there again."

He pauses and looks at me from the corner of his eye. "Do you want to go there for fries or to make fun of people?" He laughs a forced laugh. It is meant to ease tension, not really to convey that something is funny.

"What?" I ask, genuinely unsure.

"You don't remember?"

I think back and see us sitting at the table for two. As I think of this, I suddenly remember the woman standing at the door. "Are you talking about your girlfriend?" I tease.

"Yes, and that's as terrible now as it was then," he retorts, and I know that he is serious and I am stunned and I don't understand. I try to recover, not seem surprised and hurt.

"Are you serious?" I ask.

"I *am* serious," he says with apparent earnest.

"That was a joke," I tell him, wondering why I have to tell him.

"I know," he says, smiling and glancing at me as he turns into the parking lot of the restaurant.

"You're upset about that?" I ask, concerned.

"I'm not upset."

I wait a moment, then reply. "You wouldn't be mentioning it if you weren't upset."

"It's not that I'm upset. I just thought it wasn't so nice."

His vehicle glides into a spot near the entrance as I say that I was kidding, and feel myself getting red in the chest and face, tears forming in my eyes and my throat and my heart. "I would never have been rude to that girl. I was just making a harmless joke."

"Okay," he says, then adds, "I understand."

"No you don't," I tell him.

He puts the car in park, turns off the engine.

"Ready?" he asks.

I want to tell him that I am not ready and that he should fuck off and take me home and also that I'm sorry and that I admire all of his moral fiber and that I absolutely cannot stand it at the same time.

"You still want to have dinner with me, even though I'm so mean?" I'm teasing, and then again I'm not at all. I'm never going to be good enough, not for anyone.

"You're not mean. We just have different senses of humor. It's fine."

I think about that and say, "I'm not sure that it is fine."

"For me?" he asks.

"For either of us," I say.

He uses my name then, and I hate that. I really hate it.

"It's okay," he tells me. "I just felt sorry for that girl."

I consider this for a moment, having not before.

"I was just teasing a wardrobe choice," I tell him. "Not her as a person."

He laughs, more sincerely this time it seems. "Well, the wardrobe is part of who she is as a person, I think," he replies.

"Right. I guess I was separating the two," I explain.

He raises his eyebrows and softens his face as he looks across the front seat at me. "Well, that's good. I feel better about that."

"Why do you feel better?"

"I feel better because if you were just picking on clothes that's not the same as picking on a person."

I'd like to tell him that what would make me feel better is if he would not be late again, ever. I mean, since we're trading shit we don't like here, I might like to trade that. I don't though. I don't say that because I'm trying to keep my feet on the ground and not get so easily bowled over by things. I'm trying not to let every word mean so much and I'm trying not to be bursting with self-doubt and pain. I'm trying not to need to protect myself because maybe I'm not in any danger.

I'm trying not to let the outside in.

I say, "Right. I understand."

"Right," he says. "It's not the same thing."

That's for sure, I think. It is not the same thing.

"It was such a good night," I tell him. "Wasn't it?"

The sound of my voice seems too much, like a slice in the beautiful silence, and I wish I could take it back, stay quiet. Some things you just don't have to talk about, but I always do, and I wonder if he hears how my voice shakes a little.

It has been just over a month since we pulled into that parking spot and he challenged me about the girl and her T-shirt. It is October thirty-first, Halloween. We are lying in his bed after taking off our costumes and changing into sweatshirts and pajama pants and eating dozens of bite-sized candy bars as we sat on the couch listening to music and watching orange flames in the fireplace.

"It was," he says as he reaches for me and pulls me into him, my right cheek resting on the left side of his chest. Above his heart.

With the quiet outside and the warmth under the blankets and the sweet memories of this fall night, I feel more safe and grounded, more securely planted in my own life than I ever have. Ever. I realize it has been this way for a week now, maybe longer, and I wonder if a week is enough time to make something stick.

I know that it is not.

I feel overwhelmed then, overwhelmed with something that seems like grief, but I'm not sad, not grieving. Or am I? I don't know what this is and I want to talk more because if I talk it might help ease this mounting anxiety, this worry built of some sort of fear, but I don't know what I'm afraid of. I think I have just always been afraid that there is something to be afraid of.

My words break the gentle quiet again as I ask him what his favorite part of the night was because I just want to make sure this is happening, that he feels it too. I may have a new sense of safety, of being securely planted, but the roots are not deep.

"Rocky," he says. "Definitely Rocky."

I laugh and start to chant the theme song again and he joins me as we remember how the neighbor was dressed in his wife's white bathrobe with gym socks and sneakers, boxing gloves on his hands. A group of teenage girls approached our two yards and immediately their group leader began to belt this out. The other girls quickly joined her and then so did we, and our neighbors too, and it instantly became one of those moments. It became one of those simple beautiful moments that for me is never quite simple. I'm always filled with too much emotion, with a feeling I can't quite name that is like a strange mashing together of love and fear and hope and sorrow. It forms something I don't know how to carry around without getting hurt, and I don't know how to put it down either.

I want to talk more, about this night and what he feels for me and more things and more things, but I know I can't. I can't tear everything wide open and try to sort out each detail because as much as I think that will make me feel safe and sure, it never works. I have to remember that it never works. It just leaves a mess instead, and so I need to let things simply unfold. I need to sit back and let it all unfold and it will take time and I'm not comfortable with time and not well practiced at patience, but I'm trying. I'm trying something different.

CHAPTER SIXEEN

It's Over

I am completely aware that what I am doing is not rational and that it is motivated by fear and that I should not be doing it, but still I am in the car at eight o'clock at night driving to his house. I'm driving to Iceland's, who five months ago did not get me at all, didn't understand my sense of humor, wondered if I was mean. Now he knows. He knows that maybe I am mean at times. Maybe I'm not all the good I want to be, but I'm getting there and he gets it. He doesn't like it all the time, but he gets it. He gets me. That's why I'm driving to his house. I'm driving there to see if he maybe loves me, or if maybe it's over.

I'm also driving to his house at eight o'clock at night because I've decided that I'm in love with him. I've decided. I know that's not really how it works. I know you aren't supposed to just decide things like this, but as much as I've learned I still haven't learned this, and so I'm driving to his house because I've been unable to admit it and so I feel us shifting. We are shifting, maybe toward something or maybe away. I don't know. I just know that we are shifting and I don't like shifting. I like things to be steady and still. I like to hold on.

So I have to tell him. I have to tell him now, at this very moment, on a Tuesday night when I should be in pajamas on my own couch because we didn't have plans to be together tonight, but that's part of the problem. I wonder why. Why didn't we have plans? When you love someone shouldn't you be with them every moment, full of all sorts of fire and heat, consumed?

As I turn the corner onto his street I wonder if maybe I'll find out he doesn't love me after all or if I'll find out that I don't love him either. Maybe I'm just scared and I want something different and he is my something different. Maybe he's too different though, and maybe I'm going there to tell him that.

I pull to the side of the street and park. Quickly I get out of the car. I lock the door and scurry to the first step that will take me up the hill to his front door, but I'm halfway up the steps when abruptly I stop.

What the fuck am I doing? I'm planning to go in there and say something like, "I love you. Now what are we going to do about it?"

I was actually planning to do that and now I realize with alarming sadness that I cannot. I simply cannot. I am so ill-equipped, so broken. I have no idea how to just let things unfold as they should, let the natural course of events be my guide. No, I have to start fires, heat it up. I have to be filled to bursting with this other person. I can't allow awareness to softly move in, reveal itself little by little. I have to completely tear everything open and lay it all out, know every last detail immediately. It is less of an unfolding and more of a coming undone and I just can't. I can't. I know better.

On a yoga mat with my brow to the earth and my arms outstretched, I've learned to get quiet and still and notice and I've noticed. Under hands on a Reiki table, I've felt pain pour out of my heart and something like peace settle around my feet and I've settled.

But I haven't.

I hear a sound and look up. He is opening the door, about to step onto the porch. He is smiling at me. I take in a deep breath and blink my eyes, open them wide, try to keep the tears from falling down my face.

And then I just turn around. I turn around and call over my shoulder that I forgot something in the car, and scurry back down the stairs, rush to the driver's door and open it. I pretend to be rooting, but really I'm just hiding because I'm ashamed of myself for being frantic and unsure, for never getting it right.

I look up. He's going back into the house and I'm thinking how less than two months ago he gave me a beautiful Christmas card that said our time together had been some of the best he'd ever had and that he hoped our first Christmas would be one of many. I've read those lines over and over and I've read its closing too. Head over heels. Before signing his name, he'd written, "Head over heels." And I thought that could only mean one thing. But still, he has never said it.

Then again maybe he did, and maybe he said it a week ago too, when he signed a Valentine card with the words "All my love" and attached it to a little box, a ring box. I noticed right away, its small square shape like a beacon. I'd had a little box like that once before, but then it was gone.

My hands had trembled opening that new box, listening to the familiar creak of the tiny hinges on the lid. When the inside was finally exposed, a small gold crown had stared up at me. It sat atop a heart and two joined hands, all molded to a ring. It was his mother's ring, he'd said, the claddagh ring his father had purchased for her in Ireland thirty years before. I'd gently removed it from a slice of velvet that held it upright, and he had told me that it stands for love and loyalty. It stands for friendship too, he had said, but he was giving it to me for love and loyalty.

We'd been sitting on the couch in my living room at the time, less than two months after what would have been the first anniversary of my marriage, and he'd given me this ring and I had wanted to tell him that I loved him, but I was scared. I was scared and so I'd waited for him to tell me, but he didn't. He still hasn't. And it feels like something is between us, something we are both afraid to look at.

I think it's our love. I think it's there, but we are afraid to look at it, to say it. We keep leaning in and moving away, leaning in and moving away, and I wonder now if our grip has been too loose, if our grip is even real. I wonder now, and so I'm in the car pretending to root around for something, but truly I'm just trying to figure a way out of this, out of the responsibility of loving someone, or maybe just out of thinking that I do. I'm in the car trying to avoid what an hour ago I so desperately wanted to come here and tell him, because now I'm just not so sure. I am never sure, and so tears threaten to move down my face and soak me in the sorrow of having changed so much and then again having not changed nearly enough, and I just want to stop all of this not knowing.

My worries are interrupted though. I get a text message. He must be texting me from inside the house because it's strange that I've been out here this long, and so I reach into my purse, dig around for my phone but don't find it. I become panicked then, and at the same time I am upset that I'm panicked, and when finally my fingers find the phone I am shaky as I pull it out, look at the screen. It is not him. It is a number not attached to a name anymore, but I know who it is and I am stunned. It has been months.

"Hi," Blue writes. "I've been thinking about you for so long and I finally got the nerve to try again. How are you? I sincerely miss you."

"Are you fucking kidding me right now?" I whisper, then slump into the driver's seat and let what seems like minutes go by, and then read the message again and absolutely cannot believe it. I cannot believe that after all this time he is texting me at this very moment, at the very moment when I am ready to tell Iceland that I love him and when I'm not ready to do that at all, and I cannot stand it. I cannot stand to think about what I've lost and what I have and what I want and what I don't want, and I cannot stand anything at all.

I close my eyes. I plant my feet on the floor of the driver's seat and notice the soles of my boots on the mat and I push them in. I push the soles of my boots into the mat and try to feel the ground beneath me. It's what I've been learning in Reiki. I've been learning to be okay and loosen my grip and know that I don't need anyone's love to prove that I am enough. I don't need anyone's love to prove anything, and I know this, but knowing doesn't make it so.

I close the phone and instead of putting it back in my purse I put it in the middle console of my car. I don't want it with me. I don't want him with me, or any of them. I step out of the car and close the door slowly, wishing now that I had the nerve to just get back in and drive home the way I had the nerve to get in and drive here in the first place.

I don't have the courage to leave though, so I turn toward his house that sits atop a hill and I go back to the stairs. I take them only one at a time now, my heart so unsteady. As I step onto his sidewalk, I try to breathe like I do on the mat, but the breath doesn't come as easily on this pavement, and I look at the spot where the girls ran across the lawn belting out the Rocky theme four months ago, and I think I'm here because I want more of that. I want more, but as I follow the sidewalk to his front porch, I wonder if it's too soon.

I approach the door and it is slightly ajar so I push it open, walk inside. From the foyer I can see into the living room where he is sitting on the edge of the couch, and he turns in my direction. He smiles and gets up. My heart settles a little at the sight of him and I finally get a deep breath and bend down to take off my shoes. As I stand back up he is at my side.

"Hey there," says Iceland. "What's this all about?" He reaches for me, helps with my coat.

"I know. I'm sorry," I say, and immediately get hot with shame. I'm burning in it.

"Why are you sorry?"

"I'm just sorry I bothered you at eight at night and acted like it was so urgent. It isn't."

I swallow hard, pleading with the heartache and self-doubt to keep their distance, to not make a bigger fool of me. I got into the car a half hour ago to drive over here and tell him I love him because it had finally occurred to me that I do. At least I think I do. I want to. Dear God, those aren't even the same things, and I have become totally convinced that if I don't admit it immediately it will somehow go away. It wouldn't even wait until morning. Tonight, it would just go away. Literally, I thought, it would just vanish in the middle of the night and tomorrow it would be gone.

Now I see those thoughts for what they are. They are delusional, completely full of fear, not grounded in any of the presence I've been trying to practice, and I'm standing in his living room just aghast at the sheer pain of being me.

"Do you want to sit down?" he asks, and I wonder what the fuck I am going to say.

What the fuck am I going to say and how could I have done this to myself? How could I have come here at eight o'clock on a fucking Tuesday night to tell him that I love him? How could I be this manic, this unhinged? How could I have a text message sitting in my car that says, "I sincerely miss you"?

We move to the spot on the couch where we have been together so many times, drinking Blue Moons out of tall glasses with oranges floating on top. He sits and picks up the remote, turns the volume down. I can still hear though. I can still hear my heartbeat of fear and doubt.

I wonder if he can hear it too.

"What's up?" he asks softly. He touches my leg then, tries to look at me, but I turn away.

I take a deep breath, let it out for as long as I can. "I don't know," I say at last.

"You don't know?" he asks gently, and I turn my blank stare from the television screen to his face, see instantly that he looks concerned, that he's wondering the same thing I am.

Why did I come here?

I have to say something. I have to say what I came to say, only now I don't know what I came to say.

"Fuck," I utter breathlessly.

"Just say it," he tells me. "Whatever it is."

"Okay," I tell him, but I don't know what I'm going to say and so I buy some time. "I'm here because for some reason I felt like I just had to tell you this tonight, that it could not wait."

He does though. He waits. I want him to say something so that I don't have to, but he just waits. This is how he is. He is steady and patient and I hate that and I love that and I know that either I get up and walk out or I say what I came here to say.

But do I even know what I came here to say?

He uses my name then. I've waited too long and so he says my name and that makes it serious and I feel like I have to talk and so I open my mouth and it just comes out.

"I think I love you," I say.

As soon as it's out I want to take it back, but not because it is untrue. I want to take it back because it sounds crazy, because this is not how you do it. I'm desperate and uncertain, grasping for something to hold onto, like love. Love lets you get a hold of it, a nice firm grip, and I want to hold on. But I went about it all wrong. I always do.

He takes his hand from his lap and moves it behind me, wraps it around my waist and pulls me in a little. Then he says four words. He says four words, and at first I think I don't hear him correctly because they are not what I am expecting.

They are not, "I love you too." That's what I was expecting because that's what this is really about. That's what it's always been about. I want him to love me. Because when you can't love yourself you become desperate for someone else to do it, and you think if you just hold on they will. If you kick and struggle they will love you and then you'll know you are worth it. So it takes a moment to understand, and even then I don't. I do not understand.

"What did you say?" I ask him.

"I know you do," he repeats.

I wait then. I wait for more, but nothing comes. There is just the gentle touch to my back and those alarming words hanging in the air.

I know you do.

"You know I do?"

Quite simply he says, "Yes," and I don't respond. I just sit and wish I'd never come.

He continues. "I can feel it."

Well isn't that just so nice for you, I think. Isn't that just so fucking nice.

"You can feel it?" I ask.

"Yes, can't *you* feel it?"

"Feel what?" I ask because, I don't understand what is happening and all I feel is like an idiot and pissed off and sad. I am so disappointed that the only way I know to love myself is if someone else is loving me and I know that this is flawed and desperate and will not yield the love I crave, but knowing doesn't make it so. For now, I still need someone else to love me and he's not doing it right.

My Ex didn't either, did he?

"Feel that we love each other," he replies.

Wait. What? I try to process those words quickly, but it's confusing.

"So you love me too?" I ask, and immediately feel so stupid again. I cannot believe that I have allowed this to happen.

"Of course I do," he says.

I wait another moment, process more of these words that I don't understand, that I have never heard before.

"So why haven't you said it?" I ask him.

"I didn't know I needed to. I thought I was showing you."

"Showing me?"

"Yes. I guess I just thought I was showing my love for you in all the things we do, the time we spend together. I haven't felt I needed to say it."

I don't respond right away. I look at him, then down at my hands in my lap. I've needed him to say it. I've needed that.

"Are you upset?" he asks tentatively.

"I just feel like an idiot."

"Why?"

"For a lot of reasons."

"For what reasons?"

I want to tell him that I feel like an idiot because I need everything to make sense and I need to create stories and definitions and rules and I need to live by those, by those stories and definitions and rules. This doesn't do that. It doesn't make sense and it isn't part of the story I've been telling and it doesn't match any of my definitions and it breaks the rules. It breaks my heart too.

"I feel like an idiot for coming here now, so urgently, to say this to you."

"It's fine that you did. I'm glad."

"Well I'm not," I admit.

"Why?"

"You didn't need it."

"So?"

"So, I suddenly got this idea that you were waiting for me, that maybe you were getting sick of waiting, that I had to tell you right away, before it was too late."

"Too late?" he questions.

"Yes," I say. "It's dumb."

"Too late for what?"

"Like too late for you to keep waiting."

"I wasn't waiting," he says.

"I realize that now, thanks," I say sadly. "Like I said, you didn't need this."

He says my name then and I hate the sound of it. I don't want to hear my name. "*You* needed it," he continues. "So it's okay."

I needed it. I hate that. I hate that I needed this and he didn't, and I hate that I need so much and that I never get it right. I never seem to get it right and now that it's done I don't seem to feel as much either. I don't seem to feel as much in love. I was desperate with it a few hours ago, desperate. Now I'm not.

Now I don't know what is real and what I just want to be real and I need time. I need time away from this and away from him, but mostly I need time away from myself. I need to be away from myself, but I can never get that. That is one relief that never comes.

"I should go," I tell him.

"You're going to come all the way here and then just leave?" he asks, a smile visiting his mouth. My heart lurches a little and I remember why I was so desperate for him to love me.

"Yes," I say.

"All right," he says. "I understand."

"At least someone does."

"What is it *you* don't understand?" he asks me.

I inhale deeply, try to let it out slowly, be on the mat, under the Reiki hands, but it comes out fast and choppy because I hate this fucking matter-of-factness, this lack of fire and smoke and rushing. Then again, that's exactly why I thought I loved him, because all that fire and smoke and rushing was gone and I could be safe, warm.

"This," I say. "I just don't know how you can be so, whatever."

"Sweetie," he starts, and my heart lurches a little more. "I don't mean to be whatever about it."

"You might not *mean* to be, but you are," I say simply.

"Well, what do you want me to be like?" he asks.

"I don't know. I'm sorry."

"I don't want you to be sorry," he tells me.

"Well I *am* sorry," I say, my voice rising. I settle it down. "I mean, I'm just disappointed I guess, maybe not sorry. I'm disappointed that I'm not getting this right."

"There isn't anything to get right. We already got it right."

I don't have any idea what he means and then again I know exactly. I swallow hard, pleading once more with tears and heartache and shame, asking them to keep their distance. I just told him I love him and I thought he was waiting for that, but it turns out he was not waiting. He already knew. It also turns out that even though he has said that he loves me too, he has not actually said it at all.

To not look crazier and to get out of this less scathed, I tell him that he's right, but that I'm still going and that I'll talk to him tomorrow. He asks me to stay. I kiss him and tell him that we'll talk tomorrow, that I hope the rest of his evening is uneventful. He laughs and asks me to come back for dinner the next night. I say that I will, but I don't plan to.

An hour later, I crawl into bed. I pull myself into a ball with the blankets to my chin and I cry because he didn't say it back. He didn't tell me that he loved me and I am totally soaked in doubt, completely drenched. He said he thought he was showing me and he said, "of course I do," but he never said it and I wonder why, and then I remember the first time he pushed the buzzer on my apartment building. I remember how his push was softer, slower. It was not full of the same force or urgency I'm used to. It was different. He was different. Maybe this is all *too* different, and maybe I'm not.

Within moments I know that I can't sleep and I get out of bed. I move toward the spare bedroom with the green desk, that fucking green desk. I'm suddenly sick and tired of looking at it, of having it take up so much space. I want it to be smaller and less green and I want him to say he loves me and not just tell me how he can feel that we love each other. Put the words together in the right fucking order, I want to say. Put the words together so I don't have to seem like a fool at eight o'clock on a Tuesday night.

I reach for my phone. I dial my voicemail and wait for an old message. Then I hear him, that deep and gravelly voice. Like every time, it seems to wrap itself gently around me, soften my features with its clear and steady tone. He is so certain and matter-of-fact, not tragic or pleading, just quiet and still. I want things to be like this, quiet and still, and then again I don't. I need the force, the urgency. His gentle hand on my back tonight. It's always like that, a gentle hand. I want him to touch me with more than that, to be so enamored that I cannot help but feel enamored with myself, and then again, I don't want that at all. I want gentle and steady and quiet and still. More than anything though, I just want to want nothing and to think that everything is enough. Especially me.

Then suddenly I am pulling down bins, the ones in the same size and shape and color lined neatly on that top shelf of my closet. I empty purses and scarves all over the floor and start to reorganize them. I put things back in different bins and put the bins in a different order, and as I place them one by one back on the shelf, I start to feel a little better.

I don't know what to do about my heart and my head and my bullshit, but I do know what to do about bins of purses and scarves. I know what to do about those.

I listen to his saved voicemails again and I want to respond, but it is not real. It is only a recording, deep and gravelly, and I can't say anything he will hear. I can't say how I have been trying to do things differently, not to be exactly the same person, to change certain parts of me and not attract the same heartache. I want to tell him how I realize there are things that felt safer with him and I wanted things that way, but now I wonder if something is missing, fire maybe. I need to be safe, but then again I might still want to try to make it out before we each turn to ashes, before the smoke gets us. I don't know if I can have both and I don't know if I want both and I don't know if I know anything.

The next morning I wake up slowly and turn on my side to see the closet door, hoping for the newly organized bins to bring me some relief, but they don't. They aren't making me good enough and I think how they never will. Nothing on the outside is going to make me feel good enough. It's going to have to come from me. I know this, but knowing doesn't make it so, and I stretch out long like I do on the yoga mat and I try to get quiet and still and it works for a precious moment, but then my thoughts take hold again and I reach for the phone. I tap in the code to unlock it and am surprised to find a voicemail, a new one, a message he left last night, maybe as I was sorting bins.

"Hey. You might have gone to bed. If not, you don't have to call back tonight. I'll talk to you tomorrow," he says, and as always his voice wraps around me, steady and certain. He continues.

"I just want to thank you for coming here tonight, and I want to tell you . . ."

He pauses.

". . . that I love you too," he says.

My breath. It catches.

He is not tragic or pleading, just quiet and still, matter-of-fact. Like his gentle hand on my back last night, he is solid. There is another pause and maybe he swallows, collects his breath. I imagine he is sitting on the couch, in the same spot we sat in together hours before, the television silenced. He couldn't say it then, but he's saying it now. I don't know if it matters.

"Good night love," says Iceland, and I place the phone gently on the nightstand and sit on the edge of my bed. My legs hang over the side and my hands are in my lap and I'm crying and I don't know why.

Maybe it's because I can't seem to keep my feet on the ground and not get so easily bowled over by things. Maybe it's because I let every word and every silence mean so much, and maybe it's because it hurts to be bursting with this kind of self-doubt and pain. Maybe it's because I feel these broken little pieces inside of me and I don't know exactly where they came from, but they've always been there and they've always jostled around in a way that makes me wonder if I'm worth loving, and maybe because I know that being this way has cost me so much.

So much.

Just then, something about the way I am sitting and the way I am crying reminds me of that day over sixteen months ago now, only sixteen short months ago. My Ex sat in our living room chair then, two nights before I left. I see him with his legs shoulder-width apart, an elbow resting upon each knee. I see his face in his hands and I hear him and remember the sound.

I see him lifting his head from his hands and gazing at me, his face red and wet and full of anguish. I think of how I went to him and knelt at his feet, placed my hands on his legs. I see him covering my hands with his own and I hear him ask. I hear him ask how he is supposed to live without me and I remember that I didn't know. I did not know.

There was a kind of suffering in him that day, the kind I could hear and feel and almost touch, but it wasn't enough. I was not enough and so he let me go and I've never been the same. I have never been the same, and maybe I never will be and maybe I never was, even before him. Maybe his letting go wasn't what devastated me so much. Maybe I was already devastated and maybe I just hadn't noticed until then.

Pretty girls and nice houses. I wonder about those. I wonder about me. I wonder if I can pick differently.

I reach for the phone then and I dial my voicemail once more. I listen to the words of this man I know is different, without any smoke, no flame-filled heat. I've been able to feel it missing, but still been drawn in by warmth and light, content to avoid the hot and fiery mass that you can't even see through.

He says he loves me and I know I love him, but the love feels so different that I almost don't recognize it. It's not like the love who cried hot tears and asked how he was supposed to live without me. It's not like that. He loved me fiercely, but he let me go.

Still crying at the edge of the bed with my legs dangling, I listen to the voicemail once more. "Hey. You might have gone to bed. If not, you don't have to call back tonight. I'll talk to you tomorrow. I just want to thank you for coming here tonight, and I want to tell you . . ."

He pauses. I wait, my breath held, even though I know what he's going to say.

". . . that I love you too."

He does not plead.

He is not tragic.

He is quiet and still, matter-of-fact.

Like his gentle hand on my back last night he is just certain.

And then, all at once, so am I. With a suddenness that hits me hard, I am certain that it is time. It is time to stop wanting and hurting. It is time to stop regretting and holding on. It is time to stop doubting and fearing and lacking and being so fucking unsure and sad. I know that it is time and I know that knowing doesn't make it so, but maybe it is a start.

There is another pause and I imagine him sitting on the couch when he delivers this message. I imagine him in the same spot we sat in last night, but not with his head in his hands, not with eyes wet and red. Instead, he sits up straight, speaks calmly, with a clarity and certainty I need to have for myself, confirming what I should have known, should never forget.

"Good night love," he says.

Good night love.

I cry harder then because this really needs to end, this doubt and fear and lack just has to end. This regret and holding on has to stop. This wanting and hurting and aching and aching and aching just can't continue. It cannot.

My Ex is never coming back for me, and if he did I realize right now that I wouldn't go. I realize in this very moment for the very first time that I would not go. I would not.

And I cry and cry.

I cry so hard at this letting go, another letting go, this understanding that what I wanted most was for him to come for me, to ask. I didn't want to go. I just wanted him to want me to. Like Big Mistake and Blue with their constant calls and texts and emails, I wanted My Ex to let me know that I'm worth it, that I'm wanted, that I'm enough. I wanted him to answer that question about how he was supposed to live without me. I wanted him to say that he couldn't.

He's never going to though. He's never going to because he's living without me.

I get up then. I open the closet door, look toward the newly organized bins placed so neatly on the top shelf, and know that I have to know it myself. I have to know that I am enough and that nobody can tell me that. I have to know it from within, and I know that knowing doesn't make it so, but maybe it does.

Or maybe it's over.

CHAPTER SEVENTEEN
Yes

Two months later it is early in the morning as I pull out the chair in front of the green desk, the one I always thought so wonderful despite its roughness and many flaws. Now I think about painting it, as I sit down and my legs no longer seem to fit the right way. It feels too tight. The drawer that always falls out, not so full of meaning. It's just a drawer that falls out, and I wonder then. Can I let it go?

Yes, I think I can.

I pull the computer closer to me and log into my email. A list of messages quickly appears and I am appalled. The very first one is from Big Mistake. I cannot believe it.

Seven months. That's how long it's been with this man who is different and loves me and doesn't say it often, but shows me, and I love him too, so I should delete this email. I should, but I don't.

I pick up my coffee and sip, look over the rim as I read that he knows I don't want to talk to him, that two months of ignoring him makes it pretty clear. He heard a new country song though, and it was like someone wrote it for him to give to me and he can't get me out of his head. He says it is everything he feels every moment since he realized he should never have let me walk out that day.

I read all of this and I don't cry.

I already know the song. I have already cried over it, then turned my attention back to this man who would not need a girl to know what a mistake it was to let her go. I have already listened to the words about deep regret and the hurt you have to live with, the loss you try to push neatly into a quiet place inside of you that is still so loud.

I know the song.

He ends by asking if I'm single because he'd like to grab a coffee, just catch up. He writes, "I know you were seeing someone when I saw you on St. Patrick's Day (our anniversary ha ha) but I wasn't sure if it was serious. Are you still seeing someone?"

Our anniversary? Why do they do this? Why do they say things that mean nothing and mean so much and why do I still want to move toward this even though I know how it hurts? Because somehow it fills me up. Somehow it gives me the value I am still trying to give myself.

I think that I should just ignore this message like I've ignored the others, but this time I don't. I hit the reply button and ask him please not to contact me again.

I pick up my coffee and take another sip, look out over the top of the mug, and that's exactly when my instant message box pops up and I can't believe it. I cannot believe that it is not Big Mistake.

It is Blue. With his blond hair and that smell I could never quite name, he types, "Hey. Are you busy?"

I think to myself that I am busy. I'm pretty fucking busy getting my feet on the ground and not being so afraid and thinking I might be good enough even if I'm not always sure. I wonder if he's busy wishing he would have thought twice before giving me a taste of my own medicine, but I decide not to say any of that. I decide not to be tragic or pleading. Instead I will be quiet and still, matter-of-fact and certain.

I write back to him. I simply type, "I am."

Spring leads to summer and our days are full of long walks and lunches and bottles of beer on the patio he just built. Most of the time a sort of peace falls over me, the way it does under hands on a Reiki table, settling in a way I have not known before, and it feels like healing. I am healing whatever was broken or whatever I just wasn't using properly, healing the constant thoughts of fear and lack and shame and self-doubt.

But am I really?

Iceland and I speak of our future together. We talk about it on the way to a tour of homes in our city and while we make pizza at his house on Wednesday nights. We talk about it when we watch football and play chess and pull back the blankets before getting into bed.

We talk about it, but we don't.

There are no concrete terms. We don't make any plans. We don't say when or how. We don't really say what the future will be, but rather simply suggest that there is one, a future. It's hard for me. It's very hard.

I want to press. I want concrete terms and plans and when and how and I want to know everything, every single thing.

But for now I don't push. At least not the way I'm used to pushing. I try to let things just be, to unfold naturally and not have to tear it all open. I try to trust, to know that I am okay no matter how things turn out, no matter who loves me. But knowing doesn't always make it so.

Today is the twentieth of July, the anniversary of the day Iceland's mom died three years ago, before I even met him, when I was still getting married. It is unseasonably low humidity, so the fresh rose petals I bought will stay that way for a while after I lay them at her grave. My hair should stay fresh too. Just like the flowers, my hair won't wilt at her grave when I meet his mother for the first time.

I am home just a few minutes after picking them out, the perfect bag of yellow rose petals, the ones I've made painstakingly certain have no other colors mixed in because only yellow seems right today. Iceland will be here soon and we'll leave for the cemetery, but first I put the bag on the kitchen counter and go to my basket filled with all sorts of goodies for packaging gifts. I rummage through the flowered bags, tissue paper, bows and boxes, looking for gold ribbon to go with the yellow petals, but I find only a very small strip that is not nearly enough to tie around the opening of the bag, and I huff and curse and fear that it will never look right because I really want gold. But then suddenly I realize. I realize that I am holding on too tightly. It is just a bag of rose petals and a ribbon to close it and I need to let go, choose differently.

I rummage again through the ribbons and spy a long strand that is pink and glossy, but I keep looking, keep holding too tightly, even though I know. Finally then, I come to another longer piece of gold and I am relieved as I take it to the bag of petals on the counter and it fits perfectly. I tie it so that long strands hang beneath the loops of the bow and then with my scissors I get them to curl sweetly, and I think it is beautiful, what I imagined. Not pink.

Sunlight pours in through the window and I pick up the bag and grab my purse, then step across the living room toward the door, where I slip on my shoes and put my hand on the doorknob as suddenly I remember. I remember that moment last year when I'd opened this same door and my mom had stepped toward me and taken me into her arms. I remember how I'd followed her out and down these same steps and through the same front entrance and to her car, where I had sat in the passenger's seat crying.

The weather and the light and the sounds and my movements make this feel almost not like a memory, but like that same day all over again, and I shake my head. Literally, I shake my head to rid myself of these thoughts and feelings that are scary, but not real. Then, just as quickly, it is gone. Like a ghost, the memory has vanished, and I know that it is because I am learning not to let pain make such a home in me anymore. It is costing too much.

The warm sun hits me as I enter the parking lot of my apartment building and go to my car. I open the door and get behind the wheel, place the bag of yellow rose petals on the passenger's seat. I start the engine and turn on the radio, expecting to wait for him today, as I do most days. I accept that he's always late, but then again I don't, and just as I am wondering how long it will be, he pulls up next to me, surprises me as he often does. His passenger window is down and he calls to me.

"Hi babe!"

I'm so happy to see him as I open the door and get out of my car. I step to the window of his vehicle and place my arms on the opening. Looking at him, I try to gauge his heart today. He smiles.

"Hi lovie," I say, smiling gently back. "How are you?"

"I'm good," he says, with his signature soft smile and that pure look in his eyes.

"You sure hon?"

"Yes," he replies simply.

He is not tragic or pleading, just quiet and still, matter-of-fact. Even with the anniversary of his mom's death, things are what they are. That is what he is teaching me, and I am an eager learner. I need to learn this. I need him to teach me that sometimes things are what they are and not everything has to mean something, and that perhaps I can be okay even when things around me are not. Perhaps.

"I'm ready then," I say. "Lead the way."

I turn to get back into my car and he calls to me.

"Nice butt, hottie!" he says, and my heart flutters the same way I imagine these yellow petals will flutter on the wind soon, spreading all around like sun. I shake my hips at him, then turn and look over my shoulder, smile in a way that doesn't tell him nearly enough about how much I need that. I need his reassurance and approval, though I do not want to.

We each pull out of the parking lot, taking separate vehicles because we have our own things to do afterward. We'll meet back at his house in the evening, have dinner, spend the night together, the entire weekend probably. It's been quite some time since we spent a Friday or Saturday night apart, probably since that Friday five months ago, a few days after he'd called and said he loved me in a voicemail.

For twenty minutes I follow closely, until eventually he puts his blinker on and turns into the grandest wrought-iron gates I've ever known, ones that lead into what is by far the loveliest cemetery I've been to in my life. It is regal almost, and I find myself not surprised. This is what I have thought of his family many times, that they are regal, refined, so poised and polite. That is how his mother was too. I know it from the stories and the pictures. She was so much grace, and I wonder what she would have thought of me even though he says she would have loved me. She would have, I think. I know how to get people to love me. I just can't seem to get them to stay, what with my heavy expectations and all.

We drive slowly around a bend and then another, until finally we come upon a spot with a line of trees along the back of it and another line along one side. That's when he pulls off to the edge of the paved path and parks. I pull in behind him, and within moments he is out of his car and turning toward me. I reach for the bag of golden petals, then step out of my own car. As he approaches me I hold them up and ask, "Do you think we can scatter these?"

He looks at the bag in my hand and puts his arm around me. "Sure," he smiles.

We turn now, arms around each other, and start walking to her spot. We have hardly covered any ground when I see the gorgeous flowers that have been placed in a big pot to the right of her stone, and I feel like I knew.

Yellow.

"Oh my gosh," I say to him. "Who brought those flowers?"

"My dad has that done," he answers.

"Well, they're beautiful and just the right color!"

"The right color?" he questions.

"Yellow," I say. "It will look so pretty with these same petals, don't you think?"

"It will," he says.

"It's funny, I almost mixed some pink in, but then decided not to," I tell him. "Now I'm glad I didn't."

"My mom would like whatever you brought," he tells me. "Just the way it is."

His mom would like whatever I brought, I think. Just the way it is. Still, I'm glad it's all yellow.

We come to her graveside and stop, look down at her name on the stone and then become silent. We just lean into each other and look at the stone and I don't say anything. I think I should let him have this time with her, but then doubt creeps in and I wonder if I should say something or do something, until I remember myself under hands on a Reiki table and I let peace settle around me and it makes sense. It makes sense to be still and quiet.

After some time, he shifts, and gently I turn to look at him, find a small smile on his lips. He's remembering maybe, so

I start to look away, to give him more time, but he looks at me and asks if I want to scatter the petals now.

Holding the bag between us, I reach in and gather a small amount in my fingertips. I prepare to let them go and scatter neatly to the earth around her spot, but the wind becomes gusty and suddenly takes them from me. They blow in all directions, and at first I am disappointed and think their scattering will be ruined, but then, just as suddenly, I let that thought go. I remember not to hold so tightly. Do not hold so tightly, I think, to thoughts or to rose petals or to anything really.

"I guess we're sharing these with some other residents," I say.

His smile grows and then he too reaches into the bag, and we walk slowly around his mom, sprinkling yellow rose petals. Many drift away, spreading the gold glow beyond her place, but most surround the stone that says her name. Taking turns, we continue reaching into the bag and scattering petals, until soon the sack is empty and we stand back and look at them. We see them lying all around and blowing away too. They are so pretty and look just right with the big pot of yellow behind them.

"That was a good idea," he says. "Thank you."

I smile and step in close to him. He raises his arm so that I can fit under it again and I wrap both of my arms around his middle and turn toward him as we stand looking at his mother's place. It is beautiful and filled with yellow and I still have a fleeting thought about how I'm glad there's no pink, but I bring my attention back to the glorious yellow and I imagine her just like that. Glorious yellow.

It is in just that moment that I see something though. I see one little spot. I see this one little spot among all of our yellow petals and my eyes get wide. My eyes get wide because it is not yellow.

Even after all of my careful selections and my only wanting yellow and not pink, a small lone rose petal must have glided into my bag without notice because there, among all of the carefully chosen petals, is one that does not match. There is a single pink rose petal.

"Oh my gosh," I say to him, pointing. "Do you see that one pink petal?"

"Oh, cool," he answers.

I wanted only yellow and not pink, no pink. But there it is, a single pink rose petal among all of the yellow, and it seems to call out to me like a well-placed message, and it seems to tell me that I can let things unfold and that not everything has to be a certain way to still be okay, to still be beautiful.

Pretty girls and nice houses, I think, and my throat starts to close with many years of shame and uncertainty.

But then I let that go too. I let it go. For now.

That evening I lean back on his couch, the same one he was sitting on when I arrived unexpectedly just five months before on a Tuesday night. The beautiful July day has turned into a warm dusk, as we drink Blue Moons from cold glasses with shots of orange juice in the bottoms and orange slices floating on top. He's also hung one orange slice over the edge of each glass and they look so beautiful, like maybe we shouldn't be drinking from them, messing them all up.

Iceland takes another sip of his drink before setting the glass beside mine on the black wooden coffee table, and I look at our glasses next to each other, like a pair meant to be where they are, side by side. The most gorgeous light from the setting sun is casting a soft glow on them and the feeling of warmth and sweetness that was already filling me seems to overflow now, soak me in it.

I get a little scared.

"We shouldn't drink these," I say, half teasing, trying to distract myself from the worry of losing it all. "They look so beautiful. I don't want to mess them up."

"Oh, that's silly," he says laughing.

"Look at them though," I say. "Isn't it such a perfect picture?"

"It is," he says, "and so are you."

His words give a sharp nudge to the doubt that always tries to settle in. They move it aside to make room for something more, for joy I think, and I look at him and find him looking back at me with an intensity I don't often see. There is so much warmth in his eyes and it matches the summer heat in the room and the July sun that's been on my skin all day. I tilt my head toward him and speak. "I'm definitely not perfect."

"You are to me," he says, and I'm surprised. We've had these moments before, but not many, and there is much time in between. I never know when they will happen, when he'll startle me like this, take his love out and present it openly rather than letting it simmer quiet and calm.

It's not that it isn't always there. It is, just below the surface, a warm and steady pulse, but I treasure these moments when it's right before me, a little more proof of what I should already know with certainty but don't. It will take a long time to clear out all of this self-doubt, the fear that I'm not good enough, that nothing is. It's the same fear I now know probably helped drive My Ex away. I've been reading about it in his old messages, noticing it in all that we were.

It's hard to change what you say and do, what you think. It's really hard. But so is not changing.

I lean in and kiss him. He tastes like Blue Moon and orange juice, like sunshine and rose petals. I want to stay here forever in this house on this couch with these pretty glasses full of cold beer. I want to stay right here, with my heart completely intact, self-assurance finding its way in and making a home. I want to be more than I think I am. I want to be enough.

I hear his words again.

You are to me, he said.

Three Years Earlier

"Hello?"

"Hi there. I'm calling from the Dr. Phil show," she said, then told me her name and asked for me by mine.

My breath caught. "This is," I tried to say.

"Hi there," she said again. "I'm calling because your story has been selected to appear on the show. Do you have a moment to talk?"

My breath. Caught.

Desperate, I had written to the Dr. Phil show just two months before, asked him in a brief letter to, quite simply, help fix my relationship the way I had watched him fix so many others over the years. Then I'd written that if he couldn't fix it, he could end it instead. I'd written that. If you can't fix this, then I need you to end it because I can't do it myself. I had written that letter and then a woman with a California number was calling and Dr. Phil was going to fix us and I was completely filled with hope and despair.

"Yes, I have a moment," I said.

"Great," she said. She repeated that my story, our story, had been selected to appear on the show and that they wanted to tape it in just three months, October. She said we would need to fly there and I said that we could, but really I didn't know.

Then she asked more questions, personal questions. She asked if he'd ever cheated or if I had. I told her that we had not because we hadn't. Not yet.

"So he just doesn't want to get married," she seemed to ask and state at the same time. "He wants to live together and participate in your family and your life pretty fully. You share expenses and celebrate holidays and eat dinner together every night and all of that, but he just doesn't want to get married."

She wasn't asking. She was telling. She was telling me what I had written in my letter and it was difficult to listen to and I had a hard time talking so she told me to take my time.

Finally I said, "That's about right."

Quiet tears rolled down my cheeks as this woman from the Dr. Phil show continued to speak to me about my relationship, then asked that I send pictures of us to her, and I told her that I would, and imagined them displayed across television sets, happy faces that couldn't possibly need help. But we did, and Dr. Phil believed in us. He believed that we were messed up enough to need help.

"Do you think you can get me those photos in the next week or so?" she asked.

I swallowed back a handful of heartache and said, "I do."

It is the afternoon following the Blue Moons and rose petals, and I am sitting on the couch with a peanut butter and jelly sandwich. Reruns of the Dr. Phil show are on when I'm hit with the memory of that phone call, and I wonder how many times I will have to let go of this pain before it is gone for good, and I wonder where it even comes from. Is it all from My Ex or is it something from before, something I don't even remember? Is it me? Is it just fucking me and my fear of not being enough because someone else is always prettier and because my childhood house filled me with shame that I'm still drenched in?

How did I even know to care about those things? Who taught me that?

A lump forms in my throat as I remember the woman from the show telling me about my letter, about my life, about this pain that seems to still have a grip on me, this pain whose source I think I might not even know, that might run deeper than these men in my life and deeper even than me. It's like it comes from another life I don't remember, an instinct to hurt. Do I want to hold onto it or let it go? Do I have a choice? I think I do, but I just can't seem to make it every time.

We never went. To the Dr. Phil show. We never went because he said he would not display all of our troubles for the entire nation to see and that it was bullshit for me to even suggest it. When I cried he said he was sorry and I let him be sorry and I let us limp along for over two more years.

It was over two more years before it ended.

Kick. Struggle.

But has it ended? Has it really?

I love Iceland, this man with his mother buried in a beautiful cemetery, whose love for me simmers constantly, quiet and calm, and yet one mention of the Dr. Phil show and my heart feels ravaged. From the outside in.

Unexpectedly the phone rings then and I draw in a deep breath. I sit up. I look to see if it is him and it is. I dry my tears. I answer.

Iceland tells me that his plans for the afternoon have fallen through and he's glad because he would rather be with me. He wants to know if I can meet him in a park we both love, take a long walk on the trails and have a late lunch in the grass. He will pack it. I should just bring a blanket.

I hear that whisper again, the one that speaks of a sorrow that has always been there, is just now trying to name itself. But I hear him too, a voice that lets ache start leaking out of my heart. It is a voice of comfort and trust. It is steady and certain. It is safe and true.

But am I?

Hours later we are sitting on a blanket in the grass after a long walk through the trails in the park, tired, refreshed, hungry. It is three in the afternoon and the sun is warm and welcome on our bodies, the blanket soft beneath us. We take out the sandwiches he made and the thermoses he filled to the top with iced tea, pass out napkins he tucked neatly under little bags of pretzels. I pull out slices of cucumbers and chunks of baby carrots and I am so filled with abundance and joy, ways I am learning in my Reiki sessions, my stretches of healing. I almost don't know what to do with it all though, where to put it. This happiness takes up a lot of space. It is bigger maybe than pain.

"How amazing is this?" he asks without really asking. His sandwich is in his hand and he's chewing with his face turned toward the sky.

"It's so amazing. I wish we could do this every day."

"Me too," he says, and turns his gaze to me. "I'll just settle for being with you every day though."

My breath. Caught.

I hide it by telling him that every day is a lot of days and he says it is not enough and I hope he means that. I hope even if the days are not enough that I am, that I am enough. I want to say that to him and I want to say so much more, words I don't even have names for, but I can't find my voice because I don't want him to know either. I don't want him to know that I don't always think I'm enough and that I really want to be and that maybe I'm not as strong as I seem. I don't want him to know that I'm filled to overflowing with this new love, yet pain taps gently just below my heart, reminds me. I feel bad about that, how it seems to come from another life I don't even remember, like an instinct to be hurt. I want to let it go. I just haven't been able to.

I smile and tell him that I love him. "I love you too," he tells me.

I open my mouth to say more, but I don't. I turn away. This hurt seems like a secret I need to keep.

"You okay?" he asks me in that voice, deep and gravelly, the texture of it seeming to wrap gently around my face, soften my features. It is with those two words that the pain memories recede, stop tapping and whispering. I look at him and smile.

"I'm great," I tell him.

"You sure?" he asks.

He doesn't press, just acknowledges, waits. He acknowledges and he waits, and though this is something I am still not used to, this lack of tragedy and pleading and self-absorption, it feels right. It feels new and strange and scary, but right. Like other times, there seems hardly any emotion at all in the tenor of his voice or in the words themselves, but it is there. It simmers beneath his ease, his certainty. I feel it and I need it. I need it today and the day after this and for all of my days, and suddenly I feel that this is what I must have. I feel certain of it, steady and clear, different. This is what I must have for all of my days and so I answer him.

I say yes.

CHAPTER EIGHTEEN
I Don't

May 18, 2008

I've taken the dining room table apart myself this time, having learned how from my dad almost three years ago. Just like it did then, the table lays upside down on the floor, its legs and chairs beside it. There are bins packed and pushed up tight against the walls. My entire life again, down to boxes and tables, suitcases full of clothes. I think it's going to be different this time though. I do.

And I don't.

Still, as I step back to survey the space, make sure there is room for the movers to get around, hoist my things into their arms again and carry them out, I am not surprised as I begin to feel a strange sense of loss. Even among all that I have found, there is still so much loss.

I look at the empty space of the overstuffed white chair I just sold, picture My Ex sitting it in, his head is in his hands, crying and shaking and asking. And I ache.

I don't ache for him though. I don't hurt because I want it back or am still sorry he's never called. I hurt because loss just does that. It hurts. Even if what you lost is better off gone and you finally know it and you wouldn't answer even if he did call, it is still a loss, and loss can stick for a while. It can crawl right up and make a home in your heart. I don't think we're built for loss, any of us. I know I'm not. But we do survive it.

The buzzer sounds then and drowns out those pangs in my heart. That fucking buzzer, I think, and laugh out loud. I won't miss that thing. I won't miss a lot of things.

I go to the door and push the button that will let them in the building, then turn again to see everything, to see what I *will* miss about this place. There is so much I will miss about this place I never wanted to be, about these rooms that held me when I needed somewhere to land, rooms that allowed me to still make a home even through all of the pain, even with a windshield having fallen completely into my lap.

It's still there, the pain is, but I don't feel so full of it anymore, overflowing. I have it in me and I carry it around. I still take it out and look at it too much, but I know it's not me. It's just a part that has played a bigger role than it deserves, and I have learned that here. I have learned to know better, and knowing doesn't always make it so, but sometimes it does.

There are footsteps right outside the door now, heavy but welcome, and I greet them as they enter the living room and begin looking around, making plans. I look around too, also making plans, and then one asks me if everything is going and I start to say yes. Until something stops me.

I look down the hallway, straight down the hallway and through the open spare room door to where the green desk sits against the window looking back at me, and something occurs to me that has not occurred to me before now.

I think suddenly that I can't take it with me. The green desk. I have to leave it behind. I have to let it go.

Just then my phone rings and it's Iceland, his voice wrapping around me when I answer, softening my features. "Hey sweetheart," he says, his words gravelly and deep. "You ready?"

"You still think you have room for me?" I ask, teasing, but not.

"Plenty," he says.

I ask him to hang on then and I press the phone against my heart as I tell the movers to pack everything except for one item. They should pack every single thing except for one.

The green desk.

"Okay, so you don't want this desk loaded?" he confirms, pointing.

I look back down the hallway. I see the green desk sitting with its top bare, drawers emptied and placed beside it. My eyes fill with tears, but not because I want to keep it. It's just because loss can stick for a while. It can crawl right up and make a home in your heart, and peeling it off really hurts. It really does.

I breathe in.

I let go.

I turn away.

"I don't."

Just Three Weeks Before

We were finishing breakfast in his kitchen, at a table against the wall and under a window, with bright sunlight casting a glow on the old linoleum, the white 1980s counters and cupboards. It needed a makeover. We'd already planned it, modern wooden cabinets and a stainless-steel sink mounted in a sleek earth-toned counter top. We envisioned creamy tile floors and a new stove with five burners, buttery walls filled with Public Market prints. Still, even without a makeover it was clean and warm and felt like home.

"Are you ready for this?" he asked.

"I think so," I said, "but we'll find out, won't we?"

He smiled and raised a glass of orange juice to his lips, and suddenly I wanted to hurry, to gulp down that last piece of toast, chug my milk and rush upstairs to get dressed. I wanted this project to start so it could be over and I could stand back and enjoy the results. I had no need to for the journey. None.

I knew it wasn't right though. I knew even before I knew, even before the yoga mat and the Reiki hands had been teaching me to slow down and let things unfold. Still, I felt so ill-equipped to trust that there was a natural course, a soft awareness that might gently move in and reveal itself little by little. Instead, I was driven by a need to completely tear things open and lay them out, know every single thing.

I had the need, but I didn't always fill it anymore.

Sometimes I could quiet down and wait, trust.

Sometimes.

Of course, it wasn't just this project I wanted to unfold, the taking down of wallpaper, painting new colors to go with the life we talked about living. I wanted to get going with this life too. I wanted him as more than a boyfriend. I wanted to stop figuring out whose house to eat dinner at, stop forgetting my toothbrush, stop "sleeping over." I wanted to know that this was it, and I wanted that because I wanted him, and I wanted him to want me, and I wanted things I didn't even know I wanted because I just wanted. And so for weeks, that old familiar urgency had been living in me. It had been filling my veins and my breath, making it impossible to fully experience each moment because I was so distracted with where they were all leading, with *if* they were leading at all.

I knew it was dangerous too. I'd learned. I'd learned in my head, but not in my belly, way down deep in that basement where I was still unpacking all the junk I'd been stuffing down there, and so I pushed. I prodded and hinted and questioned and one day, two months before breakfast in the outdated kitchen, he'd asked me to move in with him, to this home with wallpaper that had to be taken down. It was the same house on the hill that I had walked up on the night I decided he needed to know that I loved him.

"I can't," I'd told him. "I'm sorry. I've done that before. It doesn't work."

I was so scared that this time would be just like that time, even though this time was nothing like that at all. He had said that he understood, not tragic or pleading, just matter-of-fact, certain. He'd said he understood and that was all he'd said, and I was left wondering what exactly he understood. I wouldn't ask though. I wouldn't ask, but I would plot and worry and fill my veins and breath with more and more fear. I knew he could feel it too. I knew my fear was seeping into his head and his heart, but it had such a strong hold on me. And even though I'd learned enough to measure my words and mask my distress, I couldn't get it to not be.

I was thinking about this again when he asked if I was okay and I looked at him across the breakfast table. "Oh, sorry,"

I said. “Yes, I’m fine, just really looking forward to this,” I told him, my voice soaked in sarcasm.

“I can totally do it myself, babe. Seriously. If you don’t want to I understand.”

“Nope, you’re not getting rid of me that easily,” I teased.

“I never want to get rid of you,” he responded, and I nearly choked on my last sip of coffee.

“Never is a long time,” I said.

He smiled at me, eyes soft. “Not long enough,” he told me.

I titled my head, a smile spreading across my face, some of the fear leaving in my exhale, pumping away from my heart. Let it unfold, I thought. Just let it unfold.

After another beat, we both stood and picked up our plates. We stepped to the counter beside the sink and set them down, then turned toward each other. I stepped into him, kissed him lightly, then pulled back. He grabbed me though, moved me in again and held onto me. He held onto me and I held onto him and I tried to just have the moment and not need to know what it meant. I tried to not need.

After a little while that was long and quiet, he kissed me tenderly on the neck. Then he released his embrace and reached out with one hand, smacked me hard on my rear end.

“You effer!” I yelled, pushing him in the chest.

“Stop procrastinating and go get dressed,” he bellowed. “Don’t you know we have wallpaper to take down?”

I hope we have a lot more than just that to do, I thought. And I hope we get started soon so this worry lodged deep in my soul will dissolve, this worry that I’m not enough, but if you love me and marry me to prove it, then maybe I will be.

And I hope I can stop needing that, stop needing everything from the outside in. I hope I can find the love for myself that I always seem to be trying to get from somewhere else, and just trust that I will be okay no matter who loves me and who doesn't.

I hope I can.

"Oh my God," I moaned, and heaved an enormous sigh. I plopped down onto my ass, slid up against the wall. "That was only supposed to be a couple of hours!"

"Well, it was. A couple of hours and a couple more. Maybe another one," he teased, then joined me on the floor.

I rested my head on his shoulder and said, "I'm going to die of starvation and dirtiness, just die. I never thought it would end like this."

He laughed at me.

"So let's get up," he said, eagerness in his voice, a sort of delight that caught hold of me and caused me to lift my head, look toward him. "We'll get lunch, take it to the park or something."

"Are you freakin' kidding me?" I said mildly. "Look at me."

"There's nothing wrong with you," he said. His tone, as always, certain, matter-of-fact.

"I look like I have not showered in days. My hair is actually frizzy and it's only April. My hands are covered in wallpaper glue and I am not even wearing earrings!"

"Oh my God, that's disgusting," he said. "No earrings!"

I shoved him. "Seriously, I can't go anywhere like this."

"Babe, it's a beautiful day and we've been in this dining room busting our asses for five hours. Let's go!"

"Oh my God, I have no choice. I'm starving. There's no time to shower."

He stood and reached his hand toward me. I took it and let him pull me up and into him, where he kissed me softly on the lips and said thank you. He said thank you for spending your entire Saturday in this mess with me, and I told him there wasn't anywhere else I could ever be.

And there wasn't.

“We did not just eat that entire pizza,” I stated flatly.

“I’m afraid we did,” he replied, then tossed his last napkin into the empty cardboard box that fifteen minutes before had held our large three-topping pizza.

“That’s great. So not only do I appear un-showered with frizzy hair and hands covered in wallpaper glue, but I’m also fat!”

He replied matter-of-factly, “Don’t forget that you aren’t wearing earrings either.”

“Oh, shut up!” I screeched.

He flipped closed the lid of the box with the tip of his fingers and started to gather our used napkins. He secured the top on his own soda and then swung his legs over the picnic table bench and stood. “Let’s go,” he said to me. “We need to walk.”

“Walk?” I questioned.

“Yes. Let’s go up to the reservoir, do a few laps. We’ll walk off this pizza.”

“Oh God no. I’m exhausted and dirty. Let’s go home, to your house I mean, and shower and sleep.”

“Sweetie, come on. It’s still sixty-five degrees outside and sunny on only April twenty-seventh. We could be getting an ice storm right now. Let’s walk. You’ll feel better.”

I heaved a dramatic sigh and swung both legs over my side of the picnic table bench. “I would rather die,” I said tragically, “but I’ll go.” I started to help him clean up.

“That’s my girl,” he beamed. “Put that down though. I’ll get this. You relax in the car.”

“Yeah, I’ll rest before this stupid walk,” I said, my words moving around a sly grin.

“Yes,” he said. “You deserve it.”

And I hoped he was right.

On our third lap around the reservoir, I finally started to feel less huge, but still gross. The bloat in my stomach from five slices of pizza had diminished to a manageable mound that fit a little better in my dirty pants, the ones covered in wallpaper solution. My fingers, still grubby from hours of scraping glue, were a little cleaner, but my eyes felt gritty and my hair was frizzy and I longed for a shower and the sheets of our bed, his bed really.

It was right then that I started to feel self-conscious and hoped he wouldn't look directly at me as we walked. I wondered how I could have left the house like this and then add half a large pizza and a sixteen-ounce bottle of soda to the mix. I reached up to redo my ponytail, make it a little neater. After that I pinched at my cheeks, trying to give them back some of the color that had surely been erased by so much sweat and dust.

We were walking quietly side by side and I felt what I always could in his presence. Ease. I felt ease and a sense of letting go and, ironically, I wanted to hold onto it. I wasn’t sure how to have that without him, and my mind filled with thoughts about how for weeks I’d prodded and hinted and questioned about our future, but still couldn’t figure out what it would be. We had talked about moving in together and how I could not do that without marriage, the proposal of it at least, and I’d hated saying that, felt somehow desperate and needy. Still, it was real, something I had to admit. I wasn’t going to make the same mistakes. I at least had to make different ones.

He had said that he understood and then he had not said anything else. He had not said another word. For two months.

All-too-familiar pangs of anxiety began to grip me then, hold firmly to my belly and pump up to my heart and my head, or maybe the other way around. Maybe they started as thoughts, swooped down to my heart and belly, settled there and fluttered their heavy black wings. I could never be sure, but either way I tried to release it.

"So my lease ends soon and I'm going to start apartment hunting. I don't think I want to stay where I am."

Hint hint. Prod prod.

"I thought you were willing to go month to month when it ends?"

"I was, but I'm rethinking that. It's more expensive to do it that way."

"I know. I get that. It gives you time though."

I wondered what I needed time for. We had been together for a year and a half and that was enough for me to know I wanted to be with him and I didn't need time and I wanted to say that, but of course I didn't. I had at least learned that much. I'd learned to measure my words, but I'd not learned to measure my fragile heart and wild thoughts and so I said it silently, in ways I was sure he could feel even though I didn't want him to. But then again, I did want him to.

The wings of worry continued to flutter. I tried to swallow them, let things unfold naturally and just trust that I'd be okay, but I couldn't yet. I couldn't be quiet and still and wait. Instead, I was again trying to tear things open and lay them out, see all of the details immediately. I knew that I needed to slow down, but I had not yet learned how. I always had to move.

"Well, I think it's been long enough," I said, prodding, hinting. "I don't want to stay there. No amount of time is going to change that."

I want to be with you, I wanted to say. I want to be with you so I can be good enough because I still only know how to be that from the outside in. I want to make sure you want me, but I can't push because I have to trust and not need a plan and just believe that a plan will arise even if I don't orchestrate it, and I know all of this. But you know what they say about knowing.

Quiet filled me then, and I tried to keep these thoughts to myself, remember what I had learned from the others. I'd learned that it wasn't all their fault when we'd come so completely undone and my heart had broken into so many pieces. They'd felt my doubt and fear and they'd been afraid of it, and I had to stop doubting and fearing. Doubting and fearing myself mostly.

"Yeah," he replied. "It's time."

We were quiet longer then, only the sound of our feet hitting the pavement on our fourth lap around. I knew he could sense my worry and my wondering, my need to tear everything wide open and know every last fucking detail, so I tried to make it better.

"It'll be fine," I said. "I'll figure it out."

My voice was carefree, but that's because it wasn't mine.

"So hey," he said. "Let's go to Spot, get protein shakes."

"Are you kidding me?" I cried. "We cannot possibly ingest one more thing today."

"I need something sweet and we haven't been to our spot in a while."

Our spot. Spot Coffee. The place we met in person for the first time after a couple weeks of online dating, of carefully placed words in Times New Roman and pop-up windows late at night. I'd had a flight leaving to visit My Big later that day, but I'd agreed to meet him because it had felt as though it needed to happen at that moment. Again with the urgency. Right from the beginning. Urgency.

That had been a year and eight months before. I'd gotten there first and was waiting in the indoor balcony near a window, a hot mug of tea cupped between my hands. I saw a large BMW SUV pull into a spot along the curb of the building and the man in the driver's seat looked like the pictures I'd seen online for the previous weeks. He'd looked like Iceland, and I'd watched nervously as he'd fiddled with things in the car and seemed to take an eternity before opening the door, slowly stepping out. And of course, I'd wished for him to move more quickly.

I'd placed my mug on the table that day, stood up with forced slowness and descended the stairs leading from the balcony to the large open area below. It was filled with tables and sofas and old dressers and people coming and going, and filled with all of my fears too. Then, just as I'd reached the bottom step, he'd emerged through a small group that had been waiting in line for lattes and sandwiches, and he'd recognized me immediately, stretched out his arms and said hello in this way, with this look. It was so different. Right from the beginning he was so different, not trying to mask his uncertainty, but seeming to unabashedly let it show. He just let it show, and as I stepped into him I was filled with the scent of the simplest soap and something like oatmeal and something else too.

Ease. I was filled with ease.

We'd pulled back then and held gazes, and his was a look both confident and humble, and I didn't know what to do or what to say or what I had just found, as he suggested that I go back to the balcony and save our seats while he got in line to order. I had agreed, and turned toward the stairs with that pure scent of him hovering around me, and I was disoriented, startled by how he wasn't like anything else, and unsure how I could even know that so soon.

"Babe," he said, breaking my reverie about that first day. "Wanna go to Spot?"

I breathed in, still remembering how I'd taken the stairs two at a time back into the balcony and over to the old blue armchair I'd been sitting in. I'd taken one sip of my tea, but right away I could not sit still, and I'd set the mug down again, walked over to the railing that overlooked where he was standing, found him with his back to me, hands in his pockets. His jeans were loose, but not loose enough to hide his trim frame. His T-shirt was fitted around his lean arms and he felt large, steady, certain.

Even from those first moments, with little more than soap and oatmeal to go on, I had known that he was different and wondered if maybe I could be too.

“I cannot believe I am in here looking like this,” I said to him, after we’d left the reservoir and headed to our spot, gotten in line for strawberry protein shakes.

“Sweetheart, you always look good. It doesn’t matter what you do.”

“That is not true,” I argued.

“It is,” he said.

“Have you seen this disgusting ponytail?” I asked.

“Well no, because I was distracted by those ears with no earrings.”

I punched him in the arm as we stepped up to order our drinks, and when our order was complete we moved to wait at the other side of the oversized bar.

“Let’s go home with these,” I suggested.

“What? You love Spot,” he said.

“I know,” I told him, “but I’m starting to feel so exhausted, on top of looking this awful.”

“How about we get a sunny seat at the bar along the window?” he asked.

I softened. It seemed important to him, like he wanted to just keep moving, like something was pushing on him. That wasn’t like him. It was like me though, so I understood.

“Fine,” I said. “I do love being here with you. Do you remember the first time?”

“Of course,” he responded. “I could never forget the first time I met the love of my life.”

My heart caught in my throat and I swallowed back easy tears as I leaned into him and he put his arm around me, pulled me in and kissed my forehead. I nestled under him, and despite the wallpaper glue and the dust and the pizza, I still smelled the oatmeal and the soap. I looked up at the balcony and remembered walking down those steps, seeing him for the first time in real life, not in pixels on a computer screen.

"Our drinks are ready," he called, and I was pulled from my memories of us.

We took our shakes and headed toward the window seats he'd chosen, walked past the stairs that led up to the balcony where I'd been sitting when I'd seen him pull up to that curb. I remembered more about the T-shirt then.

"Oh my God! Remember the Willie Nelson T-shirt you were wearing the day we met here that first time?"

"Yup," he said.

"That was such a cool shirt. I think I noticed the shirt before anything else," I said, "except for maybe your teeth. I noticed your teeth."

"Yup. You love my pearly whites."

"And what do you love about me?" I asked, as we approached our stools at the long bar in front of the window, set our protein shakes down in front of us.

"Oh boy," he replied. "Here we go."

"Come on. Is it so hard to name three things?"

"Oh, now it's three?" he asked.

"It's always three," I reminded him. "That seems like a small list considering all you have to choose from," I teased.

He laughed and said, "I love your frizzy ponytail," then took a sip from his drink and looked away, hiding the smile.

"See, I do look disgusting!" I wailed.

"Oh stop. You do not."

I sipped my own shake and could not hide the grin that started at the corner of my mouth and turned into a full smile, then a hearty laugh. He started laughing too.

With sarcasm I said, "I love how you have no problem busting my balls right now, but a year and a half ago you almost broke up with me because I sort of made fun of the way a girl was dressed."

"Uh, these are two different things."

"Nope. Not different. You are no better than me now."

"Oh great, you've brought me down to your level," he teased. "You take pride in that?"

"Great pride," I responded.

"How about you just drink your shake?" he suggested.

I reached for my drink, pink and frothy, and as I brought it to my mouth my text message indicator went off. I pulled my phone from my purse and saw my sister's name across the screen. I looked over at him.

"Go ahead," he told me. "I'm gonna run to the bathroom."

He kissed me, then got up, and I watched him go, all dirty and disheveled from our day, but still as handsome as he was the first time we met, at the base of the steps not far from where we were sitting. I turned back, took another sip from my shake and opened my sister's text.

"Hey!" it read. "Are you guys still taking wallpaper down? LOL."

I wrote back, "Thank God no. At Spot now."

"Aw," she wrote back. "Your spot."

"Yup. We're leaving soon though," I wrote. "I'm dirty and exhausted. I'll call you later."

He came up beside me then, pulled his chair back out. I looked up and wondered about him. He seemed unsettled, not himself.

"One sec," I said to him, looking back down to read my sister's farewell and exit my messages.

"There," I told him. "Done."

I tinkered a moment more with my phone, but didn't look up as I asked him if he wanted to finish his drink while we walked.

"Sure," he said casually, but with something else in his voice, something odd that mixed with the gravelly sound.

I looked up.

And there, all of a sudden, something was sitting on the counter between us. All of a sudden, on the counter between us, there was a box.

A small, square-shaped, dark blue box.

With padding in its frame and two tiny hinges in the back.

It sat on the counter between us and it looked so familiar.

And yet like it looked like nothing I had ever seen before.

All of a sudden.

A box.

There on the counter between us.

I looked at him.

He looked at me.

I looked at the box.

I looked back at him and he held my gaze with a beautiful mix of confidence and uncertainty and I held my breath, looked back at the box.

I could not believe it was there and I could not believe I was not tearing it open, desperate to know every single thing immediately, desperate. Instead, I just looked at him and he looked back at me and nothing seemed to beat but my heart.

And then immediately I started to hear words that seemed to speak to me from inside that box, and they seemed to say that I was loved and I was enough and I was okay and I was worth it. That's what they seemed to say to me until all at once they didn't. All at once something else interrupted. More knowing words tried to step in, to speak a greater truth to me.

But it was harder to hear. I had to lean in. And so I did.

I leaned in and listened closely and it spoke. It said that really, a ring could not tell me that. A ring could not say that I was loved or enough or okay or worth it. Not now. Not then. Not ever.

"Are you going to open it?" he asked, and the sound of his voice triggered tears that lodged in my throat and felt like they were made of fear and doubt and shame, burdens that I had always carried around and that I looked at too much, but that I had been trying so hard to put down. They were made of things I sometimes felt, but things that were not all I was. They were made of girls who were prettier than me and a house that I was never proud of, and so I couldn't be proud of myself either, or so I thought.

And they were made of more things. More things and more things and more things, things I didn't really understand, that I couldn't even name, but that made me feel like less. They were made of things I struggled to get out from under, and so I sat motionless with that box on the counter between us and thought about how when you can't love yourself you become desperate for someone else to do it, and you become desperate for everything to make sense, to create stories and definitions and rules to live by, and you think that if all of that lines up, then you'll know you are worth it. Then you'll know.

So now do I know? The question landed firmly in my belly and fluttered its heavy black wings and I wanted to be more than that. I wanted to be more than someone who needs a ring on my finger to feel like enough.

But I didn't know if I was more. I just did not know.

And I don't know how long I was like that either, motionless and lost, when finally the sweet smell of soap and oatmeal floated into my senses and I reached for him and I held on and he did too, and I wondered again what such pain was all about and if it was like this for everyone. I wondered if everyone felt everything as deeply as I seemed to, a cold hand constantly squeezing and twisting and breaking the heart, a strange mashing together of love and fear and hope and sorrow that forms something I have never known how to carry around without getting hurt. And I have never known how to put it down either.

Pretty girls. Nice houses.

Not everything has to mean so much, I thought. Maybe I am enough.

Suddenly then, I became aware of the space we were in, the people and sounds and smells and light, and it felt like I was just entering, emerging from someplace else, from a long journey that I didn't want to be on because I always just wanted to get to the end. And this was what I thought the end would be. This was it.

Only it wasn't. There was a knowing settling in, and it said that this was not it.

This box.

Just sitting there.

On the counter.

All of a sudden.

I know this is not the end, I thought.

I do.

And then the apartment is empty except for me and the green desk. This green desk is all that is left to get rid of. Just this. But not really.

And as I trace my fingertips along its top I wonder about things that don't need wondering. They just don't need wondering. What they need is for me to plant my feet firmly and breathe in and know. I need to know.

I need to know that when you can't love yourself you become desperate for someone else to do it, someone else to love you enough to know that you are worth having. But I need to know for myself that I am worth having.

And then my phone rings and it is my sister because she knows. All of it. Every single thing. She always has.

"How ya doin'?" she asks.

"I'm good," I tell her. "Thank you."

And my thank-you is filled with so much more than those two words. It is filled with all the words we have said to each other over the years, so many years, maybe since we were little girls. It is filled with words about love and pain and anger and joy and being okay and not being okay at all, not being one fucking bit okay.

It is filled with words about self-doubt and fear and rejection and disappointment and shame and not being enough and then thinking that maybe you are. Maybe you are enough and maybe you can love yourself even in heartache. Even if nobody else does.

But maybe you can't.

I still do not know, but I am trying to know, and I am wrapping all of these words up into one huge package of the most love I can give, and giving them to my sister, giving them to everyone. Giving them to myself too, I hope.

So many other things seem to be receding now, letting me out of their grip a little, but not because of a ring, not even because of a love. It is receding because of courage. I have been finding the courage to look at myself and notice, really notice and do things differently, not every time, but as often as I can, and that kind of courage moves you forward. It leads you into bigger things, and bigger things bring more courage. I am finding more courage. I am finding more.

But it isn't over yet. It is not over. This is not the end.

Heartache has been with me for too long to just go away because of a ring on my finger or some courage I can sometimes find. No man or marriage can bring the self-worth and confidence I still crave, and I know it is dangerous to think for a moment that they will. I also know that knowing doesn't make it so and I will have to be careful, very careful.

I will have to keep my feet on the ground and hold onto something I felt in that very first Reiki session and in every one since. I will have to hold onto awareness, the power of hearing and seeing my own life and knowing when I'm fucking it up and at least trying to do it differently, trying to know that I am enough. I will have to hold onto the power of standing in my own space and counting for something, no matter who loves me back, no matter if anyone even loves me at all.

On a yoga mat with my brow to the earth and my arms outstretched, I've learned to get quiet and still and notice, and I've noticed. I've noticed that I have to be right with myself. I really have to be right with myself. But I've noticed that being right with myself is so hard. It is so fucking hard.

I know all of this as I listen to my sister's voice and I also know that knowing doesn't make it so. Knowing does not make it so, but it is a good place to start.

"Hey," my sister says. "Do you think this is where your book will end?"

I am at the door by then, away from the green desk, away from a lot of things, and I put my hand on the knob, pull it open and look out. I think how long ago it was when my mom came to get me and my bag full of mismatched clothes and sorrow. How long ago, I hope.

Still, when I answer my sister, it is in a voice that is not tragic or pleading. It is just matter-of-fact. Certain.

"No," I say. "I don't."

Acknowledgements

It seems to me that the many words of this book came more easily than the few needed here, in this one page of appreciation. How can I possibly name each one of you, and express what you have contributed? There are not enough pages for all of your names. There are not adequate words to show my thanks. This book has been a work of nearly seventeen years, and I did not do it alone.

So, I hope you will know who you are and what you have done to help bring these words to light. You are my family and my friends and some people I hardly even know. Maybe you have read excerpts. Maybe you have read the whole book. Maybe you have let *me* read the words to *you*. Maybe you have not known one syllable of this story, and yet still believed in it. Thank you for messaging me in multiple ways with your encouraging sentiments, and for sitting across from me with your wine or coffee, your love and support. Thank you offering me the courage to keep going and to believe that these words deserved print, that *I* deserved it. Thank you seems less than enough. Some things are just too much magic for mere words. This is one of those things.

I am grateful and I love you,
Jeannette

About The Author

This is Jeannette Maloy's first published work. She wrote it almost in its entirely between 2005 and 2009, and has spent the following years revising, editing and wondering about publishing it.

Jeannette has many roles and could be labeled many things, but has always felt, above all else, that she is a writer.

She is grateful for the presence of good friends and colleagues, and especially for her supportive family, including loving parents, two sisters and one brother.

Together with her husband (Iceland) and sweet fur-family, Jeannette lives in Canandaigua, New York.

Made in United States
North Haven, CT
12 December 2022